I Hear You Emma

A Journey of Intimacy

DIANA ST. JAMES

I Hear You Emma
Copyright © 2019 Diana St. James
All rights are reserved
ISBN: 978-0-9895033-1-0

Published by

Big Hat Press
Lafayette, California
www.bighatpress.com

Prologue

This book describes the deepening intimacy I developed with my extraordinary horse, Emma, and the discovery of abilities that she possessed and used to help others. Due to her astounding sensitivity, Emma was far more aware and attuned to worlds beyond our senses. As our lives unfolded, I continued to be surprised by what she could do and how she affected the humans in her life.

I Hear You Emma picks up the narrative where my book *Emma Speaks* ended. While it stands alone, it omits the introduction to telepathic animal communication that *Emma Speaks* provides and assumes acceptance of that capability. As in *Emma Speaks*, the experiences that I share can be considered unusual and the reader may need to suspend belief, but I hope would acknowledge the source and accept it for the gift that it is.

The arc of this book ends with Emma's retirement as a riding horse and with her new life to simply love and be loved.

Human characters including veterinarians and employers have been combined, their names changed and descriptions altered. The dialog with the animals and my experiences with them are described as they happened.

Acknowledgments

I am most thankful for and appreciative of my readers, who because they were intrigued by Emma's life, have consistently nudged me to finish and publish this book.

I am forever grateful to Emma for her kindness, generosity and unconditional love. She taught me how involved animals are in our lives in ways we could never imagine. She opened my heart and healed deeply implanted wounds in the core of my being. Through her love I evolved into a better human.

I am blessed by my husband Geo, who supports my love of horses and my need to share Emma's story.

Chapter 1

Loving a dangerous horse is not a choice I would have made. But we all know that life has a way of guiding and at times forcing us down exotic paths we would have never imagined. Matters of the heart seem to be the most potent agent of change. So here I am, a middle-aged woman, inextricably linked to my horse, Emma, who is subject to unpredictable, spontaneous, violent attacks of fear. Picture this: nostrils flared, eyes glazed over and eleven hundred pounds of muscle, bone and hooves blindly charging away from an unseen horror.

My situation might have made sense if I had been born on a ranch and was savvy about troubled horses. Not me. I was born in New York City and have lived in cities or large city suburbs ever since.

Sitting at my round oak kitchen table, teacup in hand, I reflected on how fate roped me in by my heart, a fragile and vulnerable organ given the abuses of my childhood. How fortunate I was that Emma found me and drenched me in complete and unconditional love. That nourishment did more than open my heart. Discovering telepathic animal communication changed my perspective on how I relate to animals - a profound impact to my life. Hearing Emma directly, knowing the complexity of her emotions and receiving her wise counsel led me to regard her as a being with equal rights to happiness. I came to regard her as a soul with a voice, a voice I first heard through the translations of an animal communicator and then directly through my own deepening connection.

And if a horse who spoke wasn't enough, what made Emma most extraordinary was her paranormal capabilities that never ceased to surprise me and offered me experiences far beyond what most of us consider part of the "normal" world. Every time I thought I had plumbed the expanses of her powers, I was astounded by what my mind, bounded by mortal thoughts, could have never envisioned without her help.

What a harsh twist of fate that Emma, the horse I was closest to, the one with whom I shared a deep karmic connection, was plagued by episodes of anxiety that made her unsafe. The unpredictability of the attacks added to the danger. Was this God's way of weaning me off horses? I hoped not.

Besides an all-encompassing, compassionate heart, Emma also delighted me with her extraordinary beauty. I got her as a five-year-old when she was still undeveloped. Now at ten she was filled out, muscled up and looked the athlete. Her exquisite sculpted head with a perfectly centered white star was connected by a delicate throatlatch to a long, naturally arched neck. The softness and liquidity of her vibrant brown eyes revealed the gentleness within. Her black mane and tail and black points set off the mahogany brown of her coat. She was all thoroughbred at 16.1 hands. Refined, powerful, elegant. Breathtaking.

I set my teacup down and gazed out my window at the shimmering leaves of the trees flanking the street. My life felt split in two. At work I lived in the corporate world as a financial services management executive. My career was driven by reports, statistics and performance – hard measurable facts. My experiences at home made me feel as if I had walked through the looking glass into an alternate reality with a whole different set of rules. I often found that passing between these two worlds left me incapacitated while my mind reoriented to manage the transition.

I pushed against the chair back seeking something solid. Warm sunshine streamed through the kitchen window full and strong with a bounty of golden summer light that tempered the edges of my apprehension, a low-level anxiety that seemed to be a permanent part of my psyche. A couple of squirrels huddled in the sycamore tree across the street, scolding the neighbor's cat. They had made their home in that tree for as long as I'd lived in this house. Too bad the stately old tree, now suffering from disease, was scheduled to be removed. My gaze followed the squirrels skittering through the branches before returning to the real estate want ads of the *San Francisco Chronicle*.

A couple of months before, I had come to the realization I could no longer keep Emma in a boarding stable environment. She would be relaxed one moment munching her hay, the perfect vision of the sweet-tempered horse I knew to be her real self. Then with no discernible inciting event, her eyes would go wild and she would run and scream in terror. She couldn't be reached in that state. She was fleeing for her life. For the last two years these panic attacks had been confined to her stall and adjoining paddock where she would race the fence line of her pen until she somehow escaped from her inner demons. Recently her attacks had expanded to the outdoor arena when I was riding her. The frequency and severity of the episodes were also increasing. Getting her safely back to her stall to run it off was more difficult than I had wanted to admit, until one day after a severe attack another boarder took me aside. She shared her concerns about the risks I was taking - not only for myself and Emma but for others at the barn especially the children who visited. After much deliberation I decided the best solution was to move from my suburban house in a family community and purchase our own home, a home that would accommodate a special needs horse.

Several of my friends asked me why I kept a horse with unpredictable and perilous behaviors. I would have been able to walk away from Emma if she wasn't my soul mate, if I wasn't as connected to her as my very breath. But, this kind of deep love, perhaps because of its rarity, made me do strange things. So now I was jeopardizing my financial well-being by looking for horse property in the bay area east of San Francisco, well known for its expensive real estate. To get adequate property would mean earmarking a large portion of my take-home pay to a home mortgage. That meant plenty of belt-tightening in all other areas. Little room would be left for major car repairs, vacations or a well-heated house in winter. The fact that I was afflicted with Chronic Fatigue Syndrome and could be ill for months at a time added another risk variable.

Despite the imagined deprivations, I smiled. This home would be a huge present. All my childhood I had longed to own a horse. I was in my mid-twenties when I was finally able to manage my first purchase. Then I harbored an even bigger dream of having my own place where I could keep horses. For a couple of years while living in Virginia, my apartment was adjacent to the pasture where my horse and a couple of others were boarded. For hours I would watch the gentle swish of their tails and the nosing of blades of grass as they hunted for the most tender, tasteful shoots. How soothing it was to listen to them snort or softly nicker while I rested in the evenings. At that time, I was a private school teacher whose salary ensured such an aspiration would remain fantasy.

With some luck and after going to night school to get my MBA, I had been promoted to executive management and 1995 was a good year for my company. I was pleased I had finally achieved the financial resources to even be able to consider a horse set-up. The purchase would mean I would have to continue at high-paying jobs with generous bonuses. As much as I enjoyed the benefits of the compensation package, being a corporate officer and the head of a marketing and product development division of a Fortune 500 company had its stresses.

My eyes returned to the newspaper. I perused the want ads scanning the write-ups for what might fit our needs. We needed a quiet residence of any size or age, a warm barn, turn out space for Emma and a flat area where I could build an arena with cushy footing.

An arena was needed to continue in my dressage career, a sport often referred to as "horse dancing" with its requirement for a closely woven partnership. My passion for this sport was as strong as ever. I didn't need to take Emma to horse shows to compete, exciting though that might be. Training her to be a more flexible and powerful athlete was what I needed to do to be whole, to create beauty, harmony and unity. Dressage was my art form. The joy it produced enlivened something at my core. The deep-seeded high I received when Emma and I were connected left me living for the next ride. That kind of union is transcendent. Without it I would wither, since my work life offered little artistic or creative nourishment.

My exploration for our new home had taken me all over the San Francisco East Bay including ranches without a reliable source of water, acreage perched precariously on hillsides and a retired ostrich farm with a few rogue birds still running around. Finding nothing of interest, I put the regional newspaper aside and pulled out a small local paper that the news delivery person had left on my doorstep. The real estate section listed an ad for horse property that included a level field. I reached for the car keys, bounced into my Mustang 5.0 convertible and pointed my wheels towards that open house.

Just a few short miles away, I pulled into the driveway of a lovely ranch house within commuting distance of work. The home sat on nearly two acres of usable land in Lafayette with a small barn, space for an outdoor riding arena, a turnout paddock and trail access to Briones Park.

Although bigger than I needed, the house had charm. There was a spacious eating area off the kitchen overlooking the backyard. The front was enclosed by a white plank fence and a generous lawn surrounded the driveway. The barn had two stalls and a large tack room where I could store hay. The side yard had a professionally installed putting green that might be fun for picnics. I picked up the marketing flyer and headed home.

My fingers punched the numbers for my real estate agent. She was a friend and knew that I had a special relationship with Emma. Even though doing so was new for her, she was willing to ask the sellers if I might bring Emma onto the property to see how she would react to the energy of the land.

The sellers agreed and the following weekend I trailered Emma over. I opened a side gate to the property and led her across the newly plowed field towards the barn. She took long, even strides, moving her neck left and right, taking in the area. She peeked into the stalls and sniffed the ground in the connecting paddock. From a previous boarding situation, I knew Emma was sensitive to the energy of the land and wouldn't thrive just anywhere. I cleared my head, concentrated and did my best to tune in to her feelings. I sensed she liked the warm dirt beneath her feet and was giving me her approval.

For sure Emma would have more to say about the property than I was able to hear. Even though my intuition told me that Emma liked the home I had found, I still needed the validation from another source. The purchase was too big an investment to risk a mistake. When I got home, I would call Carol, an experienced telepathic animal communicator.

I loaded Emma and hopped into the truck. Emotionally I was like a little kid. Just the thought that I might fulfill a long-held goal amped up my excitement. I bounced up and down on the truck's bench seat. Squeak, squeak went the springs and squeal, squeal went my heart. I knew that the strength of my emotions might be called excessive by others, but, hey, that was me and I'd been living with it for over forty years. I wondered if Emma shared my excitement.

I was grateful for Carol in our lives. She had been there for us over several years. As my own communication skills got better, Carol insisted that I no longer needed her. I just couldn't quite trust my own capabilities. Besides, Carol had said that when someone is emotionally involved with an animal, the communication might be muddied. Well, I was emotionally involved with my horse and in getting horse property.

Once Emma was snuggled in her stall at the boarding stable, I unhitched the horse trailer, dove into my truck and rushed home. I threw my body into the wing-backed chair in the family room and snatched up the phone. Although I had been doing it for years, I still felt a bit strange calling Carol in her home six miles away from me to have a telepathic conversation with my horse who was hanging out in her stall at the barn nine miles in the other direction. I shrugged, burrowed deeper into the cushions and dialed the phone. Carol picked up after a couple of rings and I explained the situation.

"OK, give me a minute to tune into Emma," Carol said, her diction clear and her tone, direct.

I quieted, knowing it took a couple of minutes for Carol to connect to Emma. To hear an animal's voice and have a clear communication, she had to release her mind of its rambling thoughts and the day's pressures. She had to let in and believe in that subtle energy Emma sent and separate it from random ideas that flitted through her mind. Animals sent pictures, words and feelings. I waited while Carol's breathing slowed. I struggled to suppress the irritation that manifested with these pauses. Patience. Hmmm.

"She's joined us," Carol said at last.

"Hey, Emma, what do you think about the property I took you to visit?" I said, with a strong and hopeful voice. My words vibrated into the emptiness of my family room devoid of other living ears. I wondered if I would ever get over the awe of these communications. "I'm optimistic that this home will work for the both of us."

"Emma is giving it hooves-up," Carol said.

"What?" I had visions of Emma pushing up daisies instead of eating them.

"Hooves-up is the equivalent of thumbs-up," Carol said, laughing. "Emma is making a joke by imitating one of your gestures."

"Alright, ha ha," I said with a bit of annoyance. "Does Emma have anything else to say?"

"Diana, this is wonderful," Carol said. "She says she thinks she can be happy there. No more emotional excesses."

Emma's response stunned me into silence. I had a hard time believing those words. For the last few years I had exhausted every resource I knew to bring peace to my horse. Her most recent challenge, her anxiety attacks, drove my emotions off the chart. What she felt, I felt. The intensity made me crazy.

"My God Carol, you know what we've been through," I finally said. "Do you think a solution could be this easy?"

"I have no idea," Carol said. "Emma doesn't know either. It sounds like a good start. She's looking forward to the move. Wait..."

My wristwatch clicked the seconds by. I turned my hand to inspect the face of the watch and followed the second hand as it crept from ten to twelve to two.

"She's saying something about her current barn," Carol said.

"I'm listening," I said, pushing the receiver against my ear.

"Emma says that the owner of where she is boarding now is really stressed and it sets the tone for everyone who lives there. She thinks the woman is close to having a nervous breakdown. She's very brittle."

"Oh gosh, I didn't realize it was that serious," I said. "The owner has been bombarded with some really tough life events. After a valiant fight against cancer, her husband died leaving her to raise their two children. She's been a little irrational recently." My gut wrenched with culpability. How could I have missed the influence of the barn owner on the horses? I knew the energy of a place started at the top and influenced all the beings associated with that space. I had enough of those experiences at my jobs. The corporate philosophy at the highest levels of management set the tone for the whole company and it affected everyone, even those in entry-level positions. Why would horses be different?

"Emma says the owner's difficult moods impact the horses and increase tension," Carol said.

"OK, I'll move her as quickly as I can," I said, reliving my own memories of the constant turmoil and violence that permeated the atmosphere of my childhood home. I knew all too well what that did to my anxiety levels.

"I know you always do your best," Carol added.

"Emma, I'm so sorry," I said. "Why didn't you tell me sooner?" I could feel guilt multiply its little tacky feet on my skin.

"Remember, Diana," Carol said, "It's like when she had a toothache. When it comes on slowly, she accepts it as normal and doesn't think to mention it."

"OK, I know what I need to do now," I said, relaxing my shoulders.

I thanked Carol, hung up and called my real estate agent to start the negotiation process to buy the horse property. I was overjoyed to have a path forward. That night instead of picking up a book, I quieted my mind and slowed my breath. I sat still in my living room and let my musings take flight into a variety of delicious visions. My very own place with my very own horse. A safe place where Emma could regroup. Where I could do the sport that elevates me to emotional heights. To have this dream manifested kept adrenaline energizing all the cells in my body. I thought I might vaporize with all the delight I was feeling.

After midnight, I eased into bed. The minutes ticked by until my physiology settled. As I drifted off to sleep, I pictured Emma cavorting around the new place, smiling and bucking with glee. I felt the hay in my hands as I fed Emma her breakfast and the weight of her blanket as I slipped it off, freeing her to enjoy the sun on her back. I saw her head hanging over the fence waiting for me when I drove home from work. I imagined the contentment I would feel in living with her.

I wished I could have drifted off to a peaceful sleep wrapped in delight. But I couldn't ignore the needling I felt creeping up my spine. My life didn't tend to evolve that way.

Chapter 2

When the homeowners and I finished a couple rounds of counter-offers, I found myself paying more than I had wanted. With the vision of a happy horse in my head, I made the decision to put my signature on the sales agreement for our ranchette. I giggled whenever I used that word. City girl that I was.

Next, I needed to secure financing. The mortgage paperwork stared up at me from my kitchen table. I shoved my back against the chair as if the support of the oak slats would reassure me I was doing the right thing. My eyes stopped at the loan amount and accompanying monthly payment. I winced, picked up my pen and started filling out the application.

Halfway through the forms, I put the pen down. I could feel stirrings that needed expression. Now that our home was nearing reality, I wanted to get busy with plans for the move. Suffering from Chronic Fatigue for more than a decade, I knew that planning and preparation were essential to economizing my energy and protecting my health. Checklists and action plans were necessary tools for me to live more than a bed-ridden life, given my debilitation. If I could spread out the tasks needing to be done, I could conserve my energy for the move. I wanted to be ready to plunge into action as soon as the sale closed.

I grabbed a scratch pad and began my list. I had to decide what type of fencing I wanted to put up and which kind of mat should be purchased for Emma's stall. The automatic waterer needed repair and the opening to Emma's stall from the hay storage area needed widening. I would have to buy a reciprocating saw to cut through the wood. I needed to do research on how to construct a riding arena. How should the foundation be built? What kind of footing is best for outdoor?

What living with Emma would be like piqued my curiosity. I couldn't imagine being any closer. But then again, she had managed to surprise me in so many ways. Once, out of the blue, she orchestrated a telepathic conversation with my first dog whose passing away a decade before still brought tears to my eyes. She said it was her job to set up the connection. My dog wanted to contact me to tell me that I didn't have to anguish over the decision to put her down. When she could no longer chase squirrel or cat, she was no longer dog. She reassured me that she had asked to be moved on to her next life and that I always heard her.

On a relationship level, Emma and I had grown as close as couples who have lived together for decades and are able to read each other's minds and finish each other's sentences. I knew I couldn't distinguish my thoughts from Emma's. An incident from a couple of months before stood out in my mind as a good example of how close we'd become.

At the place we were currently boarding, the owner had a habit of letting her horse loose on the property. Most of the boarders didn't appreciate how her horse barged into the barn with a haughty demeanor and created a potentially unsafe situation for those of us who groomed our horses in the aisles. Because the owner was emotionally fragile and would sometimes verbally abuse the boarders, no one wanted to approach her about keeping her horse confined.

One day when I was brushing Emma in front of her stall, the owner's horse marched in with a bravado that irritated me and sent a flash of anger ripping up my spine. In a spilt second, I pictured Emma kicking this horse and felt the satisfaction of putting him in his place. No sooner had that thought whizzed through my brain than Emma thrust up her hindquarters and planted both hooves on the horse's chest. Shocked and stunned the horse backed out of the barn, clearly chagrined. I was delighted that he got the "attitude adjustment" he needed and at the same time relieved that Emma had left no marks on his coat, no signs of a wound. Emma clearly had restrained her kick to a warning blow.

The next time I talked to Carol, Emma took the opportunity to inform me that the vision in my head hadn't been mine at all. Emma had sent me the image of her kicking the horse as her way of asking for permission to teach the horse some manners. My emotional reaction to the picture had given her the answer she had needed to continue with her plan. This kind of interchange happened often enough to teach me that I couldn't be sure who originated any particular thought. That gave "not knowing your own mind" a new meaning. This phenomenon was unsettling for me. Emma would always protest by saying, "Why does it matter whose thought it was?"

As much as I enjoyed reminiscing about these lessons Emma had taught me, I had to get back to the drudgery of paperwork. I finished filling out forms for the loan application. Relieved that it was done, I tilted my chair back on two legs and stretched. I couldn't stop a grin from spilling across my face.

Buying the horse property was the most exciting home purchase I'd made. I wasn't used to fulfilling dreams on such a major scale. I felt as if I had won the lottery. When all the roof, termite and other inspection reports had been submitted and the necessary compliance work completed, I removed the contingencies.

Each day after work, I went out to the boarding stable to see Emma, to discuss the intended improvements with her. She seemed to be interested although was probably being polite.

A few days later my loan was approved. That was the last hurdle in the purchase process. Given the clear path forward to buying our new home, I drove out to Emma's boarding stable in a particularly good mood. I levitated with anticipation and delight the entire way. We would only be in escrow for another couple of weeks. I had a hard time corralling my excitement.

Ever since I put an offer in on the house, Emma had been relieved of her panic attacks. She was once again my sweet, capable dressage horse. Riding every day had a multiplicative affect to calm my nerves and raise my endorphin levels. Maybe there was something to getting our own place. Did I dare to believe that a lower stress environment might be the balm Emma needed? Might the move do something that a variety of healing methodologies and vet schools couldn't?

When I slid out of my car, Emma greeted me with an eager whinny and energetic head bobs. I saddled her up and led her to the outdoor arena. Something about her walk made me pay more attention to her gait. As soon as I entered the arena I clicked her up to a jog and ran along beside her. Her head bobbed each time her left front foot hit the ground. If only it was just a tiny nod.

"Oh, no." I turned and shuffled back to the barn. What now? It seemed as if every time I got her fit and working well something happened. Maybe it's only a bruise or an abscess on her foot I reasoned. I'll call the vet when I get home to set up an appointment.

The day the vet was to arrive I padded around the barn. The late afternoon sun drenched the barn in diffuse, amber light. Despite this gentle atmosphere with its backlit motes calmly drifting through the tawny haze of the barn aisles, my anxiety refused to soften. My apprehension about life's unpleasant turns heightened whenever Emma was lame. A deep breath filled my lungs with air scented from the pine shavings used as bedding in the stalls. I tried to quiet myself. There was plenty of time before the vet would show up. More deep breaths. Grooming Emma would keep me busy until he arrived.

A sigh escaped when I saw the familiar dust-feathered car creak into the parking lot, raising fine silt from the gravel. The familiar ensemble of a camouflage-patterned baseball cap and Eddie Bauer vest identified my vet as he eased his six-foot frame out of his car and stood up and arched his back. He nodded when he spotted me standing in the barn aisle.

"Don't panic, yet," he said in a reassuring tone. He had had plenty of experience with my emotional life.

"Knowing my luck." I said.

The vet looked at me and shrugged. He knew that I'd had some issues with Emma's feet in the past. I hadn't shared with him my experience with my previous horses, so he didn't know that my first horse went incurably lame after six weeks and my second horse after three months and on it went. I had reasons to be skeptical. My stomach knotted ropes around the carrot I had been gnawing and stomach acid etched my esophagus. I couldn't help it. I was always waiting for the next announcement of bad news.

The vet asked me to lead Emma outside and across the parking lot. He watched her trot on the hard ground. He only needed to see one pass and followed me back to her stall. He opened the black leather bag he had put down outside her door. The metal hoof testers came out. He picked up her right front foot and applied pressure in a methodical way to the sole of her hoof. She flinched a little bit with each test. Then he picked up her left front foot. Each time the vet squeezed the handles of the hoof tester, Emma jerked her head up and wrested her foot away.

"I'm going to remove her shoes and take X-rays," he said.

"That doesn't sound good," I said. More knots, more acid. I was amazed that I still had an intact stomach wall. I watched him unclench the nails on Emma's hooves and pull off her front shoes.

"I'll know more after I see the films," he said, walking towards his car and the portable X-ray machine he kept as a tool for field diagnostics. The open hatchback revealed bandages, syringes, medicine bottles, a stainless-steel bucket and other veterinarian paraphernalia jumbled together in a haphazard manner but arranged in a system he apparently knew well.

He hooked up his machine to an extension cord that easily reached the outlet. With the efficiency of one who has done it multiple times, he positioned each of Emma's front feet on the plates and took several angles. When he completed the X-rays, he headed for his car and in his usual clipped manner called out, "I'm coming back to the barn in a couple of days. Call my office for the time."

On my drive home I tried to keep my spirits up. My very bad habit, one that had relentlessly taken up root in the core of my being, was always to think the worst. Emma could have tweaked something and it could be gone in a couple of days. But that's not where I dwelled. Her condition was most likely something horrible. Navicular, arthritis, or some other incurable disease I had yet to discover. I did my best to console myself into believing that it might be a stone bruise and Emma's lameness wouldn't last but a few weeks.

The day the vet was scheduled to arrive I waited in the parking lot, pacing back and forth and flipping glances down the road for his aged brown car. At least I thought it was brown but with all the buildup of dirt and road grime it was hard to tell. When the temperature got too hot, I went inside the barn to Emma's stall. Although I was staying attentive, I didn't trust my ears. Scraping open the stall door I peeked out of Emma's stall every couple of minutes to check the sunbaked parking lot. My vet arrived within a few minutes of when he was scheduled. His car door rasped open, its hinges resisting the rust build up. He approached me avoiding my eyes. My muscles froze.

"Her pedal osteitis, which you know is an inflammation of the bones in her feet, has gotten much worse," he said, scuffing his boot in the gravel. "You may have to accept the fact that Emma will need to be permanently retired from work. She won't be your riding horse."

I gasped. My vet didn't sugar coat the message. Well, here it was. The other shoe had dropped.

Because Emma was quite lame and not just a little off, my vet felt rest would reduce the pain in her feet but would most likely not restore her as my sport horse. He reasoned that we were already doing everything we could with her medication and specially designed rubber shoes.

I must have dumbed down my senses. A full minute passed before his message wheedled its way into my brain past the defense mechanisms I had erected. When I absorbed the ramifications of his message that nothing else could be done, I went numb. I knew that I was looking in his direction, but I couldn't make out his face. I didn't hear anything else that he was saying or if he was even talking. The ever-present chattering song birds went silent. The breeze stopped rattling the corrugated metal roof of the barn. I tried to focus my eyes on a wisp of hay on the floor, but it started to blur.

Then I felt my vet's hand on my shoulder; its warmth seared through my body directly to my eyes. The tears started to flow and then my chest shuddered. As I looked up, I saw the vet walking out of the barn. As he disappeared, I sank into a depression. I didn't know why he left so abruptly. Later I would learn that in the morning he had put down an injured horse. He probably had had enough emotional pain. But I didn't know that then.

When the breeze dissipated the last bit of dust stirred up by his car, I returned to Emma's stall. I lay my head against her neck and the tears splatted from my cheek onto my blouse. Emma leaned her shoulder into me and the warmth of her body nurtured me.

"Oh, Emma," I croaked. "I thought we had this worked out. I thought we had successfully managed your foot issues. At least, the vet thinks with rest we can make you comfortable. I don't want you to be in pain. I'm so sorry you have sore feet. I'm so sorry that this condition was created by thoughtless humans when you were a foal. I'm so sorry that you continue to suffer."

I put my arms around her neck and stroked her shoulder. When she turned her head to me, I noticed the wrinkles around her eyes and that the whites of her eyes appeared under her eyelids. "Please don't get anxious," I whispered. I ran my hand over the star on her forehead and down her muzzle. I kissed her eyes. Time seemed suspended as I basked in her love.

A noise startled me and broke my immersion in the emotions of the moment. I removed Emma's bucket from the hook on the stall wall and went to the storage room. I hoped by offering her some grain I might divert her attention and soothe her distress.

I retreated to my car and headed home. Once within the protective walls of my bedroom, I let loose. My pillow muffled the wailing my lungs created. Each spasm of my rib cage rushed to expel the frustration and disappointment I was feeling. Horses weren't pets for me. I had horses in my life to ride. My sport was my creative outlet, my physical exercise and a way to connect on a deep level with another being. My despair plunged down a bottomless hole. My emotions ricocheted between anger, depression and grief. My fists hammered the down pillows on my bed.

When the outburst of emotion was exhausted, I curled up under my bed covers. I tried to move from the pain in my gut to the rational part of my brain. I always had a hard time explaining how I felt about riding to my non-horse friends. Most had never even heard of dressage. For me it was about performing a refined set of movements like ballet. I joined my horse in a relationship not unlike dance partners. In our six years together, Emma had advanced in her training so that riding her was an ultimate joy for the both of us. We both appreciated the competency we had achieved.

So, what would I do now? Buying this expensive horse property limited my options. I couldn't afford another horse or the upkeep to share someone else's horse. Besides, there's nothing like having an exclusive one-on-one relationship with your own horse. With the treatment plan that had been working so well I had hoped that I could continue riding Emma for years. I had visions of making it to the highest levels in dressage.

I shuffled into the living room and slumped down into my easy chair. Staring at the cloudless sky, my body froze in place as the day darkened around me. The timing felt particularly cruel. I felt as if I were in free fall and could spot nothing to grasp, nothing to slacken the descent.

Events in my early home life ensured that I had a plethora of abandonment issues. Any form of loss was hard for me to process. This situation seemed particularly bitter. A lame horse didn't need horse property with enough land for a riding arena. She couldn't stay in a boarding facility either. I would need to find a suitable retirement home. That thought made me flinch. Separation from Emma? How would I do that? One step at a time, I reminded myself.

In the morning I would call my real estate agent and see if the owners of the property would release me from the sales contract.

Chapter 3

Rejecting the commute traffic on the freeway, I cruised along the frontage road. After a few turns and stops, I let out a sigh when my car eased into the driveway of my suburban home that had generously offered me refuge for the last seven years. What a relief to leave the corporate political machinery behind after a tough day at work. I padded through the house, made a quick pit stop in the kitchen, and grabbed my comfort foods. My cushy chair in the bedroom received my tired body as I flopped down into its embracing arms. I released all the tension that I could consciously control. My corporate life strained my values and need for harmony. At home I desperately needed peace and support.

I was grateful that I had been able to process the emotions Emma's lameness created. I surrendered to the idea that Emma would no longer be my riding horse. That very morning, I had thrown up my hands and said "OK, God. I accept Your will." All I could do was keep moving my feet.

Shortly I would head out to the barn to hand walk Emma for a half hour. Even though she was lame she needed some mild exercise. It is unhealthy for horses to be confined for too long. The last time I was at the barn, I had sensed something was troubling her. I couldn't quite understand what she was saying, so a call to Carol was in order and I wanted to do that before I saw Emma.

I was grateful that Carol could hear Emma's voice with more clarity and detail than I could. And sometimes I was just too tired to do the work of clearing my mind and connecting to Emma telepathically. To get Emma's messages directly was rewarding. Receiving sensations in my body that Emma was sending at the very moment she was feeling them couldn't be more direct, immediate and clearly understood. But I was exhausted.

I dialed Carol's number.

While the phone rang, I fiddled with the outside of the Dr. Pepper can between greedy snatches from the Cheetos bag. To assuage my guilt for consuming the fat, salt, sugar and chemicals, I promised myself dinner would be healthier.

Carol answered the phone and after the obligatory greeting, went quiet. I knew what my part was. Think of Emma and concentrate on her to summon her to Carol and me. By now I was quite familiar with Carol's process and what she would be doing when the phone was silent – the quieting and clearing of her mind.

"Emma wants to know what you're going to do with her," Carol said.

"What?" I stammered. "What does she mean?"

"She knows she isn't going to be your riding horse anymore," Carol said. "She's worried about her future and her life and she's picking up your stress."

"Emma, we both know that some people slough off their horses when they no longer serve them. I can understand why you might be concerned. That behavior is hard for me to grasp. I will never sell you or do anything you don't agree to. I want to be able to respond to your needs. I have committed to doing my best to make you happy. I wouldn't do anything without consulting you."

"I'm not sure she totally buys that," Carol said.

"For goodness sakes," I said, a seed of exasperation sprouting, "I've stood by you through your difficult periods with health and your emotional recovery work. What proof do you need? And you know that with my Chronic Fatigue Syndrome, my health is always dicey. I can be laid up for several months at a time. Even when I was extremely ill, I managed to take care of you. You're important to me and now we're going to have our own home, so I won't have to find you a retirement facility."

"Oh, are you still moving to the horse property?" Carol asked me. "I was afraid to bring it up."

"I got the call today from my real estate agent," I said. "The owners of the property won't let me out of the contract."

"I'm sorry to hear that," Carol said.

"I took a while to process that news," I said. "I have mixed feelings. If I weren't getting the horse property, I would still need to find somewhere to move Emma. Finding an appropriate home that would meet her needs might be a challenge. It just seems that the timing is particularly cruel."

"So how is it going to work for you?" Carol asked.

"I won't build the arena I had planned," I said. "I'll just do the few things needed to make the property ready for a horse. There's been no horses there for several years. I want to make a home as nice as possible for Emma. What else can I do? I would have preferred having the choice of another solution that would leave me with more financial resources and options. But that's not happening."

"Emma is so relieved that you aren't going to get rid of her," Carol said.

"Emma, I promised you I would never sell you," I repeated, putting more force into my words. "I wouldn't do anything that you didn't agree to. How many times do I have to say that? Yes, riding is important to me, but you are my best friend. You are important to me, too."

"I know you want to do dressage," Carol translated for Emma. "I feel ashamed. I feel I've let you down."

"Oh, Emma," I said, my voice softening. "You've always done your best. What happened isn't your fault. You didn't choose to be lame."

"I think she's still feeling bad about it," Carol said.

"Let's do our best to enjoy our new home," I said, popping in another handful of Cheetos.

I hung up the phone and my body sank deeper in my chair. My arms felt like they had weights attached. I wished I liked the taste of gin or vodka and could find oblivion from the frustration and disappointment I was feeling – a pricey new horse property and no riding horse. The easing that a glass of wine would provide would have to do. I could manage a small glass. I didn't like wine either, but I did like the affect – the world always seemed rosier.

I roused from my chair. I needed to go to the barn and walk Emma and think about the preparations I'd need to make for the new home. What had once seemed so joyful now took on a mechanical feel and each problem that inevitably came up was met with grumbling. I was still trying to come to terms with the fact that Emma couldn't be ridden. I knew it wasn't her fault. I was angered by the situation and at God. I just couldn't picture my life without riding.

My feelings reminded me of a recurring dream that had haunted me throughout my childhood. In that dream I came upon a herd of horses grazing in a sunny meadow. I would hop on one to go for a ride. As soon as the horse started to move I would slide off his back and fall to the ground. No matter how hard I gripped, I was never able to ride the horse. I would awaken feeling empty and cheated.

These dreams had echoed my waking life and had reminded me that my experience as a child felt hard and cruel and what I wanted would always be out of reach. I knew that I didn't want to be sucked back into the emotional space created by those dreams. I dug into the corner of my being where inner strength was nestled and yanked myself out of my depression. I was determined to come up with ways to make it a positive experience.

For a time I envisioned what it might be like to get a second horse. Several people suggested that I might be able to afford another horse now that I would have my own place and didn't have to pay board anymore. The two acres of pasture didn't offer enough forage to feed one horse, never mind two. I would still have to buy hay and bedding. Even if a miracle happened and an accountant could show me the way to afford another one, a part of me knew that I didn't have the physical energy to manage the care of two. What if I got another special-needs horse? What if I got sick again?

Maybe Emma's friendship would be enough. She was loving and could be quite entertaining with her antics and humor. She was capable of touching peoples' hearts in special ways. Who knew what other experiences might be in store for me when we lived together?

Chapter 4

On a sunny November day, the Bekins moving van eased its behemoth mass into the one-lane private road bordering my new home. Like a squadron of ants, the movers formed a line and marched the furniture and boxes into the rambling four-bedroom ranch house shaded by a cluster of mature elm trees. I had forgotten how much stuff I had until the movers emptied the van four hours later.

Once everything was bedded down in the house I could deal with the highest priority chores - hook up the refrigerator and washer/dryer and more importantly figure out why there wasn't any water. Another one of those unpleasant move-in surprises. Next, I unpacked the boxes that had been earmarked as necessary for daily life. Got to have a couple of dishes, a pan, the cereal bowl and spoon and a teacup.

I worked all day to finish the unpacking. I had taken a full week off work to give me the time needed to get settled. Within two days my belongings were organized well enough and I went to sleep with a sense of accomplishment.

The next morning, I woke up in a brighter mood. I channeled my energies into the preparations for Emma's arrival. The metal fence posts and rubber stall mats had been purchased and reposed in the bed of my dented and weathered F250 pick-up truck anticipating their new assignment.

Always there to assist, my friend Elaine came over to help with the tasks that required an extra set of hands. I laughed when I compared our fashion statements. I was in dirty blue jeans, a slightly wrinkled gingham blouse that fit loosely over my shoulders and shredded tennis shoes that clung to my feet. My close-cropped blonde hair was shoved up under a sun-bleached baseball cap. Elaine wore a pair of pressed beige chinos, a white starched blouse with a notched collar and polished boots that gleamed from good care. With red hair radiating copper highlights, shining blue-green eyes and a readiness that outshone the best Girl Scout, she would amp up anyone's energy level. And she was giving up a Saturday afternoon to help a friend. A true champ.

First on the agenda was installing the mats. I maneuvered the truck as close to the barn as I could manage. Totally stoked and summoning all our energy we tried to lift the top mat out of the truck. The two of us struggled to raise the mat from its brethren and drag it over the lowered tailgate. We felt like the Keystone Cops fumbling, falling, and lurching to wrestle the unwieldy mat. We laughed each time the mat flopped back down joining its mates, seeming to enjoy its victory of immovability.

Both of us were independent businesswomen who had owned our own homes for some time. We weren't inept and thought of ourselves as handy. We might not have the upper body strength of a man, but we could figure this out. We nodded at each other and sat down on the truck's tailgate for a minute. Our two minds wheedled out a plan. We would stand the mat up vertically on its narrow edge and flip it end over end until it fell off the truck. We high-fived each other when the first mat plummeted to the ground with a dust evoking thunk. Once on the ground we continued the maneuver. Get the mat vertical and roll end over end. On the uneven ground both of us had to bolt from side to side as the mat precariously leaned too far one way. The plan was a success. With the fourth mat in the barn we sighed with relief and laughed. Why was it so hard to move four lousy mats?

Fortunately, the installation was easy. Elaine's battery-operated hand drill made short work installing the two-inch wood screws. In no time the four mats were secured to the oak plank floor.

The next weekend Elaine came over again. Exuberant and effervescent as ever, she greeted me with a warm hug. Her shoulder length red hair was held in check by a crisp cotton scarf tied at the nape of her neck. My hair, in need of a wash, hid under my cap. Today we would work on fencing the pasture that bordered Emma's paddock. We marched over to the truck and found unloading the posts a much easier task than the mats had been. With the posthole driver in hand we set about sinking the twenty posts that it would take to run the full length of the property.

We thought it would be more efficient if we took turns sinking the posts. Elaine did one, then I did one, then Elaine again. On my second post we couldn't help but notice that I sank the posts with such force that it only took me about three good whacks with the driver while Elaine took close to ten. I guess I was working out my frustrations and anger. Elaine, retired fashion model that she was, filled out a perfect size ten and had about the same muscle mass as I did, so it wasn't about who was beefier. Since I seemed to be such a pro, I took over the job of sinking the posts while Elaine did the fetching and held the T-posts in place.

Each time I started the whacking of the next fence post, Elaine leaned back in awe. I hadn't thought about it and didn't realize that I was carrying that much exasperation and annoyance.

"I've never seen you like this before," Elaine said, balancing the fence post she was holding.

"You're right," I said, laying down the tool. "I try hard to think positive. I don't have a way of releasing unpleasant feelings when they build up."

"What's going on, besides your horse being lame?" Elaine asked, turning to face me and shielding her eyes from the sun.

"A lame horse is a really big deal," I said, taking off my baseball cap to shove a few escaped strands of hair back up. "It's easy to underestimate what it means to me. Much of my life has been about my need to ride. It's my way to decompress. I've ridden all my adult life. This will be a new experience - not having a saddle horse. It leaves a big hole."

"What about work?" Elaine said, unscrewing the cap of her water bottle. "You could invest more of yourself there."

"I feel trapped," I said, jamming my sneaker into the dirt. "With this property I need a big salary to maintain the mortgage and my expensive avocation, namely Emma. I like the work itself and it suits my skill set."

My voice trailed off, leaving an unsaid "but."

"Where's the problem?" Elaine asked and tilted the bottle back taking a dainty-like sip.

"An occupational psychologist once told me I don't have a defense against unscrupulous politicians," I said, gulping down the remaining water from my thermos. "He said I wasn't well suited for corporate life. In many ways I'm naïve and because I don't know how to maneuver the power plays. I feel a lot of angst and insecurity."

"I thought you liked a couple of your previous jobs," Elaine said, wiping her hands on the cloth I offered.

"I did," I said. "I wasn't as high up on the organization chart then. A recent *Wall Street Journal* article rated Marketing Vice Presidents of financial institutions as one of the highest risk professions. I guess it makes sense that my frustrations and anxieties have accumulated into some intense feelings."

"What's your boss like?" Elaine asked.

"Let me just say that the culture isn't any more dysfunctional than my family was."

"Lord, that isn't saying much," Elaine said, grabbing the next post.

"I'm conflicted," I said stretching and then picking up the driver. "The work is interesting, but the environment is definitely toxic."

Elaine grabbed the next post and we resumed our rhythm. Once we traversed the pasture with the posts, I collected the box of insulators I had stored in the barn. Hopscotching across the pasture we snapped two of the insulators equally spaced a couple of feet apart on each of the posts. The last insulator was secured just as the sun had indisputably retreated from the day. Cool air oozed behind the receding rays. Elaine took out a cotton handkerchief and dabbed at the powdered dirt and the glisten of moisture on her face. After a big hug, she picked up her toolbox and headed for home.

Anxious to finish the job and determined to use up the last bit of light, I retrieved a spool of wire from the barn. Stringing wire was a quick way to build a fence. The current that surged through the wire would dissuade Emma from poking or prodding against it – she had had experience with an electric fence before and knew to stay away. If she forgot, the charge was a gentle reminder rather than an electrocution. If she accidently ran through the wire, it would break before it would cut her. I snugged the wire between the posts, giving the wire a quick wrap around each of the top insulators. When I reached the wood fence I spliced the wire to its mate on the top plank. The other three sides of the pasture had had wire strung on the wood plank fence from a previous owner. Next I completed pulling the wire on the bottom insulators and joined the two tiers. The electrical circuit was complete. My job was finished. Darkness had consumed the field, so I wasn't able to survey my work. Knowing it was done would be enough for today.

I sighed with pleasure. We had accomplished a lot. I wouldn't need to hook up the wire to the current generator until Emma moved in and I had devised some sort of gate.

I took a deep breath and released my mind from "project management mode." The pause in work gave way to an exhaustion that was scary. My knees trembled and I felt a spasm in my arms. Drat! I had worked for too long and too hard. The absorption in finishing the project made me oblivious to my body. I had forgotten to leave any gas in my tank.

"Please," I asked of the evening breeze, "I don't want a Chronic Fatigue relapse now."

I slunk back to the house, skipped taking a shower and collapsed into bed, hoping that I dodged any long-term repercussions. As I pulled the covers around me, I vowed I would be more careful in the future. My enthusiasm needed to be tempered by common sense to take checkpoints with my body.

As I burrowed into my mattress, I tuned into the sounds of the night. The rustling of dried leaves outside my bedroom window caught my attention. This home was far enough into the rural area of Lafayette that I wasn't concerned with a human trespasser. Every place has its own night sounds and I wondered what creature had come to visit. My curiosity overcame my need for rest. I eased out of bed and tiptoed over to my bedroom window. My eyes scanned the pasture and bushes for movement. Ah ha. Dappled by the moonlight and well camouflaged was a family of deer lying down under a couple of the smaller oak trees. When the breeze parted the limbs above, the moonlight spilled over the mother and her two fawns, sprinkling them in powdered silver. They lay there in perfect repose quietly chewing their cud. The tranquil scene was full of contentment and ease. If Emma couldn't be ridden at least she might be emotionally happier in her own stress-free place, visited by these gentle woodland creatures.

I slid back into bed. Though invited, sleep didn't find a peaceful landing. My mind raced once more over the checklist I had created. The automatic waterer in Emma's stall had been fixed - a simple matter of loosening the float; the hay barn had been filled with bags of pine shavings, a forty gallon can of COB (corn, oats and barley) and red oat hay - the hay that Emma would consistently eat. Nearly everything that needed to be done before Emma arrived had been completed. I was excited at the prospect of bringing her home. To her home. To her very own home. At last, I plunged into a deep, serene sleep.

Chapter 5

I parked the trailer on the shoulder of the private side road to unload Emma. The driveway wasn't wide enough to accommodate the rig and the back entry wasn't paved yet. After all the preparation and anticipation, my body quivered to finally bring Emma home. Although she wasn't my riding horse anymore, who knew what living together would bring.

Emma eased out of the trailer and moseyed up the asphalt driveway towards the front of the house. The iron scroll gates that hung from painted white brick posts were held open with a couple of decorative moss rocks. Emma's response was distinct from those she had in the past when I brought her to a new barn. Then she would stop, raise her head and neck, stretch her body up, survey the landscape and act as if she were assuming command of her kingdom. This time she eased forward with a lowered head as if she was entering a temple and was showing deference to a sacred space. There was something softer about her. I tried to connect to her feelings. What I felt in my body was a sense of wonder, a tentative exploration and a desire to soak it all up.

Satisfaction warmed my body, not only for sharing Emma's feelings. To be standing in the middle of my own place with my horse and best friend. Awesome. I led Emma through the front yard and towards the barn. I opened the slatted metal gate to her run and let her loose. The fencing of the larger pasture had its newly installed wire gate – a bit wonky but effective. The larger area would give Emma enough room to get up a good canter and zip around as she pleased.

"Here you are, Emma," I said stroking her neck. "This is yours."

She pricked her ears forward and walked towards her stall with a bounce in her step. She paused and then entered and lowering her head sniffed the shavings. She raised her head, snorted, turned her neck and looked at me.

The words "I'm home" popped into my head. I heard them the same as if I was hearing a compelling thought. Somehow I knew they came from Emma. Then a new feeling swept into my consciousness. A warm and delicious sense of well-being infused my body and meandered into every crevice. I met Emma's gaze and knew this feeling came from her. Then I had a knowing, like a strong intuition, that having her own home was good for her. Never quite trusting I'd done the right thing, this transmission was reassuring. I got shivers whenever I received Emma's communications so directly. Her spontaneous messages often came when I was relaxed and not dwelling on anything. I made a promise to train my mind to be less cluttered.

What a comfort to lie in bed at night and hear Emma's muffled footsteps as she walked around her stall. The occasional soft snort to clear her nostrils of the dust that invariably clung to the hay was a happy sound. I could never figure out what it was about horse sounds that was reassuring and soothing as a mother's lullaby. Emma's nickers embraced and cheered my heart. Perhaps it's because I never recall hearing my mother sing to me or coo or compliment or console me. I remember her crying a lot – yelling, too. Maybe that was the point. I needed to feel nurtured, and somehow through my association with horses my guardian angels were gifting me what I never got from my family. I grew up with a big hole in my heart never having known unconditional love.

Along with the calming sounds this new home offered me, came a change in the rhythm of my life. Up even earlier now, I had to go out to the barn to feed Emma and ensure her water tub was full since I never quite trusted the automatic waterer to give her as much water as she wanted at one time. When I got home from work, I cleaned her stall and paddock and fed her again. Even though she was too lame to be ridden, she showed no signs of lameness at the walk. To ensure she got enough exercise and a change of scene, I took her for strolls after dinner. We wandered down our private road and the other roads that would make a loop back home in this area populated by properties with acreage. One circle took about twenty minutes and we usually did it twice. I would tell Emma about my day and enjoy our quiet time together. We rarely saw a car and I'm sure the neighbors who happened to look out their window wondered about the nut who was out there walking and talking to her horse every night. Especially since it was pitch black by the time we got out. No sidewalks or street lights in this rural area.

Not long after Emma moved in I noticed a quiet contentment infusing me when I came home and spent time in her company. I settled into a familiar routine. After our walk, I made dinner and my lunch for the next day and retired to the family room, usually with a good book.

One day when I came home from work I found Emma standing by her stall door. She had a smug look that made we wonder what she'd been up to. When I turned on the barn lights and peered inside, I dropped back on my heels. Her stall had been divided evenly into two. In the back half the shavings were banked against the rear wall and in the front half, there was not even one speck of sawdust. The stall mats in the front half were gleaming as if they had been swept clean and then vacuumed for good measure. I have seen horses paw at their bedding to move it around before a roll, but I'd never seen anything even close to this. The division of her stall was precisely in two and the dividing line perfectly straight. I wondered if Emma had been studying geometry and the bisecting of rectangles in her spare time.

I could feel Emma's pride, but I couldn't hear her reason for doing it. I wished I knew why I didn't hear Emma consistently. But I didn't. To satisfy my curiosity I would call Carol as soon as we finished our walk and I returned to the house.

My chair in the family room summoned me and I settled down with my phone in hand. The addition of a down pillow gave my back a soft place to shelter. Accompanied by a soda I sighed and watched the moon as it rose higher in the sky and painted the top leaves of the large elm in my back yard with silver. The moon drenched the back lawn and barn roof in a lustrous glow. I saw Emma's head pop out over her paddock fence. I marveled yet again at how Emma's behavior could be so unhorse-like. I dialed the phone.

I explained to Carol what I had found and took deep breaths while I waited. How wonderful it would be if I were able to clear my mind like Carol and communicate consistently and with detail. Whenever I wanted. To receive any animal's feelings. To receive the pictures they sent. To get at a gut level the concepts they were sharing and to hear their words pop into my brain. Wow. Perhaps my mind raced on too many channels at once or maybe God knew that if I had a better capability I would probably never speak to humans in favor of speaking to animals.

"OK, Emma is on the horn, shoot," Carol said, her voice jolting me back from my reflections.

"Emma, why did you move your bedding?" I asked, speaking into the silent expanse of my family room.

After a slight pause I heard Carol laugh.

I interrupted her mirth with my impatience. "Ok. What did she say?"

"This is very cute," Carol said. "Since you two have been living together Emma has been observing your behavior. She says, like you, she was simply rearranging the furniture. She says it took the entire day and it kept her busy. Hooves aren't designed to rearrange."

I couldn't help but join in the laughter that Carol couldn't seem to squelch.

"Emma, you're adorable," I said. "But, Carol, she can't see through walls to see what I'm doing." I strained my neck to the right to see better out the family room window and judge the distance from Emma's stall to my bedroom wall. About a hundred feet.

"You're right," Carol said. "Emma is able to use your eyes to see your world. She watches what you're doing through your eyes."

"I've been exposed to so many unusual things you would think that I wouldn't find it hard to comprehend things like that," I said, scrunching up my nose in disbelief. "Oops. Wait. I forgot. You've told me before that Emma sometimes uses my eyes to see something in the distance with more acuity. It never dawned on me that she would use it … to spy on me. This feels like something out of a Superman comic. X-ray vision or something. Do you know how preposterous this sounds? Could you imagine my trying to tell anyone at work about this?"

"I assume those are rhetorical questions," Carol said, giggling.

"Every time I think I have a handle on what Emma is capable of something else crops up," I said. My skepticism over telepathic animal communication had exhausted itself after the first couple of years of talking to Emma. But the things she did went beyond talking to her and hearing her voice. So much about Emma was unusual. "So, Emma, why are you watching me?"

"I didn't use to do it very often," Carol translated for Emma. "Now that we're living together I'm paying more attention to what you do."

"That's wild," I said. "I have absolutely no privacy. I can be spied on at any time. There are no keeping secrets. So do all animals do this?" I drew the multi-colored throw on my chair close around my shoulders and chest.

"Probably not," Carol replied. "Emma is unique. She spends a lot of time attending to what you're doing. I haven't heard of another animal doing that."

"Well, thank goodness she has to eat and is distracted by other things," I said, finding a way to assuage my concern over this form of boundless intimacy. "Actually, I guess it's very sweet that Emma finds me that interesting. Thank you, Emma."

"Anything else?" Carol asked.

I heard several loud barks over the phone and then Carol shushing. No doubt her dogs wanted her attention too.

"There's another strange thing she's doing," I said. "In the past Emma has been fastidious about her manners. Whenever I groomed her at the boarding stables, she never pooped in the aisle way or grooming area. She always waited until we got on the trail or outside in the arena."

"She clearly is a student of Emily Post," Carol said, laughing.

"Since we moved into our own place," I said, "she has started pooping in the grooming stall. In fact, she sometimes poops twice. It's annoying. The pungent smell in a closed space is overpowering. Then I have to clean up and haul the mess to the other side of the barn to the manure container. I'd like to know why. Better yet, I want to ask her to stop it."

I toyed with the corner of the crocheted throw, poking and weaving my fingers through gaps in the pattern while I waited for Carol's reply. Carol's laughter jingled across the line and I smiled. It must be another Emma-ism.

"Well, she's consistent in applying what she notices about you," Carol said. "She says she's simply copying what you do. She's doing what you do in your grooming area."

A chortle exploded from my gut when I got it. When I gave it a second thought, my light heartedness took another direction. It swung into a deep understanding. How endearing to be so deeply connected to this horse. How loving that she wanted to copy my behavior. I was stunned.

"Oh Emma, I'm touched. I'm amazed," I said. I sat still absorbing the love that I was feeling. I looked over to the barn again and sent wafts of my love to Emma.

"She is rather pleased with herself," Carol said.

"Emma, that's so sweet," I said, "but it's a bit different for horses. I appreciate what you're doing, but it would be a big help if you went back to your former ways. I'm tired at the end of the day and it would be one less thing for me to do, never mind the ripe aroma splatted on the floor. Please poop in your paddock or when we go for our walk."

"I'll try," Carol translated.

"Carol, if you have the time, I'd like to ask Emma a few other things," I said.

"Sure, go ahead," Carol replied. "I had one of those rare easy days at work, so I have the time and the energy."

"Emma, how do you like this new home?" I asked.

"Now that I'm here," Carol translated, "I realize how much I was affected by the tension at our last barn. I didn't understand how deeply the environment was affecting me. I'm much more relaxed now."

"Emma, I'm so happy to hear that," I said. "I had secretly hoped that being in your own place might help you calm down."

"Sometimes I know what is best for you better than you do and now you have done that for me." Carol translated.

"What does Emma mean?" Carol asked.

"I think I know," I said. "Whenever I was debilitated with a Chronic Fatigue relapse or its aftermath, Emma would often abruptly stop our training sessions. She would screech to a stone-cold halt of immobility. No matter what I did I couldn't get her moving again. I got the feeling she knew that I had reached my physical limit. Because I was concentrating on my riding and enjoying it so much, I wasn't paying any attention to what my body was saying. Is that right, Emma?"

"Yes, I knew your body's limits better than you," Carol translated.

"On the nights Emma froze like that," I said, "I surprised myself by nearly collapsing by the time I got to my car. I often had just enough energy to get home. If Emma hadn't forced me to get off, I would have gone past my physical endurance. Getting home would have been tough and perhaps might have led to another even more severe relapse. My health practitioners warned me to never get to the bottom of the energy barrel. If I wasn't careful, I might end up bed bound for weeks or months. Chronic Fatigue is a miserable illness."

"You two are so close that it makes sense you would be in sync with each other's needs." Carol said.

"Pretty cool, huh?" I said, "Emma, I know you don't share a fence line with any horses, but there are horses two doors down. Have you made friends with them yet?"

"Yes, but I have made other friends as well," Carol translated. "I like the wild animals who pass by to visit. I like the deer, but I had to learn about them."

"How so?" I asked.

"The first time the deer showed up," Carol translated, "I shouted out 'Hi guys, how are you doing?' That didn't work. The next time they came, I murmured, 'My, how kind of you to come.' That worked much better. They make good friends if you know how to talk to them."

"Well, isn't that a truism," I said. "You did something the other day that I'm curious about. Why did you dump your water tub over? You hadn't done that before. I felt as though you were telling me that something shocking had happened, but I didn't know what. It seemed related to someone who came to visit you."

"My friend was so thirsty," Carol translated. "He was so thirsty."

"Who was your friend?" I asked, feeling totally clueless.

"I'm getting a picture of a small rodent," Carol said. "It looks like a rat."

"My friend was miserable and terribly thirsty and was too ill to get to water for himself," Carol translated.

Emma transmitted the feelings of her friend into my body. I became thirsty like I had never been, and my body ached. The discomfort made me twitch in my chair. Then I realized what I had done. My muscles froze and my breathing stopped. A distressing pang of guilt jolted through my body. My skin shivered and sweated.

"I know what happened," I said, feeling miserable. "I put out bait for the rats in the barn."

My mind tried to assuage my guilt. After all, what was I supposed to do when I had spotted a couple of major league rats running across Emma's oat hay? The image of the rats nesting in and fouling her hay and eating the grain lodged on the stalks had been a completely repugnant picture. I knew that rodents could reduce the weight of a hay bale by several pounds. I knew mice could carry the hantavirus and wondered if rats could too. I hadn't even stopped to think before I put out the d-CON.

When my body stopped shuddering, I vowed to find other ways to rid the hay barn of rats. Or I would adopt Emma's magnanimous position - everyone needs to eat - and simply live with them.

I said goodnight to Carol and gratefully sank into my bed. Yet again Emma gave me a valuable lesson. I had been so unconscious. How could I be so cruel to rats, to another being?

Emma continued to entertain me by sharing her new-found friends. When I was grooming her at night, she would let me know when the raccoons were coming. I would peek out of the back window of the grooming stall to spot the marauders scampering across the back lawn. The raccoons were racketeers, stealing and bullying their way through life. They were total opportunists who emerged after dark, looking for mischief. I called one of the ring-leaders Guido and the other Bugsy and the brute that brought up the rear, Capone. I was very careful to keep the garbage can lids secured with a locking mechanism. The raccoon mafia would need to find another victim for looting.

Fortunately most of Emma's friends weren't so villainous. The skunk was mostly shy and liked living under the barn in peace. I called him Mahatma. The hawks seemed a bit aloof and above things. The gophers were grouchy. I went out to their bunkers and asked them to leave my lawn alone. They responded with aggressive and naughty language. Maybe they weren't such cute furry creatures after all.

The first sunny day after a series of winter rains, I wondered how I might give Emma a break. I knew she had been pent up in a small space for too long and would enjoy stretching her legs at liberty. The adobe mud in her paddock and adjoining pasture kept her confined to the area that had been well covered with quarter-by-dust (fine gravel). Adobe soil melted into gloopy glue in winter and could cause a horse to pull a tendon or ligament. Nasty stuff. Because the ground in her pasture wouldn't firm up until well into spring, I decided to let her run around the front and back lawns of the house.

I closed the entry gates to the road and removed all loose hoses or other trip hazards. Emma was leaning against the slatted gate next to her stall. She seemed to know something was up. The latch slid open with a grinding sound and I pushed the gate aside. Emma was free to wander about and explore all the property around the house. Except for her first day, she hadn't really had the opportunity to check out the front and back lawn and the professionally installed putting green near the side of the house.

Emma made her way down the path and headed across the back lawn. She stopped and raised her head. She snorted and her nostrils flared wide. She dashed forward and sprinted across the back lawn, across the driveway, over the front lawn, around the barn and down to the back lawn again. She jumped the low boxwood hedge surrounding the putting green and came to a halt smack dab in the middle. She showed no sign of lameness. The adrenaline rushing through her veins was probably masking any soreness in her feet. I noticed the skid marks and clumps of grass. I'd have to replace the divots later.

Seeing Emma on the golfing surface brought back a memory. I had always wanted to ride on a golf course. When I was a kid and had rented horses at Mar Vista Stables on Skyline Drive in San Francisco,

I often rode around Lake Merced. Looking through the chain link fence at the TPC Harding Park golf course, I had longed to ride there instead of on the bridle path next to the busy road. The thought of a gallop across the undulating lawns tantalized me.

Emma stood at full alert in the middle of the perfectly manicured velvet grass. She lifted herself into a powerful vertical rear with her hind legs fully extended and her front feet reaching to the sky. Then she came crashing down and leaped straight up with all four feet off the ground as if she were rebounding on pogo sticks. She landed from her explosion and turned her neck to look at me square on. Her eyes were bright, her ears perked forward and her nostrils gently pulsed. A warm glow and a deep sense of contentment permeated my body. Emma had transmitted what she was feeling. She was bursting with joy. My body responded and tingled with bliss.

The softness of her eye coupled with the delight I was feeling was one of those happenings that you tuck away as a gift from the Divine.

Chapter 6

Our new home provided a seclusion that was devoid of interference from anybody else's energies - horse or people. Both Emma and I seemed to be able to relax at a deeper level. A few minutes after entering my property, my guard came completely down. I placed one of those inexpensive plastic garden chairs in Emma's paddock. Toy for her and seating for me. Whenever I had the time, I would sit with her. My concerns, incessant naggings in my head, would dissolve, seep down through my spine into my feet, and scurry away into the earth. At times I felt as if I left my body, losing all sense of being a human. The solitude let us connect on some deep energetic plane, creating a gratifying camaraderie and a peace I didn't experience on my own.

During these quiet times I would fill my lungs as if I was breathing in what Emma and I shared. I wondered why the scent of a horse made me feel safe. Characterizing the smell was always a challenge. The odor wasn't floral or perfume-like, nor noxious or acrid. It wasn't reminiscent of grass or corn or oats or the other horsey comestibles. What, then, reduced my blood pressure, released the tension in my gut and let me feel whole? The aroma was an airborne therapy that cascaded into my nose, gentled my limbic system and soothed the terrors of my childhood that never seemed to completely abandon their claw-like grip on my soul.

Despite the joy and completeness I felt from this special connection to Emma, we both seemed to feel the stirrings of wanting something more. We had lost the physical intimacy of riding. Emma had always said she preferred being ridden - that it offered a closeness that ground work couldn't substitute. Every time I concentrated on what I could do to assuage this need, the image never quite materialized. What I conjured up faded under a filmy screen like layers of oxidation covering the brown metallic paint on my truck. That I wasn't riding anymore was making its absence felt throughout my body, leaving me yearning for something.

I couldn't ride just any horse. That would feel awkward and unconnected - almost robotic. I needed to feel the love and the commitment of a partnership. And now we both needed a distraction to fill our loss.

Our life had settled into a predictable rhythm, so my thoughts eased into a more expansive space. My health and strength limitations dictated that I needed a diversion that wouldn't take too much energy. What popped into my mind was that Emma and I were social creatures and we liked visiting with friends.

During the previous few years we had spent many evenings on the phone with Carol, often with me exhausted in my bed sidelined by another bout of Chronic Fatigue, Carol in her home and Emma in her stall. My illness made uncertainty a way of life and I treasured these talks for the social contact. Carol was someone we had both come to love and appreciate. When Emma and I were going through some of our most difficult times, Carol's clever and often pointed sense of humor found its way into the part of me that clung too strongly to a rigid viewpoint - a viewpoint that often needed to be adjusted. Carol's easy laugh ensured that in the process of letting go, I also released vestiges of self-consciousness. She had a way of revealing the comedy of it all, so I could forgive my flaws. At the end of a telephone session I often found myself better grounded and able to face life's challenges with less emotional binding.

Because so much of our association with Carol was over the phone, I thought it would be fun to invite her to dinner. We hadn't seen her in a couple of years, so it was natural to have her among the first on the list to join us in our new home. If I heard Emma correctly, and I was learning to trust that I was hearing her, she wanted Carol to see her new digs as well.

My invitation to dinner expanded when Carol asked if she could bring Bailey along. Apparently Bailey, Carol's dog, had been asking to meet Emma for some time. There was no question in my mind - an animal friend, what a splendid idea.

Bailey was one of three dogs Carol had when I first met her, and over the years Bailey and Emma had become friends. When Emma had been lost in the foothills of the Sierras, Bailey volunteered to keep vigil. She stayed awake all night in her home in Lafayette connecting to Emma telepathically to help guide her back to my friend's cabin. Even though they had never met and only communicated telepathically, Bailey seemed to be wise and provided a stabilizing influence on Emma.

Carol let me know before she came over that she would try to prepare Bailey for the meeting. She would warn Bailey that Emma was much bigger than any dog Bailey had ever seen. Bailey at about thirty pounds and Emma at nearly twelve hundred pounds made Emma forty times bigger than Bailey. I wondered what it would feel like to make friends with someone who was forty times bigger than me and whose eyes would be about level with the third story of a building.

Carol and Bailey arrived in the late afternoon on a winter day. Carol, with her fine, straight, brown hair pulled behind her ears and blue eyes full of life, sported one of those puffy jackets that promise warmth down to sub-zero temperatures. In the San Francisco East Bay with the sun shining the outside temperature was probably all of fifty degrees. Baily's green harness set off her chestnut spots. The little brown and white splotched dog trotted over the threshold behind Carol.

Carol and I snuggled into the two white, raw silk living room chairs placed on either side of the flagstone fireplace. Bailey, her drooping ears spread out on the floor, nestled down near Carol's feet. The cathedral ceiling with its open beams gave a light, airy feel to the room and the warmth from the dancing flames in the fireplace took away the chill. The flickering light from the fire licked Carol's face with a healthy glow. What a rare gift to lean back, hang out and catch up.

"Okay, Carol," I said, handing her a glass of mineral water from the tray on the glass coffee table. "What interesting animals have you been involved with recently?"

"I have many new friends," Carol said, putting her glass back down. "I was introduced to a woman who is active in pig rescue. She has several pigs at her home, four that live in the house and several more in pens in her backyard."

"That sounds like a whole lot of pigs," I said, wondering about their bathroom habits.

"And all of them are big," Carol said. "Each one that lives in the house has his very own couch and comforter. It's great fun to visit her. I especially like the slurping sounds the pigs make when she feeds them Hot Tamale candies. It's something you have to witness."

"Rescue work is tough," I said, filled with admiration for those who do it. "I bet you've heard some grim stories."

"Some of the pigs have been badly abused," Carol said. "Letting them talk about their experiences seems to help them adjust to their new life. One pig had been confined to the front-loading shovel scoop of a tractor with no way to move and no shelter."

"How horrible," I said and shivered despite being warm.

"It's not something I enjoy talking about," Carol said, her lips drawn tight. "I have heard too many sad stories."

"Okay," I said, sitting up a little straighter in my chair, "Any favorite characters among the pigs?"

"I did meet a pig that stole my heart," Carol said, pausing to sip her carbonated beverage. "He's called Pig-a-Lot because he's so huge. This pig is particularly intelligent and emotionally sensitive. Unfortunately he's suffering with terrible arthritis and because of his pain he's confined to a cushioned pen in the house. It's too hard for him to move."

"Does he get any stimulation?" I asked. I rose and tossed another log on the fire and then turned to top off Carol's glass.

"My friend does her best to give him toys and talk to him," Carol said, "but she works full time and has all the other pigs to care for."

"Poor guy."

"I've given this some thought," Carol said. "He and Emma might make good friends. He's been getting depressed from inactivity and with Emma retired from her career she might enjoy meeting him telepathically."

"Emma's mind hasn't been challenged the way it was when she was in full dressage training," I said, feeling a pang of that loss myself. "How would this work? I know that animals talk to each other over the airwaves. I remember when we asked Emma to connect us to the goose, Mathilda, so that we could telepathically talk to the bird. But Mathilda and Emma lived at the same stable. Now that I think of it. Bailey and Emma have never met and we know that they've visited with each other. So I guess this isn't such a strange idea after all."

"Yep," Carol said. "Animals talk across species and at distance regularly."

"Emma prefers visiting with animals when she's near them physically," I said. "I remember she had a hard time leaving her stablemate Spunky, the little pony, and said it wasn't the same when she didn't live next door to him. But I guess there isn't any reason why this wouldn't work."

"I would introduce them telepathically," Carol said. "Then wait and see if anything develops. Whether they continued or not would be up to them."

"Sure, why not?" I said. "Emma could only benefit from this meeting. She has often commented on intelligent animals she's met and how much she enjoys talking to them."

"Enough of my news," Carol said, her eyes twinkling. "What are you up to? Should I ask how work is going?"

"Gosh, anything I say will seem uninteresting and mundane compared to your news." I squirmed in my chair, thinking of what I might share that would be of note next to helping rescued animals. Certainly not the trials of my everyday job.

"Finding anyone that I can relate to at work is really hard," I said and felt my back twinge.

"Why do you say that?" Carol asked.

"Folks at this company are experiencing a generalized paranoia that seems to be created and fostered by upper management," I said and sipped from my glass. "I'm not into power plays or jockeying for position."

As I took a breath to continue, Bailey stood up, looked at me and padded across the living room to my chair. She strolled right over and plopped her body on top of my feet. I welcomed the warmth of her soft belly on my thin slippers.

"Wow, that's a first," Carol said not taking her eyes off Bailey. "Look how friendly Bailey is to you. That's very uncharacteristic of her. Bailey is usually quite reserved and somewhat aloof with anyone but immediate family or very close friends. It's a big deal for her to sit on someone's feet."

I looked down at Bailey, who returned the gaze with her large, liquid brown eyes. "Thank you, Bailey, for the honor." Bailey responded by wagging her tail with the characteristic thump, thump, thump on the oak hardwood floor.

When Carol mentioned Bailey's reluctance to approach or be approached by anyone to whom she was not close, I was surprised. But I shouldn't have been. Other folk's animals, even feral ones, often came up to me as if we were old friends. Many times I'd heard from bewildered owners, "I never saw him/her do that before." Since these kinds of greetings happened so often, I didn't view it as unusual. Now I had the opportunity to ask what was going on.

"Carol, why did Bailey do that?" I said and leaned over to rub behind her ears.

"Bailey says you are very familiar to her," Carol said. "And she knows you love animals."

"Familiar as in a prior life connection?" I asked.

"Yes," Carol said.

"That makes sense," I said, "and it also explains the unusual affinities I have enjoyed from so many different animals over the years. I must have loved a lot of them in prior lives."

My stomach gurgled reminding me food was waiting.

"Time for the hors d'oeuvres," I said, rising from my chair.

Carol followed me into the kitchen. The wooden cutting board and paring knife rested on the white tile countertop prepared for action.

While I chopped the jicama and continued my conversation with Carol, I spun around and headed to a cabinet to get a bowl. I filled it with water and put it on the ceramic tile floor.

"What are you doing?" Carol said, grinning like the Cheshire cat.

"What do you mean?" I said and looked up at her with surprise. I watched as Bailey waddled over to the bowl and lapped up the water.

"Why did you get Bailey water?" Carol asked.

"It occurred to me that she might be thirsty," I said, "So I put down a water bowl. That simple."

Carol laughed and looked at me with eyelids crinkled in mirth.

"Bailey asked you for a drink of water," Carol said, leaning on the kitchen counter. "Didn't you hear her?"

"Really? No," I said. "I didn't hear a thing. I just got the idea that she might be thirsty after her car ride over here." I put the knife down to think about what Carol had said. I had interrupted talking to

Carol to get the water for Bailey. Why would I suddenly stop what I was doing?

"I'm convinced you heard Bailey," Carol said, "You responded immediately following her request. I'm sure you're getting messages, but you may not be acknowledging what you know. This isn't the first instance when you seemed to know out of thin air exactly what needed to be done. One of these days you're going to have to stop calling me and trust that you hear perfectly well."

"I always thought when I anticipated a need, it was just good timing or a lucky coincidence," I said, finishing the placement of the baby carrots on the tray. "I guess I'm still reluctant to believe that I really hear animals other than Emma. Even with Emma I'm not always convinced that I'm hearing her correctly. Sometimes I have no doubt, other times I wonder."

Many of my conversations with Emma were emotionally charged, so it's not surprising that I wouldn't trust what I was intuiting or hearing. I always felt better getting the validation from Carol. Maybe I should buck up and believe in myself.

"I understand it can get murky when intense feelings are involved," Carol said, "but you can do this. You just need to trust. Have more confidence."

"Okay," I said. "Meanwhile, ask Emma if it was her idea or mine to have you over."

"Alright. Emma, did you hear the question from Diana?"

"Duh," Carol translated for Emma, "Like where else would my attention be when the two of you are together? Yes, it was my idea and I asked Diana to have you come over for a visit. Not only did I want to see you, I wanted you to check out my very own stall. The feeling is different when it's your very own. Much better."

"And here I thought it was my idea," I said and wagged my head back and forth.

After we cleaned up the appetizers, we went out the dining room door and up the path to the barn. The sun was moving below the bottom branches of the elm tree and we wanted Bailey to meet Emma while we still had good light. Bailey looked eager and trotted ahead. As soon as Bailey spotted Emma, she froze. She looked back at Carol and I saw the startled expression on her face. She hunkered down on the ground. She raised her head an inch at a time to look Emma over from top to bottom and then left to right.

"She's so BIG," Carol translated for Bailey.

"I warned you," Carol said, facing Bailey.

"I get that a big dog is big, but she's enormous." Carol translated for Bailey, "I've never experienced anything like this size before in any of my friends."

I watched as Bailey crouched lower as though she were trying to disappear into the ground. Emma reached her nose out towards Bailey, but the dog didn't reciprocate with any gesture. She remained planted a good few feet behind the paddock fence, well out of reach.

"Emma is laughing," Carol said. "She told Bailey that it would be just fine if they remained friends only over the airwaves. She was also a little hurt at first since she didn't think of herself as particularly big, but she understands Bailey's point of view. She's not offended."

"She's not what I expected," Carol translated for Bailey. "I'm not sure that I can get over the size difference."

"Don't worry." I said, looking over at Bailey while I reached out to stroke Emma's neck. "You've been a really good friend to Emma and I bet she never envisioned the two of you becoming playmates and romping around the school yard."

We returned to the house and scarfed up our vegetarian dinner. That evening after I said goodbye to Carol and her sweet companion, I returned to the living room to enjoy the remaining glow from the fireplace embers and the heat that radiated from the bricks. My mind drifted to memories of Bailey.

When I first met Bailey, I didn't realize how important she would become in our lives. One of the deeper experiences I had with connecting to animals was a gift Bailey had given me. Whenever Carol and I were on the phone talking to Emma, Bailey had the habit of joining the conversation. She tried to be of help whenever she could. On one occasion during a phone conversation, Carol tried to describe her kitchen layout, but I had a hard time visualizing it.

"Don't keep trying," I said. "I'll come visit you sometime."

"I have an idea," Carol said. "Bailey, would you please send a picture of the kitchen to Diana?"

Immediately a picture of a kitchen popped into my head. The picture wasn't from my imagination. The image was a little fuzzy, but I distinctly saw the L shape of the counters, the countertops, cabinets and what looked like a variety of objects on the countertops. I saw the placement of the stove, sink and window. I was mesmerized by the vision that had appeared in my head. At the time I had been new enough to telepathic animal communication to be stunned into silence.

"Wow, this is awesome," I said when I could speak. "It's a little blurry but I can make out the landmarks. Your kitchen seems to have a good layout for cooking. Lots of counter space."

The skeptical part of me questioned whether this could really be coming from Bailey. Was it that easy? Just ask the dog to send me a picture? Or maybe it was my overactive imagination pulling out an image from a design magazine. The scientist part of my brain had made a note to go see Carol's kitchen and compare the images. Later, I did. From the picture that had been sent to me, I could tell where Bailey had been sitting and sure enough the kitchen had been accurately depicted.

Bailey was more than just Emma's friend. She had been my guide in understanding yet another capability of animals.

I wondered what else I might learn from Bailey.

Chapter 7

Now that I was back being social I bounced up whenever the phone rang, expecting to hear whether the next guest had accepted our invitation. One evening, I responded to one of those clamoring rings, but found myself hesitating before I answered. I couldn't dispel a queasy feeling that slowed my movements. With sluggish resolve I carried the receiver over to a chair and descended with care. My finger quivered when I pushed the answer button. As soon as I heard Carol's voice my breath caught. I knew something was amiss.

"Bailey's body is failing," Carol said. Sadness glommed on to every word. "There is no hope of recovery. Her cancer is advanced. I've made a decision that's difficult. It's time to let her go. Bailey feels she's ready and is looking forward to leaving a body that's no longer functioning."

"Carol, I'm so sorry," I replied with my voice choking. I knew Bailey had been struggling with her health recently. She wasn't a young dog, so it wasn't unexpected. Yet I was never prepared for these kinds of transitions. A profound grief engulfed me with wrenching waves of pain. Maybe it was my own issues surrounding loss that caused the strong reaction. I struggled to speak. "I know how much you love Bailey. Is there anything I can do?"

"I've made arrangements with my vet to come to the house and put Bailey to sleep in a space that's comfortable for her," Carol said, her voice, scratchy. "You and Emma have known Bailey and are her friends. I thought it was important to keep you in the loop. I don't want you to come. I'm just calling to let you know what's going to happen. Don't call me afterwards, I'll be grieving."

"Thank you for telling us," I said and pictured the little brown and white spaniel.

"If you want to think of her," Carol said, "the vet will be coming to the house at 12:30 PM this Wednesday." Even over the phone I could feel Carol struggling for control.

"Of course," I said, my shoulders stooped. "I'll think of her then and send loving energy." I hung up the phone and wrapped my arms around my chest.

I still mourned the loss of my first dog and often found myself crying when I thought of her. She was one of those one-in-a-million beings. Losing her was so painful I couldn't face getting another dog. Perhaps thinking of Bailey brought back those memories and associated feelings. Strong feelings are a double-edged sword. The joys are phenomenal, but the lows are equally intense. I clenched my jaw to stop the trembling of my chin.

I pictured Bailey's kind face and sent her my love and appreciation. I reached for a tissue to wipe my eyes. I reminded myself that we might meet again in another life.

On Wednesday, the day began with my usual routines. I fed Emma and went to work. On the drive in I rocked back and forth in the bucket seat of my car until I realized what I was doing. My body was telling me that this was not a normal day. This was Bailey's last day in her body. Towards the end of the morning I felt Emma's presence. The feeling was not unfamiliar. Just as when loved ones enter the room and you sense it before you see them, I sensed Emma was near me. I felt reassured. I felt supported.

Even though I did my best to focus on my work, my eyes kept targeting my watch, zipping back every couple of minutes from the reports on my desk. At a quarter past noon I left work to find a place where I could be alone and open myself to the world of energy. I wanted to open my heart and send my love to Bailey without interruption. I would have to set aside the protective casing I had created to survive in the corporate world. I couldn't dismantle that weighty carapace in an instant.

I steered my car to one of the back roads that led to undeveloped land. On one side, the road was flanked by oat and wheat fields and on the other, lovely, white-faced Herefords grazed on the wild rye grasses. A few minutes before 12:30 PM, I pulled onto the shoulder of the country road. When the car clock showed exactly the half hour, I intensified my thoughts of Bailey.

My breathing slowed and my eyes caressed the horizon of golden grasses, their pale blonde hues a soothing color. I didn't know what to expect but reasoned that in this quiet period I would do my best to honor Bailey. I sent her my love, my gratitude and a request that we meet again.

I wondered if I should feel anything besides my own sadness. The only things that came into my consciousness were the sounds from the ticking of my large-dial Timex wristwatch and the occasional crow. I had been gifted so many unusual experiences that I was a bit disappointed that I didn't feel anything extraordinary. After what seemed like a respectful amount of time, I drove to a local feed store to visit with the owner and her small herd of miniature horses.

The owner greeted me, gave me a knowing nod and I followed her out of the store to her side yard. We sat down in the minis' pasture on the bales of straw that had been tossed out there as furniture. I hung out, letting the breeze chase my thoughts as they randomly popped into my consciousness. The little horses refreshed me and dispelled my emotional exhaustion. An exhaustion born from a toxic work environment, my ever-present illness and the daily challenges of life.

The palomino mini must have sensed my serious mood and came over and nuzzled my hand and rubbed against me. Unlike large horses, the minis were far more demonstrative in their social behaviors. If they could, they would climb into your lap, and some of them tried. Loving on them and watching their antics lightened my heart. They could be real clowns. After a good half hour, my need to be responsible forced me to stir and head back to work. I rose with reluctance. The transition from the world of horses to the work place was difficult. How jarring to leave a world I seemed to understand and in which I felt comfortable, to return to work and immerse myself in the world of commerce, and the human interplays with which I never seemed to feel at ease or quite comprehend.

I reversed my direction, heading over the same roads I had traveled out. My Mustang 5.0 idled at twenty-five miles an hour. No one was behind me so who cared that the speed limit was more. No amount of self-talk could get me to rush back to work. I checked the clock – it was nearing 1:30 PM. I had plenty of time to get back for my late afternoon meeting. My time out of office didn't matter anyway. As a corporate officer no one kept a clock on me and besides, it was rare for me to take a long lunch.

The car coasted along the country rode and I let my thoughts drift. My mind took in the soft, blue sky that fluttered down and brushed the undulating pastureland, which seemed to rise with its grassy fingers in a gesture of greeting. With no preamble, an image burst into my awareness. This was no thought or picture I retrieved from memory. The origin was from outside of me. The image was so strong I started to lose sight of the road. I swerved over to the gravel shoulder and threw the car in park. My eyes went out of focus, so I could concentrate on the picture in my mind. I was mesmerized as it took a clearer shape. Somehow, I knew that Emma had invited me to join her in this moment.

In the vision I saw Carol's back as she was bending over Bailey. From somewhere within me I knew that the point of view was mine. Emma was across from me and on the other side of Carol. My arms were stretched out to either side in an arc and Emma was vertical, her belly facing me, with her front legs spread wide. My hands touched her front hooves and our bodies and arms encircled Carol and Bailey. I couldn't help but think how weird that was. Horses don't join hands around a circle.

Bailey was lying on her side curled up in layers of soft bedding.

Although the person bending over Bailey had thick, wavy hair and Carol has thin, straight hair, I knew it was Carol. The light that illumined the scene was a vibrant, aqua blue. Carol was wearing a garment that draped with gentle folds over the back of her head and shoulders. As I sat observing the unfolding scene in my mind, I felt as if I was being immersed into a bath of something divine. I was encased in a feeling so holy that I felt as if I was watching Mother Mary bent over baby Jesus in the cradle. The moment felt pure and full of maternal love. The intensity of this bath of love was overpowering and irradiated each cell of my body with a vibration of gentle sweetness. Then a series of beautiful, multi-colored sparks and soft patterns of muted light like the aurora borealis emerged from Bailey's body and fluttered upward. The light formed waves of pastel colors that shimmered as sheer curtains would in a gentle breeze.

At that moment I knew I was witnessing Bailey's spirit leaving her body. My shoulders shook and my body trembled in losing our worldly connection to this good friend.

Then as quickly as it came, the image that held me captivated vanished, leaving me staring at the asphalt road ahead. I sat motionless, my mind as empty as the cavernous blue sky above. My awe held me in check for several minutes.

When my emotions rebounded, they oscillated between grieving and being dazed by the power of the image I had just seen. I had never witnessed anyone's death and I felt honored to be a part – to be let in to this private moment. Emma's presence felt even stronger. I thanked her for including me in Bailey's end-of-life transition.

I shook my head, stiffened my back and took a deep breath, doing my best to snap myself into work mode. I wondered if other people had these kinds of experiences and how they managed to switch from gentle, love-filled moments back to harsher interactions. The thought of leaving this world that I had just joined and certainly preferred shocked my sensibilities. But I had to. I needed to make a living. I didn't want to shift my energies so drastically, but the goal of my employment was to carry out the corporate objective of improving shareholder equity. I turned the key in the ignition.

That night when I got home from work, I went out to the barn to feed Emma. She was waiting for me at the paddock gate. I ducked under the hot wire gate and threw my arms around her neck. She turned her head and hugged me back. I cried. Her tears were silent.

Back in the house, I debated whether to call Carol. She had told me she wouldn't be answering the phone. I don't know why I decided to make the call. The decision was driven by a compulsion rather than by a conscious, intellectual choice. Carol had already told me of her need to grieve alone. I usually respected people's wishes, so my dialing the phone was out of character. A part of me felt guilty disturbing her space. Something impressed upon me the need to tell her about the vision I had seen and what I thought I had witnessed. I would leave a message on her phone machine to call me whenever it would suit her.

To my surprise Carol picked up after the second ring.

"I'm sorry if I'm disturbing you," I said and held my breath.

"I wasn't going to pick up," Carol said, her voice sounding raspy, "but something forced me to do it."

"Well, something forced me to call you," I said. I hoped my voice carried as much compassion as I felt.

"Bailey is gone," she said, forcing out the words. "Her close animal friends and my sister were with us during the vet's visit." Carol paused. "She left peacefully."

"I had a vision of her passing," I said. "I'm still in a state of wonder as I remember the pictures Emma sent. Would you like me to share it with you?"

"Yes, yes," came the strong, unambiguous reply.

"Bailey reached out to Emma," I said, "and included us." I paused to regroup my swirling emotions and to find the words to portray the depth of the experience and how connected I felt to Bailey.

I painted a word picture of the ring Emma and I had made surrounding Carol and Bailey. When I began to describe Carol's appearance, she interrupted me.

"I had thick, wavy hair," Carol said, interjecting her thought before I could go on.

"How did you know that?" I asked in astonishment.

"In my heart I know that I have thick, wavy hair," she replied. "What you saw in your vision is what I believe at some level to be true."

"Speaking of anomalies," I said, "This experience didn't happen at 12:30 PM. Closer to 1:30 PM. I was in my car driving back to the office."

"That's when it happened. The vet had an emergency call," Carol said, "and came to my home later than planned. He had called and said he would come as soon as he could. I was appreciative he was willing to make a house call."

"That explains the timing," I said.

"I really miss Bailey." Carol said her voice softening.

"I know you do," I replied, "I miss her too. I'll keep both of you in my thoughts."

Later that week I came home to a ringing phone. I grabbed the receiver, settled into my comfort chair in the family room and tossed my mail on the coffee table.

"I have a need to let you know something," Carol said. "Last night Emma paid me a visit."

I knew that Emma was feeling deeply for Carol and her grief for losing Bailey. Sometimes I knew things with certainty. This was one of those times. I could feel Emma join me and I could feel her emotion of sadness.

"Emma came to me and took me for the ride of my life," Carol said. "I don't think I could describe it even if I wanted to. And I don't want to. I just wanted you to know she has been actively trying to help me mourn Bailey."

"God bless Emma," I said. "That sounds like her. I know you said you don't want to describe the visit, but I'm curious to know anything that involves Emma."

Carol paused before replying. "Because I really don't want to talk about what happened, I won't say much. It's personal and this is all I feel I can tell you. Emma took me for a ride off the earth and into worlds not known to us."

I sat stunned. Emma taking people to other worlds? Not on Earth? I knew she had faculties that were beyond most beings, but this seemed even stranger. Every time I got used to one of the things she could do another one seemed to manifest. My amazing Emma.

I hung up the phone and headed to the barn with a bag of carrots.

Chapter 8

I only worked a half day on Friday. I wanted to get an early start on enjoying the weekend. I sat down with a book and vegged out. An unseasonably warm winter sun shone bright and blazed in a gentle heat through the picture window of my family room. Emma was munching an extra flake I threw her in the two-stall barn out back. Semi-rural life at its best - living with your horse. I sighed with the contentment of a completely relaxed person. The phone's clamor forced me up from the delicious novel I had been reading and from the world it had invited me to enter. Disturbed, I snatched the receiver off the wall phone in the kitchen to restore the silence that had enveloped me.

"Diana, I need your help," the stressed female voice on the other end blurted out.

"Elaine. What can I do?" I said, lowering myself onto an old spindle back chair. I gazed out the bay window of my kitchen at the granddaddy elm glimmering in the sunlight. Concern and empathy dissolved my annoyance at the interruption.

"Tom is in the hospital. Kaiser," she paused. "In Walnut Creek."

My heart quaked. My body wrenched. Tom. I hadn't thought about him in a couple of years. Tom. The person who was so kind to Emma when she first came into my life. Tom. The man everyone at the boarding stable loved. And I had been one of them.

"What? What happened?" My hand clutched the receiver. My mind whirred conjuring up the worst. "A riding accident?"

I heard Elaine take a deep breath.

"No, not an accident," she said. "He has AIDs. His relatives are on their way here. From Oregon. To be with him. He's in the hospice wing." Her words came out staccato.

"What? I knew he was HIV positive," I said. "He sometimes spoke of his T-cell count which was always in the normal range. The last time I saw him he had pink, almost chubby cheeks and looked great." I gulped. He's too young, too full of life.

"The disease progressed. All of a sudden," Elaine said. "As soon as I found out he was hospitalized, I called him. He won't let me. Come visit him." Elaine's stress constricted her vocal cords mutating her lovely voice into a high-pitched, grating sound. How unlike Elaine, the mistress of composure and self-assurance. I'd never known her this upset. The tension in my body rose in sympathy.

"Why won't he?" I asked, not able to think of any reason. Elaine and Tom were good friends. The three of us had often hung out together when we kept our horses at the same boarding stable. When I left that boarding stable, Elaine and Tom continued with the close friendship.

"He doesn't want me to see him. I don't know why," she said, her speech still strained, but better controlled. "I'm beside myself. I need to see him."

Then it hit me. TV programs of late stage AIDs patients had revealed the devastation of the disease – the sores, the debilitation and the wasting. I shuddered. Elaine was currently a clothes model and had been a runway model at one time, who made her living on her looks. As careful as Elaine was in her dress she was equally careful about her environment. She couldn't bear the untidiness of a cut leaf so when it was time to trim the ivy or boxwood in her garden, she eschewed the brutal hedge trimmer, preferring to sculpt each tendril or stem by hand. Maybe Tom thought his appearance might shock her.

I attempted to picture Tom ill but had a hard time imaging him other than as I'd known him. Very much engaged in life. He was one of those rare individuals who combined good looks with a mix of endearing personality traits. Tall, with vibrant brown eyes, he enticed the ladies with a sensuous mouth that easily formed into a soft smile somewhere between an innocent hello and a sly beckoning. His laughter came easily, often associated with his gentle sense of humor. He took great care to avoid hurting anyone's feelings, choosing precise language with grace and an ease that was second nature to him. He seemed to have a boundless capacity to negotiate delicate subjects with charm and wit. He would melt anyone's heart.

"You need to do something," Elaine said. "I didn't know who else to call."

"Why me?" I asked. "Tom and I were friends once, but you've been closer to him. I haven't seen him in a couple of years."

"Because I know you can do this," Elaine said. "I'm counting on you."

"I hate to repeat myself, but what about me might be of help," I said.

"Who else?" Elaine shot back.

"Okay. Let me talk to him." I said, sighing and not at all knowing what I would say, but responding to Elaine's need for support.

I hung up the receiver and stared out the kitchen window to the back lawn and the dancing shapes of shade cast by the sprawling branches of the elm tree. My mind, unshackled by directed thought, wandered. Emotions took command and spilled out from every nook in my body.

Tom. My heart ached with my love of Tom and for the love we shared for animals, especially horses. In addition to all his engaging qualities, what made him a truly unique individual was the way he loved horses. He knew how to love unconditionally, completely and unselfishly. The maimed, the wounded, the ones that no one wanted found a home with Tom. Although he was intelligent and educated, he was not financially well-off. He would have loved to be able to set up a camp for his horses, but he was barely scraping by himself. He was a city boy who made his living on the lower rungs of the corporate ladder. Too much responsibility was hard on him, though his strong work ethic and wisdom in handling personnel issues sometimes thrust him into positions of authority.

Most of us at the barn weren't surprised when Tom quit the corporate life to teach riding and provide other services for the horse owners at the barn. What living he earned was used to support the rehabilitation of his small family of horses. They were often stabled in different barns with a variety of living arrangements. Given his limited salary, creativity was the hallmark of the way he managed to meet the needs of his ever-burgeoning herd.

Whenever Tom traveled the countryside, he kept his eye out for the neglected horse. He didn't see their scars, handicaps, psychological wounds or greying hairs. He seemed to see the glow of each horse's inner being and what they could become - he would fall in love.

Tom rehabilitated his charges with the help of dentists, chiropractors and massage therapists. After the horses had been fattened up on hay, vitamins and other supplements, he would pair them with one of his students who had fallen in love and was eager to make a happy purchase. I sighed, remembering all the providential matches Tom had made.

A squirrel caught my eye and brought me back from my memories. The bundle of twitching red fur darted across my back lawn straight to his target, stopping to scoop an errant acorn that had tumbled over from the tree next door. He looked composed and self-assured. Surely he must have the ingenuity I currently lacked. How I would convince Tom to see Elaine eluded me.

I rose from the kitchen chair and went into the spare bedroom where my books and picture albums were sequestered. The fat, red binder was crammed with photographs of friends and their horses. I fingered through the pages until I found pictures of Tom. My heart swelled with memories of his kindnesses. He was a true animal advocate and lucky for me he was one of the few people I'd ever met who understood me. I could tell him anything and he would know where I was coming from. I flipped to a random page, which held a single picture. There at the barn was the three of us, Tom, Elaine and me.

I wondered how to help Elaine. I'd sleep on it before I'd call Tom at the hospital. The new day often brought clarity to my thoughts. Please God, help me out.

The next morning I dialed the Kaiser Hospital number and the receptionist put me through to Tom's room.

"Hey, Tom," I said when he picked up. "I understand you're not feeling too well," I managed to say, relieved that my voice sounded somewhat normal.

"Oh no, I'll be back riding in a couple of weeks," he managed to get out with a weak and wispy voice.

Why does he think he's in hospice? But then again, it was just like Tom to minimize the unpleasant. He was an Olympic athlete in the art of denial. "I was wondering if I might come visit you," I asked. I held my breath, half expecting to be rejected like Elaine.

"That would be great," he said. "How about this morning?"

"Absolutely," I said, letting out the breath I was holding. I returned the receiver to its cradle and grabbed the car keys on my way to the front door.

Arriving empty handed didn't feel right. I stopped by a florist to pick up an attractive arrangement. The bouquet needed to be in full bloom. The impact should be immediate and with the flowers at peak beauty. From what Elaine had relayed, I wasn't sure how long Tom would be conscious enough to enjoy them.

Returning to the car, vase in hand full of bright, perky daylilies, I noticed that the sky was overcast and the air had a heavy, moisture-laden feel. The weather was matching my mood. The trip to the hospital gave me time to collect some inner strength and get control of my emotions before I faced Tom. I knew I loved his generous heart and felt connected to him at a very deep level. Even if it was only as two lost children who had endured early life abuse.

I dawdled, going well under the speed limit. My mind splashed from one memory pool to another. Images of Tom gurgled out from long forgotten experiences.

We had met when I had first bought Emma and had her delivered to a boarding stable nearer my house. Our relationship had grown when Tom scaled back his corporate life and began offering fee-based services at the barn. I jumped at the chance and enlisted him to turn Emma out in one of the outdoor paddocks when I was at work. Each day he would let me know how long she was able to be kept outside and which of her behaviors might be of interest. In typical Emma fashion, when she got bored she assigned ordinary objects toy status. One day she focused her attention on a nearby water hose. Apparently, she knelt, stretched her neck out under the lowest rail and carefully worked the hose free and then dragged it into her paddock, breaking the pipe and flooding the area. Witnesses reported seeing her roll in the mud with joyous squeals and then splash about in her horse-made mini-pond. Tom thought Emma was very clever to entertain herself and exhibited great creativity in the way she managed to get the hose and dislodge the pipe. A child could not have a better report card than the one constructed by Tom.

As I got to know Tom better, a pattern regarding his human relationships emerged in his behavior. The closer he got to anyone, the more he ignored them. As our friendship matured, it troubled me that one day he would act as if we had hardly met and then the next be his usual warm self.

On the days he was friendly our conversations would often delve into personal topics. On one such occasion Tom shared some of his history. He said he was troubled with bouts of severe depression and suicidal tendencies. We talked about the consequences of suicide and I shared with him my understanding of why that would be a very miserable and unwise thing to do. He went on to say he was HIV positive as a result of his knowingly engaging in unprotected high-risk sex. At this point, a thought permeated my brain with such force that goose bumps rose all over my body. I realized that if Tom could simply survive this life to a natural death he would accomplish something big. Whenever this kind of knowing came to me, I always felt compelled to share its content. I told Tom the thought I'd received. His face froze and then contorted followed by heaving sobs. His response surprised me. I felt guilty for the distress I'd caused.

When Tom's crying abated, he looked over at me and said, "I know what you've said is my truth." He gasped and then continued. "Starting when I was quite young my mother raped me over and over. I didn't know what was happening. There were other times, other things she did. I feel better now that I've told you. I haven't been able to talk about this with anyone."

"I understand," I said and reached over and held Tom's hand. Tears dripped from his face with each spasm of his body.

The closeness that Tom and I had experienced during that conversation didn't last. Perhaps Tom had a hard time trusting women. I knew that feeling. My past had scarred me too. With all my own vulnerabilities, I had a hard time trusting men.

Our friendship, never too close for too long, drifted along pleasantly for the two years that I had boarded at Pine Knoll Equestrian Center. We occasionally would go out to dinner or a movie. I once had painted a cottage he rented in his favorite color. He couldn't believe that someone would do that with no expectation of compensation. He did so much for others. Doing something for him was a privilege.

And now Elaine had brought Tom back into my life.

I parked the car in the hospital's parking lot. Tom's hospice floor was easy to find. The directions were excellent and patient names were listed on the walls next to each door. Before entering his room, I paused and prepared myself to show no reaction. I wanted to be able to absorb his appearance and quell any overt responses before he saw me. I slipped through the door. Thank God his name had been clearly displayed on the entry to his room or I wouldn't have believed that was him in the bed.

His round, boyish cheeks were gone, replaced by thin, pale skin stretched tightly over his face bones. His plump, gently curved belly was missing from the skeleton outlined under the sheet. Despite his depleted physical state, the energy in his room didn't in any way resemble a room in a hospital, much less one in the hospice wing. Brightly colored balloons, several vases of fresh, yellow flowers, and a huge bulletin board with happy pictures of his former horses and students festooned the space. Joy and love suffused this room.

Tom's niece and nephew rose from their chairs next to the bed when they spotted me. After introductions, the niece explained that Tom had just been given some painkillers. She then stretched out her arms and took the vase I had brought and placed it on the table with the other flowers. Moving towards the door, both politely excused themselves, offering me time alone with Tom. Exhausted from travel, they assured me they welcomed a break.

Tom opened his eyes and looked at me. I wasn't sure he knew who I was, but he grinned and welcomed me with a faint wave of his hand. I slid a chair close to the head of his bed and settled down. Tubes, bags, and beeping machines surrounded us. My hand rested on the edge of his bed. Each time he faded into unconsciousness, I murmured the name of God, soliciting His presence. Within a few minutes a tender love rushed over me. Gentle washes of pure, divine love bathed me and suffused the room with light. Cascading waves of divine force overwhelmed me. Gravity seemed to be suspended. My body became weightless and formless.

My gaze caressed Tom's face and my lungs expanded and relaxed to match his breathing rhythm. All the supportive energy I could muster was directed to Tom. My muscles melted into putty with the loving response. Perhaps God cannot resist His lovers. His presence felt powerful. I don't know how long I sat there, but the shadows cast by the window had migrated into different shapes.

The morphine-induced sleep eased out on kitty paws and Tom drifted into consciousness as peacefully as he had left it. His eyes cleared and he looked at me with curiosity. As soon as he was fully awake, he smiled warmly and greeted me by name.

"How is Emma doing and how is your training progressing?" he asked, eager as ever to know about the horse for whom he had taken such delight and care.

Sharing the highlights of the last few years seemed a good place to start. First, I shared how well Emma had been progressing in her athletic development. Next, I couldn't help but introduce Tom to my wonderful discovery – telepathic animal communication. I felt that concept might be something that he could embrace. Tom was fully involved in the lives of animals and might enjoy knowing the suspicion that we held was true - animals are fully sentient and capable of complex emotions.

Tom listened, fully attentive while I told him about Carol, the animal communicator who was the sister of a good friend, and how lucky we were to now have the facility to telepathically talk to the animals we loved. He smiled when he heard that telepathic communication worked using words, pictures and feelings. His questions confirmed he was intrigued by these ideas. How like him to embrace a new concept in his typical non-judgmental way.

"I can't wait to get back to the barn," Tom said. "To my horses. I miss all of them. I won't be here that long."

I ignored Tom's statement of his imminent discharge from the hospital and continued sharing anecdotes of animal conversations I'd had. He listened with all the focus he could exert. After about twenty minutes of conversation, I was not sure how much more he could comprehend. He started to drift away. Perhaps tired.

Tom's relatives returned and in silence we looked at each other with knowing. He clearly was very ill. We were all so sure that he was near death that we were pained by his insistence that he would be up and riding in no time. But then again, perhaps he was right. Stranger things have happened in life.

"Tom," I said and rose from the chair. "I'd like to come and visit you tomorrow. Will that work for you?"

"That would be most welcome," Tom replied, a wide smile beaming out an embrace. "I enjoy all visitors even though the staff here is helpful and friendly and I lack for nothing. I'm really happy to see you and to get news of Emma. I've always liked her and thought she was a special horse."

"Okay then, I'll come back tomorrow," I said. Then changing my voice to a direct no nonsense tone, I said, "Elaine is anxious to see you and I plan to bring her with me." My shoulders rose to military attention and my back stiffened. I extended my energy with as much force as I could project. At the same time, I erected a shield with the intention of stifling a negative response.

Tom took a long look at me and I stared back with all the force of personality that I had. In that chasm of quiet I held my breath and my heartbeat seemed suspended. Then almost as if he didn't have full control of his reaction, he nodded a feeble gesture in agreement.

"That's great," I said with an enthusiasm that radiated out of every pore. With a smile on my face I stroked the back of his hand. An inner sigh released the tension in my body. I knew in the way I know things to be true that seeing Elaine would be good for both. Warm adieus accompanied my departure.

As soon as I was outside of his room, my muscles reorganized. They came into a structure more capable of dealing with daily life. Not so open, not so vulnerable. To prepare for the assorted energies life brings, my mind expanded from its single focused concentration. With this shift, several emotions charged through the gateway of my heart. They swirled around and through me. The grief of losing a friend was clearly there. But it was blended with a fantastic infusion of divine force and something else, something strong but unidentified.

In the parking lot my thoughts turned to Emma. Her energy joined me – Emma was online. No, that wasn't accurate. She was present the entire time I was with Tom. What was the difference then? My mind cleared. Her energy was stronger now. Oh, Emma wants me to say something to Tom. No amount of effort clarified the content of her message. My intuition knew her message was important. I would call Carol. She would hear more than I could in my current state.

I drove home wondering what Emma wanted to say.

Chapter 9

By the time I arrived home, I realized that my visit to Tom had completely undone me. His pale, gaunt body broadcast the severity of his illness. Loss, imminent loss or just the thought of loss ripped me apart. I grieved hard and long. Probably not so unusual among those of us without family ties and who suffered from severe abandonment issues.

My family room offered me refuge from life's stressors. I plopped down on my beige and aqua polka dot sofa. My body stretched out and I watched sparse, filmy clouds meander over the elm tree on their way north. The fog had lifted yielding to a beautiful, peaceful day. I soaked up the healing vibes nature was offering up.

Deep breaths helped center me before I picked up the phone. Carol was home when I called and after the opening greetings I asked her if she had time talk to Emma. She did and listened to my account of my visit to Tom. After a few silent moments Carol heard Emma.

"Emma is glad you called me," Carol said. "She does have something she wants to tell Tom. She says it's very significant. She wants you to thank him for teaching her how to be in relationship with human beings."

"What!" I said. "What do you mean, Emma?" I sounded more demanding than I intended.

"When you got me," Carol translated for Emma, "I was terribly sad and disconnected. I couldn't see a future for myself. I was bitterly unhappy and didn't know how to be in the world. I felt that way starting when I was still a young foal. Tom was the first person to teach me about love from a human being."

I was stunned by what Emma said. Our similarities in life were uncanny. Her words resonated in my body. I had never thought to describe my early life that way, but the truth of it was an epiphany. Acknowledging truth helped free me from the bindings of my upbringing. It wasn't until I entered a spiritual path with a beloved spiritual advisor who was a master of love that I was able to do the work of deep healing. And that person was Tom for Emma.

"But Emma, I loved you from the beginning," I said, both surprised and hurt. "You are my horse. I chose you and gave you my heart."

"But Tom loved me unconditionally," Carol translated putting emphasis on the last word. "You were riding me and you wanted me to walk, trot and canter. You had expectations of me. It made me anxious because I wanted to please you. Our relationship was based on your riding me. And that meant I had to get my feet organized. When I was young, I had lost so much confidence in myself that I wasn't sure that I knew how to move."

One of those break-through understandings bolted out of the ether and plunged itself with clarity into my brain with such force that my body jerked. I knew that Emma had a wretched beginning in life, but I didn't realize how utterly broken she must have been. Every horse comes into this world knowing how to move. They must. They are preyed upon. Within an hour of birth, foals can stand up, nurse and walk. Within a couple of hours, they can run along the side of their mother. That a horse could be cut off from her own naturally given ability was inconceivable. The depth of the misery and pain needed to cut Emma off from her birthright took root in my body. I wondered if Emma was sending me her feelings. The emotions overpowered me and interrupted my breathing. My breath alternated between spasms and gasps.

"Emma, I'm so sorry," I said, when I could at last speak. "Now I get it. For you to be so detached that you had no confidence in your natural gaits meant you were really damaged when you were young. It's tantamount to not trusting that you know how to breathe. That's so basic. I'm so sorry." I felt my heart breaking and I mopped at the tears that expressed the anguish of a wounded soul.

"We would have eventually gotten there," Carol translated. "We would have reached an understanding with each other through love. It would have taken longer. Tom loved me and wanted nothing from me. He loved me in a way that made it safe for me to risk my heart. It's very important that Tom knows how grateful I am for the gift he gave me." Carol paused and I listened to her breathing before she continued translating. "Please repeat what it is you are to say because it's very important for Tom to hear and understand what I'm saying."

Emma's request whipped my sadness into the background. At first, I was taken aback that my horse was asking me to recite the message that I was to take to Tom. But then she probably knew how emotionally fragile I felt and that my mind was shattered. After repeating her message, Emma declared I had it right. I didn't have much time to consider that I had just experienced something like a role reversal before another thought entered my mind.

"Why don't you communicate directly with Tom yourself?" I asked. "You've been very successful entering people's dreams."

"Entering dreams is hard for me and exhausting," Carol translated. "I can't do it too often. But it's important that Tom hear this consciously. I will try to enter his dreams as well, if I can, but please talk to him for me. He is near death. It's very important that you see him soon."

"How do you know he's near death?" I asked, jolting upright on the sofa.

"The spirit horses are gathering," Carol translated.

"What does that mean?" I asked. "Carol, do you know?"

"Living animals can see the essence of animals who are dead," Carol said. "They're much more aware of the astral world than we are. When death is close for animals, they jump to the other side and start spending more time with their spirit friends. For them death is a natural progression of dying and rebirth. They have a sense of past lives, see departed friends, and have a calm acceptance of the circle of life. When they are ready to go, their spirit does it readily, though their body takes time and is often reluctant to relinquish its connection to life force."

"I wish it was that easy for humans," I said.

"Oh, I just heard from Emma," Carol said. "She says she was successful in entering Tom's dreams."

"Good. Emma," I said. I felt relieved and delighted. "You do such wonderful things in people's dreams."

"Be sure to see Tom in the morning," Carol translated. "He is more lucid then and he will stand a better chance of understanding what you are going to tell him."

"Yes, I'll be sure to go in the morning," I said.

"This is really strange," Carol said. "There are many voices in my head. This has never happened before. I can't make it out. There are too many voices. I can't understand what they're saying. It's making me crazy. Emma, what's going on? Who are these voices?"

"They are the voices of all of the horses who are now living and who have known Tom's love," Carol translated.

Carol seemed flustered. "Emma, can you request that they not speak to me directly? Can you be their voice? Can you tell me what they're saying?"

"Yes. I can do that," Carol translated for Emma. A moment passed. "They want Diana to take a message to Tom. They are counting on her to do that for them. They are very present with him."

I thought about what Emma was saying and remembered the joy

and love I felt when I visited Tom. "Tom's hospital room must be very full," I said. I attempted to put some lightness in my voice to ease the tension I was feeling.

"They want you to tell him that, when he dies, they will be there for him," Carol translated. "They will make a bridge to the other world. When he passes by, each horse will stand at attention to salute him. Not at attention as humans know it, but each horse will strike a pose that for each one represents the highest tribute of respect and love. There are many horses that will do this. They will be there for him and they will carry him with their bridge to the other side."

"Carol, do you have as many goose bumps as I do?" I asked.

"It's very, very important that you carry this message to him," Carol continued translating for Emma. "There are many horses who are counting on you."

"But Tom is in denial," I said, feeling tremendous responsibility to Emma and the other horses. A responsibility I wasn't sure I could carry out. "How can I tell him he's dying when he doesn't want to face that fact? He thinks that he's going to be back to his normal life in a couple of weeks."

"Diana, I know you'll find a way," Carol translated for Emma.

Emma had more confidence in me than I felt. I sat stunned and tried to digest all that was shared. For many years animal communication had been second nature to me. This experience seemed far more expansive. There was a part of me that felt honored that the horses trusted me. What they were saying and wanted communicated felt big.

After I said good night to Carol and Emma, I phoned Elaine to let her know that Tom would see her and that we should go in the morning. Her relief was palpable and her expression of appreciation sincere.

I shared with Elaine what Emma and the other horses had said. Despite her inability to accept that animals could talk she expressed her concern about what the horses requested me to convey to Tom. Elaine fully understood how hard it would be to broach a subject with

Tom that he refused to accept. That Elaine was touched by the horses' request surprised me, especially knowing that she considered this animal communication business to be nonsense.

Not feeling secure in the messages that I was to deliver, I suggested to Elaine that we drive to the hospital together instead of meeting there. I needed the extra time with Elaine to muster the support I'd need to deliver Tom his message. Elaine was happy to help me. Besides, she felt better going with me since I was the entry ticket to Tom who had been refusing to see her. She would pick me up the next morning.

First thing in the morning Elaine's navy-blue Corolla whisked into my driveway. We headed to the same florist I had visited the day before, where I had bought the arrangement of scented daylilies for Tom. With his color blindness, yellow was one of the few colors he saw and one he really enjoyed. Elaine picked out a handful of gently drooping sunflowers, their golden petals happily radiating out from the round, chubby, brown centers. While the florist was choosing the best flowers and greenery, Elaine and I looked at each other and couldn't keep it together. We fell into each other's arms and wept. We hugged and cried until our runny noses forced us apart to search our pockets for tissues. The florist handed us the sunflowers, which had been artfully mingled with willowy greens. Vase in hand, these two teary-eyed friends drove to the hospital.

When we entered Tom's room, we were greeted with an energetic welcome. His personality was back, upbeat and charming. After an exchange of warm banter and a heartfelt hug for Elaine, Tom turned to me with a bright, effervescent smile. "You'll never guess who I dreamed of yesterday."

"I don't have to guess," I said. "I know who. Did you enjoy Emma's visit?"

Tom's eyes sparkled and his smile widened to an open grin. "It was wonderful. I can't say exactly what happened. I just know it was glorious."

Tom's statement provided me with the opening I needed to deliver my messages.

"You know, Tom," I said, "I'm glad that happened because Emma has a message for you. She specifically asked that I tell you this." In the best way I knew how, I shared how much his love had meant to Emma and how it had affected her.

When I finished Emma's story, I watched Tom's face for a reaction. At first he stared straight ahead and then a wave of energy spread across his body. His face lit up and radiated joy. The room seemed suffused with his delight. His cheeks pinkened. His back seemed to get a little more strength and he sat up unaided. Tom struggled for composure and then tried to speak. He managed to drawl, "So they DO know what I'm about."

"And Tom, there's more," I said. My eyes shot a glance to Elaine, who, being acutely aware that I needed her emotional support, responded with a gentle nod and a light touch on my forearm.

"When I was talking to Emma last night, other horses joined her," I said, flipping the band on my wristwatch a couple of times. "These are all of the horses who know you. And they too want me to tell you something."

Tom gazed at me expectantly. In this sudden bloom of health, I found it even harder to deliver the message that carried the assumption of his imminent death. Tears started streaming down my face, my throat constricted. Elaine slid over and put her arm around my shoulder. I summoned some inner reserve so that I could tell Tom of the bridge that would be waiting for him. When I was done, I waited and wondered how he would absorb this message. My feet sunk into the floor as I shifted my weight back and forth.

After what seemed like a forever pause, Tom's eyes brightened, he beamed and sighed. He looked up towards the ceiling and then directly into my eyes. "Yes, I can go that way. What a way to go!"

Tom's acceptance released a wave of relief through my body.

"You're not alone." I said. "Right now, in this room, horses are here present with you. I can't see them, but I can feel them. It's as if the room is full of a herd of soft billowy clouds. If you could touch them not only would your skin feel cushioned, but your whole being would experience gentle, kind, supportive love." My goose bumps hitched rides on my goose bumps.

Tom's smile widened even more and he let out a slow sigh as he lay back on the several plumped pillows that supported his wasted frame. I felt as if I could see his body drinking in from the pool of love that surrounded him. His face radiated even more light.

"I feel great," Tom said, his face consumed by a brilliant smile and eyes that emitted waves of contentment.

We stood in silence, absorbed in the preciousness of the moment. Tom laid his head back softly on his pillows, barely making a dent. His eyes closed and a whimsical smile periodically trotted across his face. Several minutes passed before he eased into a deep sleep.

With Elaine's visit acceptable to Tom, she was able to continue seeing him on her own. She updated me on his condition after her visits.

A few weeks after my initial visit to Tom, I got a call from one of the boarders at Pine Knoll who told me some disturbing news. Tom's former horse, Polar, had suddenly died of colic with no previous history of that ailment or clear precipitating cause. I was puzzled about this. Carol had told me that animals can take on their person's processing. I wondered if there was any connection between Polar's death and Tom's condition.

I called Carol to find out if Emma knew anything about Polar's death. The timing and suddenness of the illness seemed too coincidental. Carol was at home and was available to translate for Emma.

"Emma says that Polar had chosen to die," Carol said, "so that he could accompany Tom to the other side."

I sucked in a quick breath. Polar had chosen to give the ultimate gift to Tom. My mind was stunned into inactivity. Awe swept through every cell. I sat back, giving my body the space to process what Carol had said.

When my mind snapped back, I wondered if people would ever really comprehend how much animals do for us. There weren't many people who would understand or believe Polar's choice. When I entertained these thoughts, the disparate nature of the divisions of my life seemed more acute than ever. This was crazy-making. How would I ever reconcile the diverse aspects of my daily experiences?

Carol continued translating, "Emma says that Polar didn't view it as a sacrifice, but simply as an act one did in gratitude and appreciation of a great friend."

I knew that most of the people at the barn saw Polar's death as an unfortunately timed event and worried how it might affect Tom. Even though I could imagine the grief of Polar's current owner, I felt Polar's passing was a glorious and sublime acknowledgment.

Later that week Elaine called me. She was nearly hysterical and made me swear not to tell anyone at the barn what she was about to tell me. I'd never heard such stress in her voice.

I straightened my shoulders from their usual slumped position, lowered into the kitchen chair and scooted closer to the table. I couldn't imagine what it was she needed to share. With the receiver pushed tight to my ear I listened with all my attention, blotting out the collection of random thoughts that my mind had a penchant for ensnaring.

"When I finished riding my horse tonight," Elaine said, "I took a minute to enjoy the lovely evening." Her voice returned to a more normal pitch now that she was relating her experience. "I gazed at the western sky just as the sun was setting. The color was that beautiful rich, cobalt blue that you sometimes see. I had planned to take just a couple of minutes to watch the clouds that hovered above the horizon change color from orange to pink to purple. Then without warning, I saw Polar with Tom galloping across the sky. Tom was in ecstasy. He sat astride grinning in total joy. This was not a vision. This was not in my imagination. I actually saw this with my eyes."

I pictured what Elaine described and shivered with delight. What a joyful vision. And how perfect that the disbeliever would have this experience. I wondered how it might change Elaine.

"You know I think all of this psychic stuff is nothing but hogwash," Elaine said sounding weirded out. "But what I saw was real. I'm not used to seeing strange things like you and I don't like it."

Elaine went on to describe with remarkable detail all the elements of her vision. I wasn't sure if she was trying to convince me that something profound happened. I thought it might help Elaine if I let her know what Emma had said about Polar's death. When I finished, I could hear Elaine gasp. She was planted in the physical reality of the world and up until this occurrence had never had any paranormal experiences. What Elaine had seen and what I had told her about Polar's death challenged her belief system and she didn't want to speak more about it. She reminded me not to share it with anyone at the barn. "I needed to tell someone," she said. "I'm not even telling my husband. This has me really spooked. I just want to forget about it."

After this call, I didn't hear much from Elaine. Several weeks went by and I couldn't help but wonder why Tom seemed to be living far longer than anyone's expectations. Besides, Emma had said that he was dying soon. I wanted to ask her if something had changed. During my next conversation with Carol I was able to put that question to Emma.

Carol jumped in to say, "Time is experienced differently for animals and 'soon' is a relative term. The dimension of time doesn't translate well between humans and animals."

"What would Emma say?" I pressed her.

"Humans have an arbitrary view of death," Carol translated for Emma. I could hear one of Carol's dogs bark in the background. "They view death as the moment the person stops breathing or the heart stops beating. For animals, death is a process."

"What do you mean, process?" I asked.

"A being enters the death process," Carol translated for Emma, "at a particular moment in time. At that juncture the spirit starts jumping out of the body and spending time on the other side. The body is connected to the spirit through a cord woven of many threads. With each jump, the threads of consciousness that link the spirit to the body get thinner and some threads may break. When the last fragile thread is broken, the spirit completely leaves the body and is free of it. The process can happen quickly or take months. Animals know when the process starts. When I said that Tom was going to die soon, I'd seen he'd started jumping out of his body."

I found it fascinating that what Emma described had also been described in spiritual literature. Where did she get these understandings? Whenever I would query her, she would say, "I just know."

When I next visited Tom, I went to a skilled nursing facility in Concord where he had been moved. Kaiser didn't provide long-term hospice care. Having no money for his extended needs, Tom was fortunate to be admitted to this facility. The hospice wing was funded by a woman who had lost her son to AIDS and vowed that anyone suffering from the terminal form of that disease would have a place to go. I hoped she knew what a gift that was for people like Tom.

One of Tom's enduring assets was his friends. Marjorie, a teacher of small children at the barn where Tom had given riding lessons, kept a daily vigil with him. She had put her life on hold so that she could keep him company and ensure that his needs were met. For several months Marjorie's dedication had remained steadfast. She spent much of her day at the hospice attending to Tom and even helped arrange a birthday party for him serving as hostess to the couple of dozen friends who came to celebrate.

Whenever I visited Tom, we had to be careful about the topics we discussed. Tom didn't want to offend anyone or make anyone uncomfortable. He asked that we not speak about spiritual matters or animal communication in front of other visitors or caregivers. He was hungry to learn more, so we tried to cram everything in while we were alone. He loved the stories and what they confirmed about animal behavior. He knew that this kind of conversation would upset Marjorie and we sometimes waited weeks for the right opportunity to speak. At times the best we could do was to have lopsided conversations on the phone. Alone at home I was free to speak. At his end, he was careful and only asked vague questions that were bland enough not to make anyone in his room uncomfortable yet carry enough information so that he could get the additional details he wanted.

One of the things that made Tom such a rewarding friend was his understanding of what I call my "other life." My paranormal experiences weren't strange to him. He didn't consider them fanciful. He didn't call me weird. In fact, he enjoyed them. His enjoyment stemmed from his considering them a manifestation of the way the world really operated. What a joy to know someone who could travel with you in a world so different from what others experienced.

One afternoon I found Tom in his room alone. The sun cascaded across his bed from the west-facing window.

"I've been visited by many friends," Tom said with a glow on his face. "I've been a bit surprised by the how many people have come and the number of repeat visitors."

"Do you know why?" I asked and smiled. I fully knew why. How could anyone not want to breathe the air of this rare atmosphere?

"They're coming to bathe in the love that is pouring through me," Tom said and grinned back at me with an expression that exuded sheer pleasure. "I feel as if I have been shedding my psychological baggage."

Looking at him it was easy to understand why he was so popular – beautiful, pure light radiated from his face. He glowed with the radiance often emitted by new lovers.

"Yup, the love and light coming from you is deliciously nourishing and healing. I could sit here all day."

"This makes things easier," Tom said. "What a gift to finally feel light and pure and without all of my issues."

"More gifts are coming your way," I said. "You might like to know something about Polar that I found out."

"Please, news of the horses is always welcome," Tom replied without hesitation.

"Emma told me that Polar chose to die so he could be more fully with you," I said. "I thought you would want to know how much he loves you."

"What do you mean? Polar is dead?" Tom's face went ashen.

I watched as Tom's face contorted and then grimaced. Horror embraced me with its cold, twisted arms. Too late I realized that no one had told Tom.

I sat frozen with anxiety. At that moment Marjorie came back in the room. She saw Tom's agitation.

"Polar's dead?" he said.

Marjorie snaked her head at me and told me it was time for me to leave and to do it quickly. I retreated, shaken.

Later that week Polar's owner called me to thank me for telling Tom about Polar's death. She had been left in a difficult position. Since she couldn't share her grief with Tom, she felt she would be unable to communicate with him. If he asked her about Polar, she felt she wouldn't be able to control her feelings and veil the truth. She said my telling Tom was a gift to her so that she could spend time visiting him. She said that Tom hadn't understood why she hadn't visited or called and was hurt by it.

The next time I visited Tom, it was immediately clear that he had had time to process the news about Polar. As soon as he saw me he smiled with a deep contentment. "I got it. I understand why it had to happen. I'm glad you told me about Polar."

I was relieved that the core message had made its way home to him. Because of my promise, I couldn't talk about Elaine's vision, but I somehow understood intuitively that he too had been tuned to that wavelength.

How Tom could continue to survive in his body was puzzling. His weight loss was extreme and with so little muscle I was astounded by his ability to stand and take a few steps to the bathroom. A thought kept reasserting its presence in my mind. I was concerned that Tom was afraid to die because he might consider his deliberately contracting the AIDS virus as a form of suicide. That thought was like others I'd had that catapulted into my being and demanded to be voiced.

When I next visited Tom, I waited for an opportunity to share my thought. When Marjorie left the room for a moment, I moved my chair closer to Tom's bed and leaned over and whispered, "Tom, you have lived a successful life." He didn't move his head, but instead moved his eyes to briefly meet mine. He then let out a deep sigh and closed his eyes.

The next day Tom fell into a coma and died.

I can only imagine the journey he had in leaving his body. God bless the horses. And thank God for the horse, my soul mate, waiting for me in the barn.

Chapter 10

Tom's death hit me hard and cleared the emotional theater of life's daily dramas, leaving an open space. Any big loss usually forced me to reflect on my life and check in with my emotions. My job was wearing on me and I had a lame horse. I had a lot to think about.

One wintry Saturday morning after I fed Emma, I padded around the house until the soothing cushions of my polka dot sofa enticed me to lie down. I propped my head with a fluffy throw pillow. The family room was filled with a soft light filtered through the large elm in my backyard. The breeze gently parted the leaves on the elm, sending glimmers of light to the lawn below. Good place to quiet the mind and get in touch. I watched as two squirrels dashed around the tree scolding and nipping at each other.

My mind drifted to my vocation. My job had mixed appeal. The work itself was enjoyable. The politics and machinations of my associates were anxiety producing. Things were about to get worse. A shuffling of executive staff at the highest level was in play. That usually meant restructuring and the uncertainty and angst that went with power plays. The damage done by my work environment to my well-being wasn't ameliorated by the presence of supportive friends. Friendships were hard to maintain with my being sick and having limited ability to socialize. Almost all the strength I had was used up managing my job and home life.

I knew I shouldn't complain about my Chronic Fatigue. Gratitude was the better choice. I was able to function while many others with this disease couldn't. I looked well on the surface. Good for me so I could fake it at work. But underneath I had so little stamina I barely made it through the day. Health practitioners didn't understand how I could hold down a job, never mind a high energy, high stress one. Because of my limited vitality, the scope of my life was narrowed. The options open to me were few. For any ideas to have a realistic chance of being implemented I had to consider only what I might have the ability to influence. Well, that wasn't my work environment. Getting jobs at my current level and compensation package would take a lot of effort. So, it had to be my horse. Emma was the biggest love of my life and my significant other. My question was, "Where am I with that?"

After all the years of coping with Emma's panic attacks I was most appreciative of this period of respite. And, of course, I would view it as a respite and not a cure, since my life's philosophy, one that was too often reinforced, was to be prepared for yet another challenge. Drama, trauma and catastrophe seemed to ferret me out. As my therapist had once said, "If you lived among the gangs in South Central Los Angeles, I would have a better context to understand your life's events." Lucky me.

When Emma and I went out for our evening walks, I would often pause to look her over for signs of stress. But I didn't see them. Her lowered head, soft eye, gently swishing tail spoke to her inner peace. Emma was happy. She would stroll beside me and with curiosity check out anything that had changed in the environment. She didn't pull on her halter, her lead rope rested in a soft grip in my hand. I would breathe in the rich smell of the earth made damp from moisture wicking up from the clay strata below and watch as the moon played on the shimmering needles of the Monterrey pines. My good fortune wasn't lost on me and I would say to the heavens, "Thank goodness my horse's mind is back."

Not once did it seem to bother Emma that we were away from her stall. She was calm and sensible, ignoring any fast-moving traffic that whizzed by us on the more traveled roads. How unlike her behavior at the boarding stable where her panic attacks, which had started during a trail ride, could happen anywhere, even in her stall and the riding arena.

I felt her calm in my body and I reveled in it. Her terrors had created such stress in me that I was miserable whenever she had an attack. The attacks were so severe that they had frightened me. Her eyes would glaze over and she would run back and forth in her paddock screaming. The sight was horrible and she wasn't safe. Her vacant eye confirmed that no one was home. She was not in conscious control of her actions. Her agony was broadcast by the dust clouds her storming created.

I fully appreciated that Emma's anxiety attacks had vanished when we moved to our new home. This good fortune was rife with irony. Her mental condition was a comfort, but the diagnosis of her sore feet, her pedal osteitis, made her unrideable. Her soreness was mild enough so that she could get around in a pasture and go for walks. She just couldn't be ridden. And there was the rub. My horse was happy, but I was fretting. I couldn't help that I loved to ride, that I needed to ride. Having a horse for a pet wasn't enough. I needed the physical connection of riding. I needed to do my sport, dressage. Part of me was joyful over Emma's tranquility but part of me ached, was agitated by my need to ride.

I rose from the sofa and asked for divine guidance. I felt stuck. I cleared my mind, but no answers came. Undoubtedly more practice in patience was coming my way.

By March and the end of winter both Emma and I were getting tired of the rain and were looking forward to the dry, warmer weather of spring. During the wet season the footing in the larger paddock had turned to glue when the clay soil became water-logged from the rains. Once the rain stopped, the ground would improve. The gentle slope of the larger paddock would drain and should provide a decent surface after the sun had worked its magic with a week or two of dry weather. A little heat-sourced evaporation here and a little wind-aided drying there and the ground would hold up to weight. I looked forward to freeing Emma with enough space to run around and kick up her heels.

At last the rain stopped and the sun returned. With my usual impatience I sprinted out the first warm weekend to test the footing. As I expected, the ground gave way, although not as mushy as it had been. The next weekend the ground held. I let out a huge "Hurrah!" To open the gate and let Emma out to romp in the larger area would be satisfying for both of us. We both could use some lightness and joy. Having been cooped up all winter, I could feel the ache in our bodies, ready to burst with spring energy.

The pasture was covered with a mosaic of tufts of perennial rye grass, tall fescue and orchard grass. The slender stiff spikes of the rye grass seeds and the tufted seed heads of the orchard grass wouldn't come out for another couple of months, but you could spot the bulges where they were promising to erupt. With the bountiful winter rain, the grass had quickly grown to nearly two feet in height. The delicious aroma of fresh grass, not unlike, but subtler than the smell of freshly mowed grass, attracted Emma with all the sweetness and tastes that hay couldn't match. Her nostrils flared as she sniffed the air and dropped her neck, straining to reach whatever green blade grew near the fence border.

I led Emma up to the pasture. As I was about to unbuckle her halter, a partially hidden small yellow-orange flower caught my eye. Kneeling I took a closer look. The plant was only three inches high. I recognized the lance-shaped hairy leaves and the tightly curled fernlike tip of the fiddleneck plant. Drat. The fiddleneck, a plant toxic to horses. I took a quick scan and didn't spot more of these wildflowers. To be safe I put Emma back in her smaller paddock. I returned to the spot I had seen the fiddleneck and dropped to my knees for a closer look. Huddled under the taller grasses, I spotted more fiddleneck. Lots more. Some only an inch high. A deep rage erupted from my gut. Ingested even in small amounts, the fiddleneck would slowly destroy the liver and eventually the horse. I spread out my arms and ripped out by the roots all the poisonous plants within reach. I looked more closely for any of its siblings in other parts of the pasture. To my horror there was fiddleneck lurking under nearly every tuft of the lush grass that I inspected. Further inspection revealed that the plant was only growing on the bottom half of the pasture. It seemed as if a bumper crop had sprouted up overnight.

This was unfair. Between my Chronic Fatigue and my high-pressure job, my energy and spirit were sapped by the end of the week. I spent my weekends recharging my batteries by finding joy in nature and the friendship of my horse. Now it seemed as if even nature had conspired against me and ruined this beautiful day. I had been looking forward to sharing the joy of setting Emma free to romp in the larger space. My strong emotional reaction to this setback reminded me that I was stretched too thin. Some people, people with energy, might say "Oh well," and not be bothered by this obstacle. I said a lot worse.

I saw Emma standing near the gate looking out on the pasture and said, "I'm sorry. You're going to have to wait awhile."

I returned with gardening gloves and a couple of plastic grocery bags that would collect the insidious weed. To ensure that the whole pasture was free of this rubbish from the plant kingdom, I began a methodical process of mapping out the topography into a grid. Each grid was a four by four-foot square. My watch timed my progress as I set to clearing the fiddleneck. I had underestimated the effort. Pulling all the fiddleneck out of one grid consumed fifteen minutes.

Soon the grocery bags were full and I had to return to the house to enlist the support of the thirty-gallon garbage bags used to line the large trash cans. When my stomach alerted me to lunchtime, I stood up and surveyed my progress. I groaned. Only five grids had been completed.

Once in the house, I let out my emotions and cried. If I had normal energy, the task wouldn't feel so overwhelming. Life looks different when you view it through filters of profound exhaustion. I had so little energy that I had to mete it out with measured caution, and recovery from the imbalance these unplanned tasks caused was difficult. One of my mind's post-it notes reminded me to never run out of gas and risk a relapse into months of bed-bound illness.

The part of me that wouldn't be beaten propelled me outside after lunch. My back was sore, my hands blistered and I was running near empty. My resolve forced me to not let the evil forces of the world win. That plant was going to be banished and I would work until dark. I would take breaks, I wouldn't be totally stupid, but I would persevere.

My neighbor from two doors down saw what I was doing and strode over to where I was working. I cringed a bit. She didn't seem to be a happy person and was an expert at needling. She removed her wide-brimmed outback hat and said, "When we moved in, we had to go through this same weeding process before we turned our horses out. My husband and I fortunately were retired. Even so we spent practically the whole day long for two weeks to get it all up."

"How much did you have to haul away?" I asked, standing up to stretch my back.

She shifted her weight to the heels of her riding boots, lifted her hat and ran her fingers through her long brown hair. "Let's see. I think that we took our pick-up truck to the dump a couple of times. I bet we collected about thirty to forty trash bags."

"I guess I can be grateful that my acreage is smaller than yours," I said, sighing. "You have more than two acres just in pasture, don't you?"

"Yep," she said, nodding. "Over five acres with the back field. But I had my husband to help. I let him do most of the work. You're doing it all alone." She stressed the "alone" and offered a pitying look.

"Do you have any suggestions to make this easier?" I asked, doing my best to ignore her gloating. I reasoned I might get some useful information from her. I peeled off my gloves to let the sweat on my hands dry.

"You may not have any help, but you will have it easier than we did," she said, inspecting the pile of fiddleneck I had amassed. "Because you're catching them early in the season, the plants are small and haven't had a chance to reseed or set deep roots. We moved into our place in the late summer after the plants had dropped their seeds, so we had to do the pulling up two years in a row. Be sure to pull out the entire root."

"Well, I'm relieved that I won't have to do this back-breaking work again," I said, as I struggled to reapply the bandages to my blisters.

"You poor thing, I feel sorry for you," she said, putting her hat back on. "I have to go now. My husband and I are heading out on a trail ride," she added with a smirk.

I was happy for her, but her demeanor irritated me. Why were people so attached to "one-ups"? I felt a slight tug in my stomach. Wouldn't I love to go on a trail ride? Wouldn't I just love to have a riding horse?

My next two weekends were spent filling large waste cans of fiddleneck. I finished clearing the last square late the third Saturday night. As much as I wanted to give Emma the space, I was too tired to let her out. I decided to wait until morning when I could really enjoy the experience with her.

Sunday dawned bright and serene. I popped open all the windows and the sliding glass door in the kitchen. The songbirds chirped from every tree and the breeze brought in the fresh scent of grass soaking up sun and the occasional whiff from the early blooms of my Double

Delight roses. I laughed at what I was feeling. Looking out at the pasture, I felt like a pioneer who had reclaimed the land. Pulling a few weeds was nothing in comparison to what was accomplished by our prairie settlers, but somehow, I felt I had something in common – overcoming obstacles. I knew that people who had never suffered from a severely debilitating disease wouldn't understand. Because I didn't appear sick, many people told me it was in my mind and to get over it.

When the morning chill had passed, I went up to the barn. Emma had finished her breakfast and was watching me with a sparkle in her eyes. She seemed to know that something was up. She dogged my footsteps as I strutted up the hill to the gate that led to the pasture. I unlatched the chain and swung the gate to one side. Emma stood there looking at me, testing to see if the barrier was really gone. She eyed me again and then stared at the gate resting against the uphill side. I saw in her face the moment the light bulb went on. Her eyes flashed forward, her ears pricked up, she squealed and then bounded out into the pasture. Such joy. Her mane billowed back in the breeze and her tail arched high, streaming like a proud flag. Her exuberance lit up the pasture with streaks of energetic lightning. After several passes of bucking and jumping she took up an extended trot that swept her across the ground. Her front legs stretched forward from her shoulders, each joint opened to its maximum. Her hind legs, bent at the hocks, thrust her into flight. The movement was breathtaking. I was so caught up in the moment that I didn't immediately register that she looked…sound. No bobbing head.

What? No bobbing head? That couldn't be my luck. My mind reasoned that surely it must be the adrenaline rush of her freedom coupled with the endorphin high from running that made her immune to pain. When she settled down, she would remember she was hurting.

I waited. Part of me rekindled that miniscule spark of hope that I stuffed away in my repository of forbidden dreams. Another part knew that it was too good to be true and told me to stop harboring hope. Emma and I had such bad timing in our years together. If she was well, I was sick and vice versa. Fate seemed to keep us from making the progress in our dressage training that I knew we could with such a capable athlete. We had only made it to one show and that was when I first had her.

Emma screeched to a halt and abandoned her cavorting for other pleasures. She grabbed a big mouthful of green grass and looked at me with long stalks cascading out of both sides of her mouth as she chewed. I laughed. My heart filled with pleasure and satisfaction as I watched her. She looked like an ad for contented, retired horses. Or maybe not so retired?

I skipped down to the barn and grabbed a lunge line. When I returned to the pasture, I called Emma. She marched right up to me. Hooking the line to Emma's halter I apologized for interrupting her snack and asked her to move away at the walk. Although she strode out at a good clip, I watched her as if she was moving in slow motion. My anticipation had altered my perception. I wanted to know and yet I was afraid to know. I asked her to trot. The lunge line went taut holding her to a twenty-meter circle around me. My chest muscles seized, holding my breath. She picked up an energetic, bouncing trot. There was not one hint of lameness. And this was going in the direction that was more likely to show any soreness.

The spark of hope grew to a thimble-sized flame. Before it got any bigger, my mind reminded my heart that this could be a temporary reprieve and if I put her back to work she might come up lame again. My heart quickly retorted, but today she is sound. I giggled and threw my arms around Emma's neck.

Chapter 11

The next morning, I woke up to a mind racing with disjointed images. I had a hard time holding the thought that Emma might be sound. Nevertheless, my heart embraced all the possibilities that a rideable horse would mean to me. I knew I would be graced with amazingly good luck if she didn't come up lame again. Not something I was accustomed to. Nothing seemed to breeze into my life that wasn't earned with a lot of hard work, a fact seconded by my astrologer who said that other people could coast downstream in a canoe and enjoy life, but not me. Start paddling.

On Monday I got home from work early and gave Emma her dinner. The setting sun, beginning its bow to the horizon, still provided good light, but I resisted going up to the barn. Part of me was excited that Emma might still be sound and the other part of me didn't want to know whether she might show up lame. The conflict drove me to inaction. But this day offered up an evening lit in soft hues of gold, a color so beautiful and infused with a gentleness that I couldn't resist.

Swallowing hard, I went up to the barn, put Emma's halter on and led her up to the pasture. A large insect zoomed towards me. I ducked as it buzzed inches from my head. No thanks. No bumble bee sting today. Today was going to be a good day.

I fed out the lunge line and sent Emma in a circle. My teeth worked over my lower lip before I dared to ask Emma to trot. Would she show some form of discomfort? Okay. Trot on. Her hooves lifted and then lighted on the ground with a muffled thump. The grass of the arena cushioned each footfall. Then the next diagonal pair lifted and hit with the same muffled thump. A hint of the aroma of bruised grass brushed my nose.

Once around. Twice. Her trot looked completely even. Three, four times around and then I stopped counting. Hope flickered brighter the longer she trotted. I reversed direction and turned rotating on my heels to watch her as she trotted around and around in the new direction.

I eased her to a halt and then opened my arms as I hurried towards her. I embraced her neck. "Emma, this is so exciting." She ignored my embrace and with a marked nonchalance dropped her head and snatched a mouthful of grass. I laughed with joy. The crickets joined the moment with a chorus of bliss. The raspy screech of a red-tailed hawk seemed to herald my joy.

My mind went into planning mode. On Tuesday Emma would need to be lunged again. The evenings were too dark to see much so I slipped out on my lunch hour and bought a halogen lamp. I'd aim it the best I could from the power source in the barn.

When I got home, I found that the halogen light provided enough illumination to watch Emma's footfalls. Tuesday was the third day in a row that she would be trotted. I asked her to move out and yes, she looked great to me. I squealed with delight. Developing an exercise program might be premature, but I couldn't help mapping one out.

Emma's workouts grew steadily in length until she trotted and cantered for a good fifteen minutes. Her head never bobbed, no offloading of weight to spare her feet. I wondered if she would be able to stay sound with weight on her back. Only one way to find out.

The ground was still moist enough to provide decent footing, so I didn't have to worry about the lack of an arena just yet. The big day of riding her would wait for the weekend. The glory of the sun should celebrate the occasion.

At last Saturday morning arrived and I rushed out to the barn to feed. As soon as Emma ate all her breakfast, I tacked her up and headed for the pasture. I vaulted onto the tree stump near the gate and positioned Emma next to it. My foot slipped into the stirrup and I mounted. As soon as my seat settled on the saddle I let out a sigh. Being on my horse again felt delicious as if each cell was singing the "Hallelujah Chorus." I wondered if this was what a wild bird felt like when it was emancipated from some manmade entanglement. I felt free. This was home.

Despite my joy, I was disciplined enough to take it easy. I only rode a few minutes. Emma remained sound for the duration of the ride. The next day would be telling. Would she come out sore?

After my Sunday morning ritual of laundry and vacuuming, I shuffled up to the barn. My feet plodded up the path responding to my foreboding that my hope of Emma's health might soon be extinguished. Once again I was reluctant to find out.

I eyed Emma as I led her up to the pasture. She looked bright and energetic. When I spooled out the lunge line, she broke into a lovely trot. Her steps were even. Ecstatic joy filled my heart. My mind still cautioned that one day of light exercise does not guarantee all is well. I rode her a little longer this time and she went fine. She seemed to really enjoy getting back to work.

I didn't want to get ahead of myself, but I had to ask, "Could my dreams be realized? Is this possible?"

On Monday I called the blacksmith and had Emma's sneakers, specialized horseshoes made of rubber, put back on. Time to start riding her on a regular basis and develop a training program. Each day that she stayed well, my heart grew lighter. I loved riding and I loved dressage. New found vitality energized my step and the exhaustion from Chronic Fatigue seemed to lessen with each day that I rode. Fortunately we had a few light rains to keep the pasture footing soft. When the ground hardened, I'd have to deal with not having proper footing.

As Emma grew more fit, I started taking her out on trail rides into Briones Regional Park, located in the East Bay Regional Park district. Even though she hadn't had one anxiety attack since we had moved into this home, the possibility of an attack kept me from going very far into the park. What little ground we covered was marvelous.

Her schooling in the pasture was going well. I figured that by fall she would be conditioned and fit enough to resume the level of work she had been doing when she showed up lame at Sweet Mountain, our last boarding facility. The dream of this home and living with my dressage horse was to be fulfilled. Or so I imagined.

Two months after I started riding Emma, my work life deteriorated. Fate with its love of irony was playing with me again. I shuffled out to the barn one evening after a particularly distressing day at work.

"Emma, my gut is telling me that my new boss, recently promoted into the position, is not up to the job and is using me and others reporting to him as scapegoats." I stood close to Emma and stroked her neck. The warmth from her body seemed to bolster my energy.

Emma looked at me and then returned to eating her dinner. I swore that I could hear her say, "Human behavior is so complicated." I felt her supporting me with a bubble of love and concern.

"My boss overrode my recommendation for the size of a direct mail campaign," I continued. "I warned him that his decision to increase the mailing size couldn't be defended financially. He chose to go ahead anyway in his apparent attempt to make his target number of assets booked for the quarter. I instructed my staff to comply."

Emma looked at me and touched her nose to my forearm in an endearing gesture of comfort.

"The mailing gave the dismal result I had predicted from the statistical models my staff had developed," I said, leaning against Emma's shoulder. "The president of the company called me in and demanded to know why I permitted such a mailing to go out. I could either expose my boss or take the fall. Not a wonderful choice."

I stroked Emma's neck. I could feel my mouth go dry. Loss of my job meant a change in lifestyle.

"I don't know how much longer I'll last," I said, and swept strands from Emma's forelock that had swept across her eye. "I guess I could fight for my job if I wanted to. I don't want to. I don't fit and I'm not happy in the corporate structure. I need a change."

Emma's soft chewing reduced my stress. When she was nearly done with her dinner, I said, "It's in God's hands and thank you for being my friend." I left for the house wondering if I could somehow obtain divine guidance on whether I should release myself from my employment.

A few weeks later I was roused from a deep meditation by a knocking on my front door.

"Hey, Elaine," I said when I opened my front door.

"I like what you did with the annuals in your front yard," she said. "The impatiens and begonias are beautiful."

Elaine strode in and headed for the kitchen. Her red hair flowed around her shoulders and dappled her crisply ironed camp shirt.

"Okay, what's the big news?" she said and settled herself into a kitchen chair. "Your voicemail was somewhat vague."

"I received clear direction. I quit last week." I handed her a cup of tea. "I signed my resignation papers."

"Yay, it's about time," she replied. "That seems to be one dysfunctional place."

"I know," I said and slid the honey jar over. "I can't do this kind of work any longer. I need to do something different."

"How are you going to live?" Elaine asked. "This house carries a big mortgage."

"I have some savings – my company has been very generous with its bonuses and I still have the funds for the riding arena I never built. I suppose at the worst I could tap into my 401K or IRAs," I said, shaking my foot under the table.

"Any idea what you'll do next?" she said her brows wrinkled.

"All I know is I don't want the stress that comes with executive management positions," I said. "I'm afraid for my health. I don't want another relapse."

"Wow, that will change your life," Elaine said and reached for the honey.

"It means I have to sell the house," I said and felt my hands go cold. "I didn't come to this decision easily."

"In a way I can't say I'm surprised," she said. "I've managed to avoid positions with responsibility. Takes too big of a toll."

"I've called a real estate agent to get the house listed," I said heaping an oversized dollop of honey into my teacup. "Selling it and taking time to clear my head are my priorities."

"You are a risk taker," Elaine said, concern stretching across her face. "You've had highly placed positions for some time now. This will be big change. I couldn't do it without having another job lined up."

"This is a leap I have to take," I said. "I'm burned out."

"What are you going to do with Emma?" Elaine asked easing her tea cup down on the table.

"Getting the house ready for sale will take time." I said. "And I guess in this market it will take a few months to get it sold. When it does sell, I'll have to figure it out. I don't know if Emma's panic attacks will come back if I move her. She said she was tense due to the psychological state of the barn manager. If I find a boarding stable with happier management, she might be fine."

"Keep me posted," Elaine said as she reached over and put her hand over mine, her head slightly inclined and her eyes softly focused.

As spring rolled into early summer Emma exhibited more and stronger signs of an estrous cycle. Emma's estrous cycle lasted about twenty-one days, during three of which she showed signs of being in estrus or receptive to breeding. When she was in estrus, she frequently squatted and peed and engaged in other suggestive anatomical indicators of invitation to breed. She became more sensitive to touch and could get very lazy, no doubt while dreaming of some big, buff stallion. By the middle of summer Emma's estrus symptoms became more pronounced in a way I had not seen before.

One day I found her running back and forth along the fence line crushing the ground as she ran from one side of the pasture to the other. Her vocalizations were more like screaming than neighing. They were louder, lasted longer and were of a higher pitch than a normal call of greeting from one horse to another. The sound put my teeth on edge and sent cold, icy claws up my back. I wondered how her feet could absorb that pounding. I immediately called the vet and he came out within a couple of days. He recommended and I agreed that he give Emma a shot of hormones to force ovulation. He felt that raging hormones might account for her hysteria. He warned me that she might do this again with her next cycle.

With the vet's warning still reverberating in my mind, I made plans to get alternative treatment that might last longer. Between cycles Emma was starting to show signs of high levels of anxiety. I wondered if this behavior was only vaguely related to her cycle and instead was a return of her panic attacks. I made an appointment with Kerry Ridgway. He had successfully treated Emma when she had some peculiar muscle spasms in her hind quarters that laid her up in excruciating pain and that hadn't responded to chiropractic adjustments. An opening with Kerry was possible if I trailered Emma to his home.

On the day of the appointment I gave Emma a shot of heavy sedation before I loaded her into my trailer to make the hour-long trip to Sonoma. I was concerned that with her level of anxiety she might have a panic attack in the trailer. Driving down the road alone with an uncontrollable horse in a confined space could be disastrous.

Kerry and his wife greeted me on their front lawn. Kerry's tanned face framed his bright blue eyes. He beamed out a welcoming smile and then looked Emma over. Despite Emma's heavy sedation, he could see that she was frantic and not well grounded. He was confident that his treatment would give her some relief.

When he was working on Emma, I explained that her behavior seemed linked to the seasons change and got worse in late spring and then quieted down in the late fall.

Pushing his baseball cap farther up on his forehead Kerry said, "Spring and fall are the two seasons when the estrus cycle comes out of and goes into dormancy for many mares. Emma's behavior could be linked to a hormone imbalance and not necessarily closely related to her cycle."

Feeling some relief that we might have the beginning of a solution, I said, "That's interesting. When I first got her, she hardly showed any signs of estrus. As she's gotten older, she seems to be showing more 'mare-ish' qualities. I had never planned on owning a mare for all these reasons. When I first got her, I thought I had been fortunate enough to escape changes in mood."

He laughed gently and looked at me with eyes that showed a calmness and wisdom that could only be gained from many years of life. I knew that he had suffered with ill health. He had been ill for years before he was diagnosed with Lyme's disease and by then he had been left permanently debilitated.

Kerry took another acupuncture needle and placed it in Emma's neck and said, "You know with her so heavily sedated I'm flying blind here. I think that I'm getting the right places." He placed a few more needles and asked me to walk her slowly around the grassy lawn in front of his house.

Kerry accompanied me and matched my stride. "From my experience," he said, "some mares with behavior issues are helped by having a foal. Pregnancy seems to reset their hormones resulting in a happier horse. You may want to think about having her bred."

I thought long and hard and then said, "Thank you for the

suggestion, but breeding Emma isn't something that I can picture. I can't see my way to taking on the responsibility of a foal and I'm going to have to trust that I won't have to go down that path. I barely have the energy and time to take care of Emma."

His lips turned down as he said, "I know what you mean about having enough energy to do everything you want."

"Having a foal is just too risky even if I had the energy," I said and looked down at my paddock boots. "So many things can go wrong. You never know what you'll end up with. Too many of my friends who tried breeding their mares ended up with either an unviable foal or a lifelong pet that couldn't be sold or ridden."

"Everything you say is true," he said as he buttoned his sweater. "It's a big decision and a big commitment. When a mare gives birth a lot of things have to go right very quickly, or you are looking at losing the mare or foal or both. Many of my clients try to stay up twenty-four hours a day for a couple of weeks before the mare is due to give birth. You need to be there if anything goes wrong. If you aren't physically strong that would be tough."

A couple of days after I got Emma home she appeared somewhat better, but her eyes still weren't that liquid doe-eyed soft brown. As we got further into summer, Emma's demons returned. Her panic attacks were back in full force and the timing wasn't related to her estrus cycle. I felt helpless.

When Emma was kept at a boarding stable, I would feel her distress the whole time I was there. As soon as I drove away I would get relief. Now that she was in my backyard there was no escape. With getting the house ready for sale, I was home a lot. My real estate agent had given me a list of things to do to improve the appearance of the house. So, I was painting, staining grout, pruning and repairing.

Emma's panic episodes lasted hours. She darted as fast as she could in one direction, then jammed her front feet into the dirt creating a rut with the force of her stops. She rose up on her hindquarters, spun around and then headed in the opposite direction to repeat the pattern. Her feet couldn't take that kind of beating.

When she came up lame, my heart retreated into a walnut, crinkled with a hard shell. I called out my vet again. As in the past he had no suggestions on how to treat panic attacks. For my own sanity I needed to do something. I felt powerless. Kerry felt he had done all he could and Western medicine had no solutions. I couldn't live with my stomach constantly churning as if I was descending the biggest dip on a roller coaster. Emma's periods of distress with the accompanying screams of anguish pushed me to my limits of endurance. The stress that I felt was more than I could bear.

In a quiet moment when Emma had taken a break from her distress calls, I retreated to my family room and plopped down on my sofa. My mind zipped around trying to conjure a way out of this situation. Not knowing what else to do I called Elaine as my sounding board.

"I can't live like this," I said feeling like I wanted to shriek. "I love Emma and her misery is mine and it's intense. I'm under enough pressure to get the house sold and figure out what I'm going to do with my life."

"Aren't you the one who told me that breeding her might give her peace?" Elaine asked.

"Yes," I replied. "Kerry suggested it. I can't imagine taking on that responsibility."

"Might you consider leasing her out as a brood mare," Elaine asked. "I know a couple of people who did that when their mares needed a rest and then brought them back to work after the foal was weaned."

"Never thought of that," I said, letting the idea settle in my mind. "That might work. Emma could be leased. This way she could experience motherhood, have her hormones reset and I wouldn't have the work and expense of a foal. At the end of the lease period I would get Emma back, hopefully new and improved."

"And there are other benefits as well," Elaine said. "If Emma liked being a mother and was happy she could continue her life bringing beautiful foals into the world. If lameness kept her from being ridden, she could find meaning in motherhood."

"You're right," I said. "I wouldn't lose control of her. I could never sell her. I've made that commitment to her. You've just given me a couple of possibilities with happy endings."

I thanked Elaine, hung up the phone and sat back digesting what she had suggested. My fingers traced the turquoise polka dots of the sofa. The more I thought about it the more it made sense. Emma is a classically beautiful, registered thoroughbred. Her sire, Allisando, had done well in both three-day eventing and dressage and her dam retired sound from the race track. Emma is a lovely mover and has a great disposition (except during anxiety attacks). The soreness in her front feet was thought to be related to her injuries as a foal and not to a genetic predisposition or conformation flaw.

I wondered what she would think of this plan. I made an appointment to talk to Carol and connected with her a few days later.

"Emma, what do you think about having a foal?" I asked, once Carol and I had finished exchanging our latest news.

"I think I would make a good mother," Carol translated.

"You are inconsolable right now," I said. "This might be a solution to eliminate your anxiety."

"I hate feeling this way," Carol translated, putting distress in her voice. "I'm miserable. The attacks are hard on me."

"Emma, I have to look for full time work," I said. "Meanwhile I need to get this house sold. Having a foal might be fun if I were well. Taking care of you while you were pregnant and then the care giving for a foal would be too much for me. I would like to find a home where someone would want you and your baby."

"I don't want to leave you," Carol translated putting sadness in her voice.

"It may only be for a couple of years," I said in a reassuring tone. "I will come visit you. You need to remember that I will never sell you. I will retain control of your well-being. If you tell me you're unhappy, I will get you back no matter what."

"I will try it," Carol translated, giving a sense of reluctance. "I don't want to live with this terror."

"Do you know what you're saying?" Carol asked me rather directly.

"Yes." I replied without hesitation. "I'm willing to live apart. I'm also willing to assume the responsibility of her happiness. If Emma were pregnant and wanted to come home, I would have to find a way to settle expenses with the person leasing her and would have to find her a home she liked. Even though none of that would be easy, I would do it."

"I wish all of my clients treated their animals the way you do." Carol's voice expressed the incredulity that she must have been feeling.

With the decision made, I drafted a lease agreement that would provide for all of Emma's conditions and my own. I would take Emma back if she were unhappy or if the person leasing her no longer needed Emma as a brood mare.

With a heavy heart my search for Emma's new home began.

Chapter 12

Horse magazines, equine newsletters, word-of-mouth leads and classified ads became my daily fodder. I contacted any breeder that I thought might have a suitable home for Emma. At first, I didn't feel defensive. After all, Emma was a beautiful well-bred thoroughbred with excellent conformation.

Straight away I learned that this would be no easy task. Emma was allergic to alfalfa hay and couldn't eat it, not even a mouthful. She was prone to sore feet if her feet stayed wet for too long and would need dry or sandy ground to escape the cloying adobe soil in winter. She was adamant that she would be allowed to socialize with her foal for a minimum of two years to teach the baby how to be a proper horse. She felt time with her baby was completely non-negotiable.

My calls ended in what became an almost predictable pattern. "Wow, she can't eat alfalfa hay," one kind woman said. "That's too bad. All the brood mares share the same pasture and we feed alfalfa in the morning. There's no way I could accommodate the needs of a single horse."

"What? You want the foal to stay with the mare for two years," a no-nonsense man stated. "That's unheard of. My mares are bred back to the stallion immediately after giving birth. The foal is taken away at four months, so the mare has enough energy to give to the unborn foal. This is a business."

Another breeder commiserated: "You say you want her to be able to dry her feet out in winter. My ranch is in the California Central Valley where the land is pretty much flat. When it rains, it rains. All the brood mares are kept out in pasture until they are ready to foal. I'm so sorry. Best of luck."

About a month into my pursuit I was surprised when a breeder of sport horses said he could meet my needs for Emma. Wow, I wondered if it could really be true. Too many dead ends had discouraged me.

"I'm very interested in your mare because of her breeding," Ron said with some excitement in his voice. "Her sire, Allisando, is a fabulous horse. The best horse I ever had was a son of Allisando. My heart broke when I parted with that horse. I never should have and it's one of my regrets. What a stroke of luck that your mare is an Allissando daughter. I feel as if I've been given a second chance. I've been looking for quality thoroughbreds for my breeding program."

At last I had somewhere to go and facilities to inspect. Fuel tank full and lunch on the seat next to me I headed out. I arrived at Ron's ranch in the foothills near San Miguel after driving for over three hours. Tumbling out of my car, I stretched my sore muscles to get the circulation back.

Ron first showed me the brood mare pasture. The space was large enough for the number of horses, but the steep hillside meant that the horses would never get relief from standing at an angle. There was no flat place where they could plant all four feet level. How tiring. Besides, they could lose their footing and pull a tendon or worse fall when the soil got slippery in winter. Higher ground was good for drainage, but not so steep. One lone tree provided the only shelter. I couldn't picture Emma comfortable in this situation.

"Ron, do you have other pastures for the brood mares? Perhaps one with less of a grade or that gives the horses an opportunity to spend some time on even ground?"

"No, that's it," Ron said. "I also wanted to mention that after we talked about your mare last week, I gave this more thought and consulted my barn manager. For insurance reasons I would have to have ownership of your mare. That's the only way we would take her. Of course, you'd have right of first refusal if I ever sold her. When can you bring her?"

What? Really? Why did he think he could change the terms of the agreement I had outlined? I would never sell Emma. I was annoyed. He could have told me in advance and saved me the trip. Through tight lips I managed to thank him for his consideration and let him know that I didn't think this arrangement would be workable. I accelerated my steps to the car and sped away.

The several hours it took to drive home gave me plenty of time to think. I reminded myself that this was only the first place I visited. This wasn't the time to get discouraged. The self-talk had a hard time fending off my disappointment. This placement with someone who knew of and appreciated Allisando and could meet Emma's other requirements had sounded promising.

The next two inspections ended similarly for slightly different reasons. Then by chance I ran across a friend, a vet, who could make an unqualified recommendation for a possible situation for Emma. This friend had stayed at a breeder's ranch in Nevada and taken lessons from her. I was assured that this was an extraordinary person of integrity and with a high level of care-giving. I immediately contacted the breeder and learned that she didn't feed alfalfa and was agreeable to letting Emma stay with her baby for two years. She bred her mares only every other year. Her land was sand based, not clay, and mostly flat. A refined thoroughbred was welcome in her breeding program.

I was delighted and made plans for a visit. I saved up my energy and looked forward to what might be Emma's new home. The trip started out with me well ensconced in my car, tapes playing my favorite songs from the Sufism Reoriented playbook of spiritually uplifting music celebrating Meher Baba. I munched on healthy snacks piled high on the passenger seat. Smith Valley, Nevada here I come.

My dismay began in the flat, Central Valley of California when the cruise control on my Mustang 5.0 made a popping sound and quit working. That wouldn't be a big deal for most people. I had health issues that kept me one step ahead of collapsing from fatigue. I couldn't veg out and watch the scenery. I had to keep my foot on the accelerator and my eye on the speedometer. I didn't have as much freedom to shift around. Sure enough, about another hour down the road my backside and calves were cramping.

I sank back into the bucket seat of my car and tried to change my posture as much as I could. What was I doing? If a spa were my destination, that might be different. Instead I must think up clever ways to answer questions like, "Why do you want to keep your mare with her foal for two years?" If my answer was something like, "My horse says its humanity's crime against horse to separate mothers and babies so young," I could imagine being hastily escorted back to my car. Very few people believed in telepathic animal communication. Even rarer would be to find someone who was making their living from the horse industry and who would make the emotional needs of their animals a top priority. Was all my exploration just hopeless craziness?

I left the Central Valley and began the climb up the Sierras. When I was a half hour away and a couple of thousand feet below the summit, a light rain began to fall. Rain wasn't common at this time of year and I was surprised by the sudden change in weather. The high country of the Sierras is known to be unpredictable. Back packers have found that out the hard way. Hopefully it was just a squall that would pass over leaving behind that delicious fresh earth scent.

The rain turned to sleet. The sleet turned to delicate crystals. The crystals joined hands into snowflakes. The fluffy snowflakes called their friends to join the party and they danced all around the car. The beauty and the purity of the falling flakes were enchanting.

My joy at the change in weather didn't last long with the build-up of snow on the roadway. Mid-week travel meant light traffic and no line of cars to beat the snow down. I didn't have either snow tires or chains. My tires skidded when enough snow had accumulated on the road to blanket the surface. The next time the tires skidded, the car fishtailed, and my anxiety grew. Good grief, only with my luck would there be enough snow to be a problem in July.

I called on God's help. I hadn't seen a car in an hour and if I got stuck I could be stranded for some unpleasant amount of time. These days I would be lucky if any driver would be inclined to stop and help. When my tires lost traction and whined their inability to grab the road, I worried that I wouldn't be able to control my car with the deepening snow and steeper climb that lay ahead. Not knowing what else to do I decreased my speed which was already a crawl and drifted onto the shoulder. I turned on the hazard lights but rejected the idea of raising the hood to indicate road trouble. I felt like plopping my head on the steering wheel and crying.

No sooner had I thrown up my arms in surrender than a semi-truck lumbered by me. To my delight it was pulling two trailers. Multiple sets of wide tires of the rig covered the same track and compressed and melted the snow. I threw my car into gear, turned off the hazard lights, eased on the accelerator and maneuvered the car back onto the road and into the lane behind the truck. My tires fit perfectly in the parallel tracks imprinted by the rig. I said a quick prayer of thanks to my guardian angels. Each time the road widened to offer up a passing lane, the truck driver pulled to the right to let me by. I pulled in behind him. I was not giving up my very own snow plow.

Once the summit was crested, the snow gave way to sleet and then rain. With the peaks of the Sierras behind me I could let loose some of the anxiety I was holding. My breathing got deeper. Just before dinner time I arrived at my first destination - Topaz Lake. I checked in at the lodge that had been recommended by the owner of the property I would be visiting. After an early dinner I crashed into bed.

The next morning dawned sunny and bright and with a happy anticipation I set out for the ranch in this arid, high desert of Nevada. I wouldn't have to worry about wet clay on Emma's feet here; the ground looked sandy and coarse. The directions were excellent and I had no problem finding the stables. Barbara, the owner, was waiting for me outside her barn. She walked up to me and extended her hand with a cordial greeting.

"Would you like to see me work my prize jumper?" she asked as she turned to go to a shed near the main barn. "I'm a running a little behind and would like to get him worked."

"Sure," I said as I hastened my pace to keep up with this long-legged woman. I watched as she tacked up the seventeen-hand grey gelding with a close contact jumping saddle. She was a tall woman and would probably measure a couple of hairs fewer than six feet. Her large frame was well muscled and the leather chaps over her jeans were nearly worn through. She had a peaches and cream complexion with none of the wrinkles that are characteristic of those who spend their life outside. She shoved her long brunette hair up under her hard hat and led her horse to the arena.

I took a moment to check out the land around us. The sun was starting to evaporate the water from the puddles left by the previous night's rainstorm. A deep breath pulled in the fresh smell of recently cleansed air. Even though the air was dry, I could feel moisture rising from the ground. It settled on my skin like an expensive moisturizer. The clarity of the deep blue sky made the canopy above appear to stretch out into infinity. This felt good. Emma might like this.

The area around the barn was divided into small quarter acre turn-outs. Although the dirt was mostly sand, a few clumps of grass were scattered intermittently throughout the paddocks. The rugged tufts looked as if they huddled together for protection and survival. This was not the climate for lush green blades that bent from the generous weight of their bounty. This grass was thin and wizened, as if it fought for life. Although this wasn't rich land, there might be enough to eat if the pastured horses had a large enough area. The horses would self-exercise as they wandered about looking for forage.

"I'm really proud of this horse and his accomplishments," Barbara said as she closed the gate to the outdoor arena behind her. "I bred him myself. He is by my warm blood stallion and out of my retired thoroughbred mare. Unfortunately, he inherited the head of my stallion."

I snatched a glance at his head and had to agree. The expression "suitcase head" was applied to horses like him who had overly large, rectangular heads with no remarkable features. No wonder she wants a refined thoroughbred like Emma in her breeding program. A large head wasn't a conformation fault, just not very attractive.

Barbara mounted and then trotted her horse on a loose rein. After a short warm-up, she approached the first jump. About three strides out the horse flattened, raced towards the jump and threw himself over it. On landing on the other side, Barbara gave each rein violent seesaw jerks. The horse opened his mouth and threw his head up into the air. The next time he was presented to a fence, he elevated his head before he rushed forward. The muscles in Barbara's arms bulged as she yanked on the horse's mouth. He rose up on his hind quarters into a half rear and threw his head even higher to try and avoid the pain. I cringed in sympathy for the horse. It saddened me knowing that this rider's behavior was common in the horse world and regarded as an acceptable correction. Its pervasiveness did not diminish my reaction. I winced at all that followed and was relieved when she finally got off.

"My horse is having an off day today," Barbara said as she dismounted.

I nodded as though I understood. I followed her back to the barn where she untacked the horse. I didn't want to call this trip a bust, just yet. I reasoned that even though she may not be the world's best rider, she may take really good care of her horses in her breeding program. She didn't ride those horses.

We hopped into her truck to go view the nearby pastures she had rented for her brood mares. The landscape was very different from what I was used to in northern California. As far as I could see, sand undulated to the horizon with sprinklings of vegetation. Instead of a deep Kelly green cloaking the hillocks, sage green shrubbery dotted the sand with the occasional spot of a leafier plant.

Barbara pulled her truck up to the side of one of the fenced fields that looked identical to several we had already passed. She parked her truck next to a metal gate. "Even though the pasture is a retired hay field, it manages to keep fairly green despite the lack of rain in this part of the state. With little extra feeding the horses stay in good flesh."

The two chestnut mares that she pointed to in the far end of the pasture waddled towards us with rotund bellies. Their hips were well covered with muscle and their coats shone with health. Although the two horses eyed us with suspicion, they had enough curiosity to approach us. When they were within touching range, I checked out their feet and frowned. The hooves were neglected. They were far too long in the toes and splayed out. The front foot of one of the mares was curling up and had developed a deep toe crack making the hoof look like an ungulate's.

Barbara saw my gaze and probably felt my gasp. She said, "Yes, I need to get their feet trimmed."

We left the horses behind and walked farther out into the pasture. I surveyed the field more closely. The green clumps of vegetation scattered throughout interested me. They looked too green. They looked too leafy. Pointing at one of the clumps, I said, "What is that?"

Knitting her brows and staring in the direction I was pointing, she said, "As I said this is a retired hay field." She paused and I could feel her body stiffen. "That greenery is…al…fal." She didn't finish the sentence.

Staring at the back of her head I gritted out, "Is this the only kind of pasture that you have available?"

"Yes," she replied continuing to stare at the field. "I have rented two. They are the same."

"You have no other arrangements?" I asked.

"No," she said. "That's it."

"Thank you for considering taking my horse," I said, my anger trying to burst out in a torrent. I managed enough control to say, "You can take me back to my car now. Didn't I make it clear that my horse can't eat alfalfa?"

As Barbara walked back to the truck her stride lost its elasticity. She turned the truck motor on even before I had shut the door on the passenger side. She busied herself with making the U-turn on the road.

"I never stopped to think about the forage in the pastures," she said, facing forward, her cheeks reddening. "I just knew that I didn't bring the horses alfalfa hay as a supplement. I only supply the horses with oat hay."

I clenched my jaw tighter when I realized that no apology was forthcoming. Perhaps she was embarrassed by her oversight.

Back at her ranch, I offered a perfunctory goodbye, took my leave and bee-lined to my car. A long drive was ahead of me. Near Topaz Lake I stopped and got some fast food to tide me over until I got home. I couldn't believe it. A couple of days shot, gas and hotel fees blown for nothing. This woman didn't think it through. She knew that Emma couldn't have alfalfa hay. Just because it was no longer cultivated didn't change what it was. Unbelievable how unaware and unthinking some people can be. Perhaps I might have been more forgiving if I hadn't been so exhausted or if she had acknowledged the inconvenience and expense she had caused me.

As my car eased west I searched for energy. Instead a hopeless feeling raised its ugly head and sapped what strength I had. What was I doing with my life that so much of my time, energy and money were being spent on a horse I couldn't ride? My only answer was another French fry. And because I love her.

When I got home, I dragged myself up to the barn. I fed Emma and cleaned out her stall.

"Emma, it won't work for you," I said, petting her neck.

She turned her head and nosed my hand. Her soft eyes drew me closer to her. Those brown eyes with the gold flecks could melt away my worst mood. The whiskers on her muzzle touched my hand with such lightness that I shivered. I sighed and let my heart absorb her bath of love. I soaked in these moments when she was at peace. When tiredness overtook my legs, I kissed her goodnight.

"Don't worry," I said turning off the barn lights. "I'll sort this out."

I minced my way back to the house and slunk into bed. I didn't bother getting a tissue and instead wiped my tears on my pillowcase. As I nodded off to sleep I wondered what was going to happen. The house was up for sale. I didn't want to put Emma back in a boarding stable. Was I ever going to find Emma a suitable home?

Chapter 13

The trip to Nevada had been so discouraging and exhausting that I couldn't bear to keep looking for a new home for Emma. All I wanted to do was hang out at home, work on keeping the house presentable and regroup. Besides regaining some energy, I had a lot to think about. What career should I pursue? How should I pursue getting a new job? But peace wasn't coming my way. Emma's panic attacks hadn't subsided. Her screaming ensured that the hiatus from my search was cut short. Staying home wasn't very restful with the acoustical backdrop of Emma's torments overpowering the cheery calls of the local song birds.

Coincidentally, the day I forced myself to start my search afresh, the publication, *California Dressage Letters*, arrived in my mailbox. In the classified want ads was a listing for a registered thoroughbred brood mare.

My call to the number provided in the ad connected me to Ellie, an upbeat woman with acreage above Sea Ranch in the town of Gualala on the Northern California coast. She wanted a companion for her older brood mare and a horse whose pedigree would suggest an improved chance of having attractive foals. Ellie also was in a position and agreeable to meet all of Emma's requirements. I was stunned, but jubilant. I planned to visit her ranch the following week when she had a block of free time. I was to bring pictures of Emma and a video of her under saddle, so Ellie could study her conformation and movement.

The morning I headed out for Gualala I couldn't stop sarcasm from coloring my thoughts. I wondered what lovely surprise I would find this time. I finally gave into the thought that I was on a journey and might as well surrender to the process.

Ellie's directions were clear and I found the entrance of her driveway next to the stand of redwoods just as she described. She told me she would be working in her ceramics studio in an old barn. I spotted a structure that looked more like an airplane hangar than a building that housed livestock. A weather-worn sliding door, the kind that hangs from wheels and slides along metal rails, was open and I peeked in. I was delighted to see that Ellie appeared to be a vibrant woman, probably in her mid-thirties. Her focus was on her work and I felt the abundant energy she exuded. Long strawberry blonde hair was loosely tied with a ribbon allowing wisps to escape and occasionally blow across her face. Her enamel earrings of various shades of emerald and teal brought out the green in her eyes. Her face looked open and her mannerisms were down to earth. She was wearing clay-spotted blue jeans and a gauzy tie-dyed top. I immediately liked her. She greeted me with a handshake full of warmth and confidence. First asking my permission, she took a moment to show me her kilns and her production line for the tiles she sold to various catalog merchandisers.

Exiting her workshop, Ellie led me on a tour of her ranch. The land was mostly flat with the occasional gentle swell. The dirt was mixed with sand and looked as if it would drain well. Each of the pastures provided sweeping views of the ocean. Mature oaks and pine were lavishly sprinkled around the property and provided shade in all the pastures. The grass covered the ground and was not overgrazed, which suggested good land use. An older donkey that Ellie thought came from the Bureau of Land Management would be Emma's pasture mate. Feeding them both either oat hay or orchard grass would be no problem. She didn't want the donkey to eat the richer alfalfa hay. The older mare had the pasture next door where Emma could visit with her over the fence. I liked that idea. The older mare could teach Emma about being a mom.

Bordering Emma's pasture was a spring-fed pond that according to Ellie was so clear and fresh that trout thrived in it. Almost on cue, a splash caught my attention and I spotted the rainbow gleam when one jumped out to catch a low-flying insect. Adjoining the pastures was a two-story barn that felt airy and let in lots of light. The open-beam ceiling captured the cool sea breezes and although the barn appeared quite old, the stalls were in good repair. The bales of hay stored at one end looked fresh and of good quality.

I couldn't be happier with what I saw. Fences were intact and looked safe. The views were magnificent and Ellie seemed responsible and attuned to the needs of her animals.

We walked back to Ellie's house, so I could show her a videotape of Emma that had been taken during a lesson I had with my dressage instructor. Ellie liked what she saw. With my heart in my mouth I went over the details of the lease agreement. I watched her face for any signs of resistance.

"Yes, I can live with that," she said, holding my gaze with clear eyes.

I was ecstatic. What a miracle to find such a lovely home and a kind person agreeable to all the conditions that I had outlined in the lease. We planned for Ellie to come down and meet Emma. On the way to my car I scooped up a bag of dirt. Emma would want to know about her possible new home.

As I drove back, I felt relieved. Here was someone who was easy to talk to, seemed very reasonable and would offer Emma an excellent home. At last we could move to our next step in Emma's rehabilitation. Was this the place where she could be happy? Where she could safely have a baby?

Emma was waiting for me when I got home. She pushed her nose out over the fence and grabbed at the dirt-filled sandwich bag with her muzzle. I opened it for her. She wrapped her lips around the dirt and took some on her tongue. I sensed that she liked what the dirt was telling her about the grasses that grew there, the climate and all the other things that horses know when they sample dirt.

About a week later Ellie and a friend came down to visit Emma. Ellie watched Emma move at liberty in the pasture and then when I rode her. I offered Emma to her and she accepted. When she got off she exclaimed how easy it was to ride Emma and what a soft mouth she had.

I explained that Emma's feet were a little sore from the pounding they took during her panic attacks, but if she was kept on soft footing, she could still be ridden lightly. Ellie liked Emma's conformation and thought she was beautifully trained. We finalized the agreement and arranged the day that I would bring Emma up to her ranch. Ellie mentioned she hadn't decided yet how to get Emma in foal. She would either use artificial insemination at her ranch or send Emma to a breeding farm to be bred. If the latter, it wouldn't be for very long. As soon as she was confirmed in foal, she would come right back.

I felt that Ellie was committed to taking good care of Emma and that Emma would enjoy her new residence bathed in sea breezes and with views of the ocean. Still I couldn't help but wonder what motherhood would be like for Emma. Would this reset the imbalance in her body? Would it stop her panic attacks?

A few days before I was to take Emma to Gualala I couldn't sleep. Doubts burst out of my heart and questioned me about leasing Emma - letting someone else care for the most significant love of my life. My shoulders tightened into knots and my neck cramped. I agonized if I was doing the right thing.

About 3:00 AM my eyes revolted from staying focused on the moving pictures on the tube. I turned off the television and lay in bed looking at the stars framed by my bedroom window. I tried to distract myself by contemplating what I couldn't comprehend - the size of the cosmos. After a few attempts I experienced no relief. My mind couldn't help racing back to Emma. Even though she was a couple of hundred feet away tucked in her stall, I felt her distress as real as if it were my own. Change unsettled her.

Then a thought bolted through my brain and caught in the net of possibilities. Maybe I could enter Emma's dreams - ease her anxiety about a new way of life.

I laughed. Where did that thought originate? The curtains billowed and caught my eye. The scent of roses blooming outside my bedroom window feathered in on the breeze. I laughed again. Who would understand that thought as something other than the ravings of one who had a tenuous relationship with reality? I wondered if other people lived dual lives. One in the world that most called daily life and the one where capabilities seem boundless.

The idea of entering Emma's dreams made some sense. Emma wasn't like other horses. I had learned that many times over. Animals can telepathically communicate with any human capable of hearing their voice. Emma went far beyond talking. On several occasions Emma had entered people's dreams to be of service to them. Like she did with Tom. Once Emma helped someone who was hospitalized after being thrown from the horse he rode. Emma had been concerned that this person was planning to sell his horse and leave horses forever. His injuries were serious. While he was still in the hospital, Emma appeared in his dreams to give him a bath of love and a ride that was so joyous that he reconnected to why horses had to be in his life. A consultation with a trainer helped him realize how he had precipitated the mishap with the horse. Emma's nighttime wanderings never failed to surprise me. Geographic distance held no boundaries for her love and kindness.

Because Emma could access other beings' dreams didn't mean I could. I'd never done anything like that before. I could hear the voices of animals and so could a lot of other animal communicators. Emma had the special powers, not me. She is the one who had invited me to visit other worlds and to experience them directly.

An owl hooted in the pasture next door. The whiff of skunk eased in the window and wafted away. My adventurous side took over. What do I have to lose? Turn-about is fair play.

I closed my eyes and concentrated on Emma. All my energy focused on being with her. My mind summoned the white star in the middle of her forehead. I pictured twining my fingers through the black strands of her forelock. I could almost feel the warmth of her neck as I imagined nestling my chest against her shoulder.

A few seconds passed before I felt my body go through an energy shift. I felt lighter, immune to gravity even though my body pressed deeply into the soft mattress of my bed. My hand reached for the bedframe to ground me. The summer breeze abated, the crickets withheld their symphony. My skin shivered with a sudden drop in temperature. My lungs pulled in air no longer redolent with the aromas of the summer night.

Then the moonlit walls of my bedroom dimmed and dulled to a matte black. Light played on the walls like a psychedelic show from the 1960's. Forms at first subtle grew in substance. I wasn't scared. My house wasn't haunted. Emma had sent me visions before. Visions originating from Emma had different qualities than the usual pictures in my mind that came from my imagination. My visions were like nighttime dreams - mostly visual. The visions that came from Emma sometimes involved other senses. Somehow, I knew that these images were generated from outside of me.

But this was very different. This time my body felt what I was doing as if it were completely real. I was on Emma's back - bareback. My legs rested against her sides. The muscles along her spine rippled as she moved. My hands grasped her mane as she picked up tempo. We were on a beach flanked by roaring waves and sheer cliffs.

The spray of the ocean mist blew across my face as Emma cantered along the firm sand at the water's edge. The waves flowed back and forth gently lapping at her legs as she splashed through with joyful bounds. Drops from the ocean water sprayed on my mouth and I tasted the salt. The sea-air laced with salt and the scent of seaweed conjured memories of my childhood rides on the San Francisco beach. The breeze streamed through my hair turning strands into tendrils. Emma's full-length mane rippled back from her neck and the wind playfully whipped it from side to side. It brushed my face with the softness of fine sable.

Emma's muscles tightened and bunched in readiness to bound forward at top speed. She asked me for permission and I responded, "Yes." We challenged the wind to a race. As she ran I felt as if we became a unified form with one consciousness. I dissolved into the joy and exhilaration of covering ground.

Emma's running seemed effortless and keeping my balance on her back was easy. I watched as sea birds flew from one rocky perch to another on the towering, stately cliffs. With each bright-winged swoop, they called out to each other - their voices applauding us as they joined in our play with the wind. We sped on and left them behind, hearing their distant calls affirming our shared experience.

"This is incredible," I murmured. "I'm awake, yet I have no control over what is happening. I'm riding my horse on a beach, but I'm lying on my bed in Lafayette."

I watched as if a video game played out before me. One that included sight, sound, smell, taste and touch. Suddenly Emma lifted into the air and took flight. I glanced down to see if she had sprouted wings from her shoulders like Pegasus. She hadn't and for a split second I wondered about the aerodynamics of her flight – a question primed by my college life as a scientist. I stopped my mind and returned to the experience. The wind rushed by even faster. We gained altitude on the crags that had one minute before risen above us. The ground shrank below and the cooler air caressed my skin. Wisps of cloud mist settled on my eyelashes. The bluffs retreated to barely perceptible bumps on the ground. My gaze ascended to the heavens. I was intrigued by where this vision was going. I felt a little anxiety as we soared ever higher with increasing speed, leaving the Earth behind. And then without any indication or premonition, the vision ceased. My muscles shivered. Several minutes passed while I processed what I had just experienced. I felt awed by what Emma and I had shared. When my heart stopped pounding, I fell asleep.

The next evening when I guessed Carol would be home, I settled into the easy chair in my family room with phone in hand. My curiosity about the vision I had the night before needed to be satisfied. I dialed Carol's number and waited for her to pick up.

"Carol, I'm too emotional about this experience to hear Emma clearly," I said.

"What is Emma up to now?" Carol asked.

"Not Emma this time," I said, rearranging the throw pillow at my back. "Me."

"Color me surprised," Carol said. "What did you do?"

"You know how Emma gets into people's dreams to help them?" I asked. "Well, I couldn't sleep last night so I tried to get into her dreams. She was anxious about moving up north and I wanted to calm her."

"You two never cease to entertain me," Carol said, with a soft chuckle.

"I want to know what Emma experienced," I said, my breath catching. "Did I succeed? Did I get into her dreams?"

"Give me a minute to concentrate," Carol said. A news broadcast that I could hear in the background went silent.

I could hear Carol's breath slow. My fingers tapped a quick rhythm on the chair arm. I was about to say something when she spoke up.

"Emma says you surprised her," Carol said. "She didn't know you could do that."

"I didn't know I could do it either," I said. "Yippee. So, it was me this time. I really did it." I felt as if I had accomplished something impossible. I couldn't help but wonder what an incredible place the world is. "We can do so much more that we could ever imagine."

"I was running through the waves." Carol translated, putting joy into her voice to mimic the feelings Emma sent her. "I didn't have a bridle or a saddle. Just you and me and freedom."

"Yes, we ran on the beach." I quivered with the memory of what I'd felt. "Emma, do you remember flying?"

Carol clicked her tongue and her breath whistled through her teeth. "The dream got a little fuzzy as it went on," Carol translated. "It felt really good. You stayed on without a saddle. I'm proud of you."

"Remember, you asked me to take you back to Pt. Reyes, so you could gallop on the beach," I said, mindful of Emma's request after our first visit to that park. "Unfortunately I could never seem to make that happen."

"But you did make it happen – in my dreams," Carol translated. "Thank you for this gift. We are even more connected. At a deeper level. It's easier for me to go to another home. I love you."

"I love you," I shot back, feeling Emma's love envelop me in a cocoon of well-being.

I sat back and smiled. Mission accomplished. Emma will have a beautiful new home and may now be more accepting of the move.

Chapter 14

The sun came up too fast on the day I was to take Emma to her new home. The goose bumps on my skin testified to the cold I felt despite the warm weather. I forced myself out of bed and went through my morning routine with about as much fluidity as old Dobbin. After I fed Emma, I came back into the house to make my breakfast. I nearly gagged when I tried to swallow the soggy cereal and skim milk. I dawdled at the kitchen table clinking my spoon against the cereal bowl corralling bites as if I was going to eat.

When I managed to move my feet out to the barn, I saw the flakes I had put out for Emma's breakfast. She may have nibbled a little, but it was mostly untouched. I avoided looking her in the eye when I slipped the halter over her ears. She showed no anxiety or resistance when I loaded her in the trailer. I thanked her for not making this any harder. The sun was well up by the time I aimed the truck north. All the time I drove, I wondered when I would cry. When would I lose control of my emotions? I kept reassuring myself. This is a good thing. This can only help.

The trip to Ellie's ranch took longer with a trailer and despite the tortuous turns on Highway One was incident free. Emma unloaded with quiet, even steps and we walked around the pasture where she would live. The donkey had been put into an adjacent field, so they could become friends over the fence before being put together. When I released Emma, she showed her curiosity by sniffing the ground. She strode away to inspect the landmarks and the perimeter of her pasture.

She looked calmer than I felt. No tears came to my eyes although my body was a mass of twitches. According to Emma's wishes I left something of mine with her. I put a plastic garden chair in her paddock - the white one. The one I used to sit on when I hung out with her at her stall. I gave her a cookie, patted her neck and said good bye. I struggled to look away and headed for my truck.

I drove home with an empty trailer rattling behind me. Empty of a heartbeat, the road sounds echoed in the hollowness of the walls. How odd to have no living being behind me. I was numb. My response time seemed diminished, so I concentrated on my driving. All my focus had to be on maneuvering the rig on the windy road etched in the cliffs. Once I left Highway One behind with its tight curves, narrow shoulders, flimsy railings and sheer drops plunging to the ocean, I breathed more easily.

When I reached home, I knew the drill - detach the trailer from the truck, sweep out the floor and put the manure in the muck bucket. My feet beat a robotic rhythm to the house. Settled inside my mind woke up. I reaffirmed that I would not connect with Emma for at least two weeks. She would need time to adjust to her new living arrangement. I was surprised that I had not broken down emotionally with the separation. I cried over other losses - less devastating losses. I wondered why I felt so little. I reckoned I must be in shock.

Two weeks can be a very long time. I kept myself busy with keeping the house spotless, filling the rooms with fresh flowers and making myself absent for the open houses. I allocated some time to update my resume and put feelers out for job openings. Since I didn't know what I wanted to do, my attempts were exploratory rather than targeted.

As promised, to make the transition easier, I had held to my word and had shut down my airwaves to Emma. The exact day two weeks were up, I called Carol.

"Emma, how are you doing?" I asked. "I've been concerned about you," I said, acknowledging my need for reassurance that I'd done the right thing.

"I like the donkey here," Carol translated mimicking Emma with a lilt in her voice. "He is mature and very wise and has been telling me interesting stories." We conjectured that his experience in the wild gave him lots of material.

Giving a social response to a question regarding her well-being was typical of Emma so I repeated with emphasis, "How are you?"

"This is good," Carol said. "She says she's fine and learning about her new place. She likes the person – a woman. I assume that's Ellie."

I leaned back on my chair and couldn't resist asking, "Are you getting enough to eat?"

"Yes, I have all that I want," Carol translated putting a sense of pleasure into her voice. "The food is tasty."

The mother in me felt better. She was making friends, she was getting enough to eat and Ellie was connecting to Emma.

"I miss you, Emma," I said, my tears letting loose down my cheeks.

"You will always be in my heart," Carol translated.

With Emma settled in, I could put all my energies into selling the house. I changed real estate agents and promised to make all the additional upgrades she had recommended to make the house more appealing. I knew too much change all at once wasn't good for me but staying in this place without a horse didn't make sense. I didn't have a job and I felt lonely. I wouldn't know Emma's future for a few years. If for some reason she had to come back pregnant or with a foal by her side, I would have to find another lease arrangement. I'd worry about that when it happened. Meanwhile I held onto the belief that motherhood would give Emma the emotional peace she deserved.

I had to sort out my own life. Once the house sold I would move into an apartment until I got a job. Being unemployed created some background anxiety. I reviewed my finances and calculated I had about nine months to figure out what to do with myself before I would have to tap into my IRA or retirement accounts. Besides working out the basic finances of my life I also needed to deal with the emotions of parting with Emma and with the health issues created by Chronic Fatigue. I tried to find the positive in my situation. Not working was a gift. There is something relaxing and healing about waking up naturally and not to an incessant alarm.

I had to learn how to live with no dressage and worse, no horse. A horse had been with me my entire adult life – ever since I left graduate school and got my first job. I couldn't help asking myself, "Why am I keeping Emma?" The only answer that I got back was, "Because it would be more painful to abandon her." I tried to imagine letting Ellie keep her, but I could never get very far with those pictures before my feelings erupted in anguish.

I couldn't cause more distress for Emma. I was committed to my word of keeping her happiness in my sights. I empathized with Emma and her bouts of PTSD. I could feel in every cell of my body my own childhood traumas. No one looked out for me. Among his other abuses my father had repeatedly used a bed pillow to smother me when I was a young child put down for the night. No wonder I had problems sleeping. I wasn't safe in my bed. I knew intimately about PTSD. I was criticized and made to feel worthless. I hadn't felt loved. Panic, shock, resentment and frustration had dominated my early life. There was no way that I could consciously do harm to Emma, another being who had suffered similarly. Her kind, generous and loving nature deserved to be nurtured and respected. I wanted to parent Emma in the way I had longed to be treated. When I tried to access my feelings at a deeper level, another thought came to me. To lose Emma in my life would be wounding an important part of me. The part that could give love and feel love.

In the middle of a miserable heat wave a couple of months after Emma moved north, I called Carol so that I could check in with Emma once again. I missed my best friend and with an offer on the house I knew more change was imminent. A known touch point would help center me.

"Emma, how are you being treated?" I asked and settled back into my easy chair. The air conditioning kept me comfortable as the leaves drooped and withered outside.

"I'm being treated very well by the people," Carol translated with a matter of fact tone. "There's a lady here who thinks I'm special."

"I wonder if that's Ellie's friend that I met," I said.

"It's so hot here," Carol translated, adding distress to her voice. "I'm terribly uncomfortable. It's unbearable."

"Emma, it's really hot here too," I said. I leaned back in the chair trying hard to keep my resolve and not jump to her aid. "It must be cooler where you are. The ocean water tempers extreme weather. If it's any consolation, you must be more comfortable there than you would be here." I pictured the ocean, the generous shade trees and the airy barn and couldn't understand why Emma was having such a hard time. She had experienced hot summers and this heatwave was typical of ones we've had in the past.

Just as we were about to end the conversation Carol said, "Wait a minute. Emma is trying to say something, but she seems reluctant. Emma, what are you telling me?"

"Emma, is there anything wrong?" I said, my brow wrinkling.

"I have metal shoes on my feet," Carol translated, putting even more distress in her voice.

I froze. What? I knew that metal shoes were painful for her.

"Oh Emma, you must be so uncomfortable," I said, anger infusing each word. "I'm so sorry."

"It's completely out of character for Emma to squeal on anyone," I said to Carol. "She endures all kinds of things and has always refused to rat on anyone. She never wants me to get mad. She must really be unhappy."

"Didn't you tell Ellie it would be okay to ride Emma?" Carol asked.

"Yes, but I made it very clear that Emma had to be kept either barefoot on soft ground or with the rubbery sneakers, but never metal shoes," I said, my head searching for a plausible explanation. "I emphasized that metal shoes simply didn't absorb enough concussion."

"You liked Ellie, right?" Carol said.

"I hope I haven't misread her," I said, guilt oozing a faceless ill ease throughout my gut. "She seemed very responsible and respectful of her animals' needs. She knew that Emma was an accomplished dressage horse and we talked that it might be fun for her to ride her lightly as long as Emma was comfortable."

"My feet hurt," Carol translated, putting a heavy dose of pleading into her voice.

Emma's words enraged me even further. Every mothering, protective instinct was energized and triggered a physiologic response throughout my nervous system. I was ready for action – the fight response ripped through my muscles.

"Emma, I'm coming to get you as soon as I can," I said, jumping out of the chair. "I did my best for you. I don't know how this happened. I feel horrible. I thought I could trust Ellie to care for you as we agreed."

When I calmed down, I thought about what I would have to do. The house was sold and I would be moving out. Emma would have to go to a boarding stable until I figured things out. What if she were pregnant? As soon as I found a stable for Emma I would let Ellie know I was coming to get her. I would be exercising the clause of the lease contract that let me take Emma back if she was unhappy. I pulled out my address book for local stables.

The very next day I tracked down a barn that had an opening. Fifteen minutes after I hung up the phone, I arrived at the barn and interviewed the barn owner about the stall he had available. What a miracle that I could meet Emma's needs at this place. Barns that offered an alternative to alfalfa hay and provided a paddock adjoining the stall were not common. Even more encouraging was I knew several boarders. What a relief. I wouldn't need to do my usual surreptitious interrogation to find out what it was really like to have your horse stabled there. Barn managers tended to say one thing and a somewhat different viewpoint might be shared by the boarders. I took my leave of the barn manager to go chat with a friend I saw grooming her horse. She gave me her approval of the management and facilities. I rejoined the barn owner and gave him a check for first month's board. Blood seemed to move through my body more freely now that I could fetch Emma.

When I got home, I popped out of the car to pick up the mail from the box outside the iron gates. A letter from Ellie was among the junk mail. The synchronicity gave me a chill. I ripped open the envelope.

Ellie wrote that she had made several attempts over two estrous cycles to impregnate Emma using artificial insemination. She had just received results that Emma wasn't in foal. She was concerned that Emma was barren. I knew that horses have fertility problems, but Emma had gotten pregnant easily when she had run away to a stallion when we were visiting the Sierra foothills. And that was in winter. I wasn't expecting this kind of message. Ellie went on to say since it was so late in the breeding season she wasn't interested in any more attempts to breed Emma. The vet bills and stallion fees were adding up. Emma's value was as a brood mare, not as a "hay burner." She wanted to return Emma as soon as possible and asked when I could pick her up.

As much as I had hoped this would work, there was absolutely no doubt how I felt. Emma was coming home and coming home immediately. That she wasn't pregnant provided some relief. I dialed Ellie's number and steadied my voice when I heard her pick-up.

"I received your letter," I said, doing my best to sound calm. "It's too bad that Emma didn't conceive. I'll be up tomorrow to get her."

"Oh, she's not here," Ellie replied. "She's at the stallion station in Sebastopol. It's closer to where you live then to my home. Let me give you directions."

"I just spoke to Emma and she isn't happy," I said, controlling my rage. "I was wondering if you put shoes on her."

"No, she was never ridden," Ellie said, seeming surprised at the question. "I discussed breeding Emma with my vet and he felt that I stood a better chance of a successful breeding if I sent her to the stallion instead of shipping the semen here. She went to the stallion station to be bred a couple of weeks after she arrived here."

I felt confused. A stallion station wouldn't put shoes on a brood mare. My intuition said that Ellie was telling the truth. Besides, there would be no reason for her to lie.

I wrote down the directions and hung up the phone. I was at a loss to make sense of what Emma said and what Ellie told me. My fingers couldn't dial the phone fast enough. I was relieved when Carol picked up.

After I explained the situation to Carol, she reminded me that animals don't lie. We were both puzzled.

"Emma, are you sure you have shoes on?" I asked with parental concern. "Like with a blacksmith and not just slipped over your hooves like Easy boots?"

"Yes. I am sure. My feet hurt," Carol translated putting a high level of anguish in her voice.

"I'll be up there tomorrow," I said. Anger welled up in my throat. "You are coming home."

"Diana, she is so relieved," Carol said, letting out a long sigh. "Can you feel the love she is sending you?"

I sat back and basked in the cushion of sweetness I felt.

The next day was a little cooler than it had been, but the temperature still taxed the truck's air conditioning system as I drove north. When I got to the stallion station, I saw that the barn was at the base of a narrow valley. The leaves testified to the lack of air movement and the barn received no relief from the sun. Not one tree cast a shadow on the roof. I wouldn't be surprised if the barn was hotter inside than outside in the direct sun. No wonder Emma complained about the heat. When I opened the truck door, I was engulfed in a blanket of air so hot I felt as if I had stepped into a furnace. The gravel below my feet radiated heat and scorched my feet through the soles of my shoes.

I hurried to the main barn.

The relief I expected from getting out of the direct sun didn't materialize when I stepped through the open doors of the barn. I stood for a minute inside the entrance and noticed that my sweat no longer evaporated and was making my blouse and pants clammy. I called out and Jane, a member of the support staff, came out of a doorway to my right and introduced herself. She asked me to follow her to Emma's stall. As I tailed Jane down the aisle way, I examined the stalls. I looked left and right at the horses I passed. Each looked wretched. Their faces were stressed, skin pulled tight across their brows. Their heads drooped in listlessness. Their eyes appeared sunken. When they saw me, they looked at me with pitiful, pleading expressions. The strangest feeling came over me and inhabited my body. I felt as if I had entered an alternate universe. Although it would be years later that I would visit San Quentin's death row, I recognized the energy in this barn as one occupied by tortured souls. Despite the heat, my skin crawled and the hair on the back of my neck stood on end. The air was thick and I had a difficult time breathing. Oh my God, no wonder Emma was miserable.

Jane pulled open the door to Emma's stall. I gasped. Emma was standing with her head hanging down, nose shoved into the corner. Her coat was dull and dry. She had lost weight and her ribs had lost any padding. My heart broke. I wished that I was big enough to pick her up and hold her in my arms. I wanted to rock her back and forth and reassure her that she would be alright.

"What have you been feeding Emma?" I asked, turning to Jane.

"Because Emma couldn't have alfalfa hay, she's been given only our oat hay," Jane said, flushing with what seemed to be a deep embarrassment. Her voice broke when she confided. "Because the oat hay isn't very good quality, I've been supplementing it with Calf Manna. We haven't been charging extra for that."

My back stiffened. "How much Calf Manna were you giving her each day?"

Jane smiled and perked up. "Quite a bit. As I mentioned, the oat hay isn't very nutritious."

"Do you know that alfalfa is one of the main ingredients of Calf Manna?" I said as a bolt of anger ripped up my spine.

"I know what's in Calf Manna and alfalfa is not an ingredient." Jane said, taking on an authoritarian tone.

I used all my self-control to keep my mounting furor from spilling out and consuming me. I dug deep to stay calm.

"You're wrong," I said, as calmly and quietly as possible.

"No, I'm not," she hurled back at me.

My composure returned in time for me to say, "Do you have a bag of Calf Manna on hand?"

"Yes, in the feed room," Jane said as she turned and walked back down the aisle on stiff legs.

I followed the retreating steps of the young woman into the feed room. She raised the lid of the feed bin and located the appropriate bag. She put her hand in to retrieve some of the pellets.

"See no alfalfa. The pellets aren't green," she said as she pointed at the mostly brown mound in her palm.

"Let's read the label together," I said, beyond irritation at her attitude. She found the ingredient label and started to read. Her face reddened before she spoke. "Alfalfa is the first ingredient listed. I didn't know."

"In the future you need to be more careful," was all that I said. I had wanted to say, "You stupid twit. Look at my horse, look at those ribs. Look at that dull coat. These animals are dependent on your care and your arrogance caused Emma to suffer."

I went back to Emma's stall and put her halter on. Besides my anger about the Calf Manna, the energy I felt in the barn was almost unbearably toxic. And I had only been there a few minutes. Emma was there twenty-four-by-seven.

Once I had Emma in the aisle way and out of the sawdust bedding I examined her feet. I choked on the saliva that was in mid-swallow. She was barefoot. No nail holes were evident in the walls of her hooves. None. Which meant she hadn't had shoes on her for months. Why would Emma tell me she had metal shoes on her feet? My discomfort at the discovery did not impair my haste to remove Emma from this confinement suffused with despair as quickly as possible.

Jane followed us out to the trailer. Her confident air had been replaced with a downcast face. She asked if I needed help loading Emma.

"Thank you, but no," I said, perhaps a bit too crisply. "I can get her in by myself." I was afraid of what I might say to this foolish young woman.

I led Emma to the ramp of the trailer. She pushed me out of the way and bolted in with a single bound. Even Jane couldn't miss the eagerness Emma had to get away.

Throughout the ride back Emma stood quietly. I felt terrible and apologized to her the entire time that I was driving. How could I have let this happen to her? She had to live in a place that was filled with horrors that I couldn't imagine except through the responses of the inhabitants. And being fed food that made her sick. I knew what I had felt in that barn. I knew what it was like to be powerless and subject to an environment you couldn't change. One that you could only endure.

We arrived at the new stable and I unloaded Emma in the parking lot at the entrance to the property. She had been here before for clinics, so it wasn't entirely new for her. The first place I had stabled her was only a couple doors away so the lay of the land should be familiar. I tucked her in her stall and was relieved to see that she was already looking more at ease. I hung around for an hour to talk to her and reassure her that she would be okay now. After a few more hugs I headed home to collapse.

The next day I called Ellie to let her know that Emma had been fed alfalfa.

"I'm surprised," she said. "The stallion station is run by a very well-known dressage rider and instructor. He has an international reputation and many working students. His stallions get a lot of business. His professionalism is thought to be superb."

"Did you ever go and check up on Emma after she was there?" I asked.

"I never thought to do that," Ellie said. "The instructor has such a marvelous following because of his sensitivity to horses and for understanding and caring for them. His riding style is known to be a gentler and kinder one than the Germans. My vet recommended this breeding station. What you're telling me is shocking. I had no idea. I wonder if the alfalfa is the reason why Emma didn't conceive."

I ignored her last statement and said good bye.

That night I called Carol. I wanted to get to the bottom of what appeared to be a mystery concerning Emma's lack of shoes. Much of the motivation of my life was about obtaining an understanding of how things worked or why things happened. My staff at work often mistook my questions. They thought I was trying to assign blame. I wasn't. The reason I wanted to discover root cause was to educate myself and make improvements. Simple as that. A few of them got my intentions and joined the hunt for answers.

When Carol picked up the phone, I told her that Emma's feet revealed no evidence of shoes having been put on her.

"Emma, why did you tell Diana that you'd been shod?" Carol asked with a stern tone in her voice.

"I was afraid," Carol translated, softening her voice.

"What do you mean?" I said. "What were you afraid of?"

"I was afraid that if I asked Diana to come get me and she didn't that I'd die of the deepest grief," Carol translated putting a piteous tone in her voice. "I couldn't live in a world without hope. I was deeply unhappy." Carol slowed the pace of her words for emphasis. "I couldn't even make a baby."

My heart broke. Emma's low self-esteem tore at my being. Tears burst down my face.

"Emma, you knew that I'd come get you anytime you told me you weren't happy. We talked about that many times. Why didn't you just tell me to come get you?"

"I know you told me that, but I wasn't sure that you'd come for me," Carol translated, putting sadness in her voice. "I know how protective you are of my feet. I knew if I told you I had shoes on and my feet hurt you'd come get me."

"Emma, I wish you could trust me," I said, struggling for enough air to speak. "You experienced abandonment when your mother was ripped from you, but I won't abandon you. I have told you many times I will never sell you. You are my horse forever."

Carol hesitated and then said, "I think Emma may have finally got it. She's weeping with joy."

Chapter 15

The next morning, even before I opened my eyes, my thoughts catapulted to Emma. What would I find when I went out to her new boarding stable? I knew from past experiences that Emma didn't deal well with change. But then she seemed to do fine with moving to Gualala. Neither Ellie nor the stallion station reported Emma's having any panic attacks. Maybe she would settle in and stay calm. I could try to think positive and not stress. That would be something new for me.

I didn't delay, sprang out of bed and whipped through my morning routine. The sun greeted me with warmth when I headed for my car. The entire time I drove out to the barn I felt in a weird limbo place. The emotions of rescuing Emma from the stallion station had settled down and reality's voice broke through the drama. Emma had been through much of her psychological recovery in her younger years - she had grieved, she had raged. So, hoping that she would reach emotional stability didn't seem far-fetched. Why then did she seem to be stuck with her anxiety attacks? None of the resources I employed to help her brought her sustained relief from her terrors. And now she wasn't pregnant. Her hormones and mental state hadn't been reset. Life intervened and my plans to improve her peace of mind hadn't materialized. What if her anxiety attacks came back? I had left the last boarding stable and had bought horse property because of them. I didn't have any answers. My life philosophy was to keep going. Trust in God.

I parked the car next to the hedge across from the indoor arena. As soon as I opened the car door, I heard a horse neighing. Loud enough to make its way all the way to the parking lot. I recognized Emma's voice. This wasn't the nicker that she used to greet me nor was it her scream of anxiety. This was something that I'd never heard before. I also heard a lower pitched neigh respond to her. What could it be now? I let out a loud moan and hoped no one was close enough to hear me.

My feet hammered up the path towards her stall. Turning into her aisle I didn't see her head hanging out over her stall door to greet me. I unlatched her stall door, walked through her stall and stopped at the opening to her paddock. There she was, shuffling back and forth along the rear wall, calling out every few seconds. She didn't even acknowledge me. Each time she reached the left corner of her paddock she stopped and stretched her nose around the solid wood fence to the horse next door. And in response a chestnut horse craned a short, thick neck around the wood panel that had been put up on the top rail as a makeshift separation. They both stretched their necks out and managed to rub noses together. Then Emma turned and strode away and then circled back. I couldn't figure out what was going on. In any stable she had lived, she had never responded to another horse this way.

A man about thirtyish poked his head into Emma's stall and saw me staring at this ritual of pacing and nose rubs.

"Hi, my name is Eric," he said, offering his hand. "I'm your next-door neighbor. Rather my boy is your next-door neighbor. He's quite something, isn't he?" His grin was full of pride.

I didn't think his horse was particularly attractive. He looked like a quarter horse and I had to admit my preference for the refinement of thoroughbreds. So, I chose to ignore his remark and assumed he was like many of us who thought our horse was the best in the world. I took his hand and matched his firm grip. His blue jeans fit tight around stick legs and his cowboy shirt bulged from the drooping beer belly that hung over his embellished silver belt buckle. Brown curly belly hairs managed to stage an escape from gaps between the snaps of his shirt.

"I call him my baloney pony because he's such a well-hung stud," he said, smiling from ear to ear showing two rows of gleaming white teeth.

What is it about men and their fascination with the size of certain body parts? I would've preferred to know that his horse had a sweet disposition. I did my best to stifle any displeasure from showing. Then it hit me.

"What? Your horse is a gelding, isn't he?" I said, taking off my sunglasses to better study his face. Standing in Emma's stall, he was shaded from the sun. I wanted to get a better idea of what kind of cooperation I was going to get from this guy.

"My handsome horse is a well-mannered stallion. He won't come over the wall," he said, taking a confident stride closer to me.

"That's reassuring," I said, oozing a step back and trying to keep sarcasm out of my voice. "I'm glad that he's well behaved, but I've never known a boarding stable to put a stallion and mare in adjacent stalls. This is ridiculous. The barn manager knew I was bringing a mare."

"It'll be fine," Eric said, taking a step closer and again invading my personal space.

I wasn't sure I could hide my annoyance with the situation. How ignorant of the barn manager. Mares and stallions aren't housed next to each other. Keeping stallions in barns catering to pleasure riders was uncommon. But if it did happen, the barn managers would keep geldings on either side of the stallion. I would never think to ask who Emma's neighbors were. I wouldn't ask a friend to buy me the latest best-selling novel and then specify that I wanted the book in English.

"I'm not so sure," I said, leaning back on my heels.

"Don't worry, nothing's gonna happen," Eric said as he thrust his chest forward and gently patted my shoulder.

My body recoiled at his touch, which felt condescending. Telling me to ignore my feelings was a sure-fire way to get me irritated. I could feel my back stiffen.

"I'm glad to hear that, but it's not just about physical safety," I said, displeased that I had to educate a fellow horseman in what I thought should be common sense. "My mare is in season and they are frustrating each other." I marveled at how unconscious this man seemed to be about the horses' mental environment.

"She looks perfectly fine to me," he said flashing his white toothy smile again. He adjusted his shirt more tightly into his pants and the escaped hairs were contained.

"I know my horse," I affirmed. "She's being teased and her hormones don't need any encouragement. Well, Eric I'm glad you told me about your horse. Please don't be offended if I move my mare to another stall."

"None taken. No stalls open," he said, turning to go with a quick pivot on the heel of his cowboy boot.

When I found the barn owner, he confirmed that no other stall was available and put me on the wait list for the next available one. He seemed not the least concerned that he placed a mare and stallion next to each other.

Over the next couple of days Emma's distress grew. She was out of her head with raging hormones. They had undoubtedly teased her at the stallion station before each attempted breeding, so it was no surprise that her hormones were reactive. I called the vet out to see if he could give her some relief. He was in the area the next day and could meet me at the barn.

"This is not a good situation," the vet said when he saw Emma trying to reach around the fence to touch the stallion.

"The barn manager put up another plywood barrier, so the horses couldn't touch noses," I said. "I suppose he thought he was being helpful, but it wouldn't stop the pheromones from permeating the air. This proximity is torture."

"I'll give her a shot to force ovulation," he said. "That will settle her hormones down. Once she ovulates she won't be receptive and the stallion will lose interest. But you need to move her."

"I'm working on that," I said. "This is the only stallion at this stable so any stall that opens up should be fine.

"It's always a puzzle to me," my vet said, shaking his head, "why some folks choose to keep a male horse intact when they aren't actively using him as a breeding stallion."

A couple of days after the vet's visit, Emma's frustration abated and the two horses stopped calling to each other. I hoped she could be moved before her next ovulation when she would be flooded with hormones and attractive to the stallion again. I had about three weeks to figure this out. Meanwhile, seeing her soft eye and gentle demeanor return eased the tension in my body. At least she didn't have a panic attack.

I was overjoyed when in two weeks another stall opened. Emma hadn't come back into season and I wanted her moved before she did. The stall bordered the indoor arena and was at least a good one hundred yards away from the stallion. Emma could look out from the front of her stall across the aisle and watch the horses being exercised. The resident instructor trained his clients and their mounts during the day and many of the boarders came out in the evening after work. When Emma wanted quiet, she could walk out her back door into her paddock and have a view of the hills and enjoy the afternoon sun on her back. Most importantly, Emma was between two geldings.

The day after I moved Emma to her new stall, she greeted me with her soft nicker. The sound warmed my heart. I had feared all the changes she'd been through might trigger another panic attack. What a relief that they hadn't. I wondered if something had happened during our separation. Perhaps Emma now believed and understood that I would always keep her, that I would always come for her and that I cared about her happiness. Might she have internalized a better sense of safety and peace? Had she been able to resolve some of her deep-seated terrors? Her terrors of abandonment? That would be incredible.

Then my mind got very excited. She had just had a long stall rest of a couple of months. If her sweet state of mind had returned, would her feet heal and stay pain-free absent the pounding? And if she was mentally fine and her feet stayed sound could we resume our dressage career together? The vital forces of my body soared with hope. I called the blacksmith. Who said I was a pessimist?

Chapter 16

The day after the blacksmith had put on Emma's sneakers, I headed to the barn with a renewed sense of happy anticipation. Wouldn't it be wonderful if Emma's feet had recovered?

To determine how sore her feet were I led her to the small, outdoor round pen. I let loose of her halter and asked her to move out. Her walk looked great with no signs of soreness. Although the quarter by dust that served as footing was little better than pea-sized gravel, it provided a barrier from the hard-packed adobe soil below. Given this was only a short assessment period, it didn't matter that the footing wasn't ideal. Besides, the less forgiving footing would help reveal any soreness. My tongue made the well-known clucking sound and Emma responded with an energetic trot. She threw her head up in the air and sprung around the pen with the spry movement of a youngster. I studied each footfall and her overall appearance. She looked happy - and more importantly she looked level. I didn't need to see more.

In contrast to the round pen, the indoor arena at this barn had footing comprised of Angel Island sand and shredded rubber from recycled tennis shoes. The barn owner religiously dragged and watered the arena every morning to eliminate ruts and to keep the footing from compacting or getting too dusty. Whenever a horse's foot hit the ground, the concussion was absorbed by both the fluffy sand and the rubber pieces. I loved walking across the arena. The footing didn't give way like the dry, deep sand at the beach. And it wasn't so hard as to be jarring. Instead, the arena offered a perfect balance between holding firm yet cushioning each footfall. The idea that this footing might help keep Emma's feet from getting sore had crossed my mind more than once.

I led Emma from the round pen to the grooming area. With her saddled up we entered the covered arena. Standing on the mounting block, I paused. Would the extra weight put too much stress on her feet? I reminded myself that she had gone sound before after a rest period.

I put my foot in the stirrup, swung my leg over and eased down to that place I felt I was born to sit. This feeling melted my core. What I felt must be similar to what work-weary people feel when sinking down into their Barcalounger at the end of the day. Familiarity. Feeling supported. Surrendering tension. My calves closed and Emma struck off in an active walk. To be back on my horse was sheer joy.

When Emma transitioned up to the trot, she seemed to like the footing and extended her stride without my asking. The footing cushioned her bouncy strides. I warmed her up with some large circles at the trot and canter. When her back was soft and I could stay seated in the saddle instead of posting (rising from the seat every other stride), I felt a deeper connection to her. I asked for a little more impulsion and she offered lots of suspension – that wonderful floaty, air-borne lift between strides. Wow that felt good. Even better, I didn't feel any shifting of her weight that would indicate that she was favoring one leg. No signs of the slightest soreness. Not wanting to ask for too much I jumped off Emma having satisfied myself that she was sound.

One day of riding led to another. Emma enjoyed being back at work. The dressage training suited her need to be fit and to exercise her mind. She liked the focus and concentration that the work required and how it made her feel about herself.

Whenever I walked into a barn, I could usually pick out the dressage horses. Besides being very well muscled they would emanate self-esteem and pride in themselves. When a dressage horse entered the ring, you could feel the collective "Wow" from spectators. Self-confidence oozed out of the horses and they seemed to radiate, "Look at me. Look at what I can do. I know how to do this." I imagined that a prima ballerina might have the same feeling at the height of her career when she stepped out on the stage.

Each day when I dismounted Emma, I expressed my appreciation for the ride. I patted her neck and thanked her. In return, she curved her head and neck and brushed my forearm with her muzzle. Shivers would race to my heart carrying a full blast of her love. How satisfying. And I couldn't help getting excited that we might be able to resume our dressage career.

There is nothing like the passage of time to persuade or perhaps allow an evolution in thinking. When Emma was strong enough to do a ten-meter canter circle and a twenty-meter counter canter, I was ready to trust that my dressage horse was back. I no longer used the word hope.

As Emma's strength improved, I could ask her to do more. Even with vigorous trotting and canter work, Emma showed no signs of lameness. Each day when I came out, I was greeted by her soft and present eye. I couldn't believe when four months had whizzed by. What a delicious time we shared. The interval was long enough to convince me that her wellness was here to stay. When we were at the Sweet Mountain boarding stable, her anxiety attacks had occurred every few weeks and sometimes more than one within a week. We had now gone months with no attack.

I could tell that our work was improving by the reactions of the people walking through the aisle way of the indoor arena. The comments of approval as well as the length of time they stopped what they were doing were testaments that we were creating something worth watching. The barn manager, who had never been known to comment on someone's riding, told me in private that he was impressed with what we were accomplishing. I felt great.

My riding took me to another place, a place of deep meditative calm. The seat of the saddle had melded to my shape and welcomed me like an old friend. The fresh scent of glycerin soap rose from the leather. The reins felt as if they were an extension of my hands and arms. As Emma began to exercise, her neck sweated and I could smell that delicious full aroma of horse. As a child I had wished that I could bottle that scent.

My core and hips flexed and expanded to absorb the movement of Emma's back. Being in harmony with her made it easier to sit her trot. Her back muscles invited me into a lovely place of balance. The more collected she became and as she carried more weight on her hindquarters the jarring motion of the trot was dampened and I was able to sit with little effort. A quiet seat allowed me to differentiate subtle cues. All muscles had to stay relaxed and flexible or I would lose my connection to her. A slight rise of my inside hip bone cued Emma to strike off into a canter. An infinitesimal resistance in my back and Emma would come to a halt. Gently close my fingers and flex my calf muscles and she would march backwards. We were so together that sometimes I only had to think the movement for her to perform it.

During our trot and canter work, I had to hear the sound of her footfalls. I discovered that I became disoriented if I tried to ride in the rain. The roar of the drops on the metal roof drowned out the sound of hoof beats on sand. Listening to Emma's footfalls became my meditation. The metronome rhythm of the two-beat trot gait lulled me into an alternate consciousness. I felt as if I left my body and was not aware of anything in the world except the sound of the hoof beats. What a high to once again abandon myself in my riding and surrender to the sheer bliss of being in unison with another soul.

One weekend dawned particularly bright and sunny. The beautiful spring morning added to the excitement I felt before a ride. Emma let out a soft nicker as soon as she saw me walking down the aisle. Her head bobbed up and down in greeting. The light in her eyes shown bright and the expression of joy on her face made my breath catch. I couldn't imagine a better way to be greeted. My heart flooded with love. I led her outside to a hitching post and groomed her, taking care to remove caked on dirt and bits of bedding. Next came the dressage saddle that I had looked long and hard to find. This Niedersuss *Symphonie* helped put my legs and seat in the correct position. Shoulders, hips and ankles needed to be kept in alignment. The underside of the saddle had a broad enough surface area to spread my weight out over Emma's back, so it was more comfortable for her. The saddle was now well broken in and aided my ability to ride with better balance and more security. The saddle kept me positioned in the deepest part of the seat.

The cotton saddle pad smoothed on Emma's back without a wrinkle. Then the gel pad was layered on. The saddle settled over both. The girth with elastic on both ends was more comfortable for Emma. She appreciated the padded girth and elastic ends that lengthened when she took deep breaths. She didn't like the feeling of having her breath constrained. Those of us who wear bras can understand that feeling.

When I walked around to her left side to grab the girth, I noticed that her eyes flashed worry and for a moment I saw a sliver of the white of her eye. I had no idea what that was about. Emma had never been cinchy or bridle shy. Emma tensed when I pulled the straps through the buckles of the girth. I stroked her shoulder to reassure her and eased the girth to the first hole as I usually did.

I felt the violence before I saw it. Emma reared up and crashed down with all her weight, shaking the ground as if a minor earthquake had struck, then ducked her head and thrust her hind legs straight up into the air. She looked like a bucking rodeo horse that had just been let out of the chute. As soon as her feet landed, she hunched her back preparing for another leap. Crouch back, leap forward into the air and then thrust the hind legs up. I tried to get close enough to grab her halter, but she was too fast for me. The lead rope that held her to the post gave her about three feet of play. Even with that restriction she was able to clear the ground by several feet. I had never seen her buck with such ferocity. At most I'd seen her do a little crow hop when she was feeling good, rounding her back and dropping her head, but it was gentle and more like a stretch of her back.

I knew I needed to do something. She might hurt herself. If the rope broke, she could flip over backwards and severely injure herself. Or depending on how she bucked and hit the end of the rope she could break her neck. I steeled my back and leapt to her side when she plummeted to the ground after a buck. Despite using a quick release knot, the rope had pulled so tight that I couldn't release it. I turned and in a split second unbuckled the girth and jerked the saddle off. Free of the saddle Emma's bucks decreased in amplitude.

When Emma had calmed down enough to be approached, I reached out and stroked her neck. With each sweep of my palm I used a soothing voice to reassure her. I needed to stay alert because she still hadn't returned to her normal self. Each stroke seemed to relax her further. Soon she kept all four feet on the ground. She was clearly nervous and paced back and forth as far as the lead rope allowed her.

Several minutes passed before she was able to stand still and I could trust that she would be okay. I picked up the saddle from the fence where I had thrown it and examined the saddle pad. My fingers pulsed over every inch looking for foreign objects that might have gone unnoticed. The pad had been recently washed and revealed nothing but cotton flannel. What was under it that caused such a violent reaction?

A fellow boarder who witnessed what had happened stopped

grooming his horse. "Wow, that was some show," he said as he walked up to me, keeping his eye on Emma.

"She's never done anything like that before," I said as I ran my hands over the pad, again.

"It happened to me once. I had a fairly new saddle pad and the fiber pile hadn't been crushed down yet. A sharp burr had lodged under the fluff. When I threw my Western saddle on my horse, he took one good buck and sent it flying. It took a while to find the problem. I don't use pads with thick pile anymore," he said as he leaned over and eyed the underside of my saddle pad.

"Thanks for coming over," I said as I searched the pad for the third time. "I'm not finding anything. Any ideas are appreciated."

"Let me try," he said, extending his arm.

"It's a plain quilted cotton pad," I said, offering it to him. "No pile, nowhere for anything to hide."

"Got me," he said when he finished his inspection and handed the pad back. "You better check the bottom of your saddle or the gel pad you had on."

I had and did again and still found nothing. The girth surface was smooth. I checked Emma's back. It was spotless. I wondered what to do next.

A yellow tennis ball was peeking out from my tack box. That gave me an idea. I used tennis balls to massage Emma's back. Maybe she had had a spasm of some kind that caused an uncomfortable cramp. An overturned bucket served as my stool. With the ball in my palm I mimicked what the chiropractor had shown me. My hand eased the ball into her back along her spine with a kneading motion. Emma loved her massages and seemed to be enjoying it now. Her back showed no signs of soreness or tension.

Relieved that whatever caused her behavior had passed, I picked up her pads and replaced them on her back. She stood quietly. Next, I ran my hands over the pads putting pressure on them. She did nothing, not even a flick of the ear. I picked up the saddle and lowered it onto her back with care. Still nothing. I took the girth and attached it to one side of the saddle. When I came around to the other side and picked up the girth to fasten it to the saddle billets, her body tensed. I watched Emma's eye as I eased the girth up to her belly. When the girth put pressure on her belly, the whites of her eyes showed and she bunched up her hind legs. I let loose the end of the girth and whisked the saddle off. Once again, I inspected the girth and pad all over. Still nothing. I reasoned to try one more time. Isn't the third time the charm? I buckled the girth on the right side and then ducked under Emma's neck to the other side. As soon as I got the girth to the first hole on the saddle leathers, she gave no warning and exploded into bucking. Ready this time, I let loose of the girth and whipped the saddle off her back.

"Emma, I'm totally clueless," I said over my shoulder as I carried the saddle to the tack room. "I wish I wasn't so emotional and could hear you better," I said, coming back to her side. I stood by her shoulder and rubbed her neck. Relief spread through my body when Emma's eye eased back to its usual soft appearance. "Thank goodness we have Carol to help me understand."

Not knowing what else to do I turned Emma loose in the round pen so that she could get some exercise and work off any excess energy. Riding would have to wait for another day.

Inside the welcoming comfort of my home, I threw myself onto my family room sofa and called Carol. While the phone rang, I watched the squirrels scamper across my back lawn. These furry creatures played with abandon and seemed to be worry-free. But then they hadn't chosen to be domesticated and join with humans in relationship.

"For all of the nine years that Emma has been mine," I told Carol when she asked me what was up, "she's never had a problem being saddled. Why is it suddenly an issue?"

"Emma, Diana says you acted up when she put the saddle on you today. What's going on?" Carol asked.

I waited, wondering the reason and knowing that Emma always had a reason for what she did.

"Wow, she's full of rage." Carol said with surprise in her voice. "Emma, what are you angry about?"

Worry wrapped its cold fingers around my stomach as I catalogued what I might have done to cause this. I couldn't remember anything different in my routine. Could I have been doing something that escalated an irritation until she couldn't stand it anymore?

"Diana, I'm not sure what she's saying." Carol said, sounding perplexed. "Something about a mean man."

"Emma, has someone done something to you?" I asked. "My friends haven't warned me about any strangeness at this barn. My previous horse, Fortune, was frightened of the men who cleaned his stall, but Emma hasn't shown any aversion to people. She's very social."

"It happened when I was two years old," Carol translated, the pitch in her voice rising. "A man came to the pasture where I was living. Up until then I had been left alone. He caught me and tied me to the side of the shed where the hay was stored. Now I know that he had come to teach me how to be ridden. But then I didn't know what he wanted. He was in a hurry and didn't explain things to me, so I got confused. I tried to be good."

I heard Carol gasp. Then the phone went silent. My impatience made me speak when the pause lasted too long.

"What's Emma saying?" I demanded.

"I was getting nervous," Carol translated, "so he slammed a club on my forehead."

The staccato rhythm of Carol's words hammered into my brain. My rage whipped by adrenalin rose to a fury.

"I was dazed," Carol translated. "I couldn't move. He put the saddle on me and cinched it up really hard. It frightened me. I didn't think that I would be able to breathe. I panicked. He hit me again. Next, he put the bridle on my head and forced a metal bit into my mouth. I had never had anything in my mouth before. I didn't know what was going on. Then he got on me. I was still stunned or I would've bucked him off."

My muscles hardened into rocks and my free fist clenched. "Carol, this is awful."

"Diana, Emma feels she was brutalized," Carol said. "Because she was stunned, she couldn't fight back. She was powerless. She felt betrayed by her own body."

"A cruel weaning, the injury to her feet when she tried to join her mother, ignored in her pasture and sickened from the hay she was fed and then this," I said hurling the words out.

"When he got on me he dug in his spurs," Carol translated. "But I didn't know what that meant. All I knew was that it hurt my ribs and my skin. When I tried to run away he yanked on the bit in my mouth. The metal pressed against my gums and the roof of my mouth. It really hurt and was sore for days. It hurt to eat. I didn't know what to do to avoid the pain. He kept asking me to do things I didn't understand and he called me names. He called me stupid. He came back several times and did the same thing over again. My anger grew, but I couldn't do anything. I was relieved when he didn't come anymore. I didn't care if I never saw another human."

The tears were streaming down my face. "Emma, I'm so sorry. That's a horrid experience. Why didn't you tell me about this before?"

Carol translated, the words choking in her throat, "I didn't remember what happened. That period of time was a black hole."

I dropped my shoulders and sunk back in my chair and tried to calm my emotions. "I'm so sorry, Emma. Humans black out memories as well when things are too awful to remember. My sister has several years during her childhood without any memories."

"How about you?" Carol asked.

"No, I was conscious for all of it," I said. "I can't help but be amazed how Emma is able to love like she does. How do horses do that? Where do they find all that forgiveness?"

"And to answer your question, I don't know." Carol said. "Emma has more to say."

"…I'm so sorry I bucked when you saddled me," Carol translated mimicking sadness. "I couldn't help it. The memory of that man came back to me in a rush of feelings and I had to act out."

"Emma, don't apologize," I said, my heart spasmed in sadness. "That you remember what happened to you is important. It's part of the healing process. Because you're feeling safer and you are stronger you can let these memories surface. I believe in the wisdom of the saying that the truth will set you free."

"I'm so lucky you are my person," Carol translated. "I know I would have died if you hadn't gotten me."

My tears welled up again, "Emma, it's my good fortune to have such a wonderful horse as you. You've taught me so much. Just think of all the wonderful experiences we've shared."

After I hung up the phone, I reflected on Emma's recovered memory. I saw it as a positive sign that she could remember and process the traumas from her early life. Maybe that's why she hadn't had an anxiety attack in a long time. She might be further along in her psychological recovery. Might this be proof she had taken a big stride in her journey towards wellness?

My body sank deeper into the sofa. The simple materiality offered me comfort. Emma had started her psychological recovery work in earnest a couple of years after I had gotten her. She began by processing the shocks and atrocities of her weaning and early life. Her abandonment issues seemed to have lessened. She no longer dissociated from her body. She had completed a lot of her grieving. She had passed through months of rage attacks. And now she has uncovered an abuse that had been hidden away in the depths of her subconscious. I was so proud of her for the progress she'd made. I knew what it took for me to travel that road. I'm in awe of anyone who takes on their recovery work and sticks with it long enough to come out the other side.

The next day when I went to the barn, I was careful to take my time saddling Emma. I had experienced cold-backed horses before, with their intolerance of being saddled quickly, and knew how to move with deliberation. I stroked her neck, murmured reassurances and gave her numerous treats throughout the process so that she would have better associations with being saddled. If I took my time and fed her Mrs. Pasture's cookies, the saddling process was tolerated without any bucking, although I could see rage and terror flit across her face.

I could only wonder if she had gotten through the worst of the insults that stood between her and an extended happiness. Each time she made progress, I held that thought. Maybe this time she is on the other side of her internally generated emotional prison.

Chapter 17

No caregiver could be prouder of her charge than I was of Emma for facing her demons and doing the work to be well and emotionally whole. Good thing that horses were known to have a strong life force promoting health. With a little bit of coaxing and a whole lot of treats, Emma's saddling improved - though I still had to be careful. The episode with the saddle reminded me that I could never quite know what she was going to do from one day to the next.

Every time I gave Emma's continued soundness of both body and mind any thought, I felt like I had been the recipient of a gift from a benevolent force. Even though Emma had experienced a flashback of abuse and reacted in a violent way, I was relieved that she didn't show any signs of returning to her seemingly random panic attacks. The issue around saddling seemed to be an isolated incident.

These respites were fully appreciated. In my life I tended to be skeptical of any drops of kindness that splashed my way. Two different astrologers using their own words had given me the same message – don't expect anything to come your way, anything you get will be due to hard work. One was kind enough to suggest that my life was patterned much like Chiron in Greek mythology - the healer who was abandoned as a baby by both parents and then as an adult suffered from a painful wound that would never mend. His career goals changed from making war to learning as much as he could about the healing arts. My life's mission, like Chiron's, was to heal others. So, I guess it shouldn't have surprised me that shattered animals found their way to me. I had a basis for understanding their pain.

From our life together, I knew all too well that Emma's happiness could change at any moment. How fortunate I felt as the weeks passed by and Emma was happy and the fully capable athlete I knew her to be. The weeks slipped into months and I praised my luck that my dream horse had been returned to me. I could only speculate why she hadn't had a panic attack since moving to this boarding stable. Perhaps a combination of maturing, feeling safe and now the realization of the source of her repressed rage helped get her past her anxiety issues. Post-traumatic stress often originates if the body can't exercise its physiologic response to action. When the man "broke" Emma to saddle, she couldn't flee or fight. I wondered if this could have been the inciting incident that created her panic attacks.

Emma's body had developed enough that we were able to train movements we hadn't schooled before. Her physique reflected the dressage work she was doing. Her muscles rippled under a shiny coat and although she was a refined thoroughbred it was not a stretch to call her brawny. Her topline was round and her loin and gaskin muscles radiated strength. She had the beginnings of a canter pirouette. Her hind end had enough power to keep her rhythm while she lowered her haunches and shifted the weight off her shoulders. The size of the circle that she made pivoting around her hind end was a still a couple of meters, but she executed it well. I conjectured before long before we would be able to reduce the size of the circle and do a proper pirouette. Our progress was thrilling.

Emma was doing so well in so many ways that when one of my friends at the stable asked if I wanted to go with her on a trail ride, I couldn't resist. I felt as if I was being serenaded by *The Sound of*

Music. The hills enticed me to cavort in the grass. The young nun Maria needed to romp in the great outdoors and so did I. A handy rag removed the dust from Emma's Stubben all-purpose saddle. I tacked her up and followed my friend as she rode down the driveway, across the road and through the gate that led to miles and miles of open space and riding trails. The air was clear and I breathed in the clean smell of fresh, spring grass. The sun's warmth with its radiating fingers spread across my back and massaged tension away. The wild mustard was in full bloom painting the hillsides in a bright, brilliant yellow, a yellow so radiant it would uplift any reluctant heart.

With each step Emma took, my joy soared and I felt my consciousness unfurl and stretch out to the crest line of the rolling hills surrounding us. My being felt so expanded that I could embrace every living thing in sight: the humming insects, the red hawk soaring above, the ground squirrels skittering across fallen tree trunks. I imagined I knew what lambs experience when they are let out of the barn after being locked up all winter. I wanted to kick up my heels and squeal. I couldn't have been happier. I figured this is why the cliché of the cowboy kissing his horse and riding off into the sunset had such staying power.

The red hawk was joined by another; they rode the air currents higher, gliding in slow circles above my head. Off to the right on the facing ridge, Hereford cattle, red coats ablaze, grazed on the lush pasture. They looked peaceful and content basking in the sunshine, bathed by the gentle breeze and cocooned by the temperate weather.

About a mile from the barn all my senses snapped back into my body like a taut elastic band let loose. I sensed a change that was too subliminal to either quantify or qualify. Was I imagining a shift in Emma's energy? My antennae raised on full alert. I couldn't see anything startling. My friend's horse plodded ahead of us unperturbed, calmly negotiating the turns in the single-track trail.

I was about to shake off the dread when I could feel a slight shortening in Emma's stride. She craned her neck high, abandoning the long and low frame of a relaxed horse. I gently worked the bit, vibrating it in my fingers, closed my calves and asked her to lower her head and stretch her neck down and out. I breathed in relief when she quickly responded and resumed the loose rein, even-paced languid dawdle with her neck horizontal to the ground.

A few strides later, her head shot up. She flicked her poll as if to rearrange her forelock. Two strides later she tossed her head and neck up and down as if she was trying to dislodge a ferocious biting fly. Her body started shaking. Then I knew I might be in trouble.

"Emma is coming undone," I called out to my friend on the small, black Morgan plugging along ahead. "I need to go back."

"Do you want me to go with you?" she responded. "Would that help calm Emma? My horse has a way of giving other horses confidence."

"From my experience, no," I said, turning Emma around. "Besides, her anxiety may be contagious to your horse. Go ahead and enjoy your ride."

I took a deep breath and settled deeper into the saddle. This wasn't going to be fun.

There wouldn't be much time to get Emma to the barn before the terror would take over and blot out any hope of reaching her mind. Controlling her was going to be difficult. Despite my growing anxiety for the safety of both of us, I couldn't let my body telegraph my rising concerns. If I communicated any distress, it would signal fear to Emma and exacerbate what she was already feeling. I used all my self-control to force my muscles to stay loose though my own mind was warning me of all the disastrous possible outcomes. If I tried vaulting off her this far from her stall, I might not be able to hold on to her. She might bolt off at full speed and run through fences and other obstacles that got in her way, hurting herself or others.

I needed tact and all my knowledge of Emma to decompress this situation. I had to read subtle cues and respond appropriately without exhibiting anything except calm. Decisions of whether to sit tight or act were based on knowing her limits. When she started tossing her head, I knew I had to work the bit in a very particular way. If my hands moved the bit too quickly, I might escalate her rage. If I moved my hands too softly, I would be ineffectual in distracting her and keeping the dialog open. If I did it just the right amount to be felt and at the right rhythm, I could keep her four feet on the ground - albeit at a rushed and jerky pace.

I reminded myself I had no problem staying on a galloping horse. My skeptical mind reminded me that I would be challenged to stay on a horse that, running at full speed, changed directions with no warning. If Emma decided to make a sharp right turn and I was preparing for a left turn, I would be thrown forward and hit the ground going somewhere around thirty or more miles an hour. Smashing into the ground would be damaging enough, but I could hit a rock, a tree trunk or fence post. I had seen far too many badly injured or paraplegic riders to not know the risks.

I had to stay fully present and use my body and intuition to feel where she was emotionally. The first big challenge was getting her out of the park lands. I had to be hyper vigilant to anything that might set her off. Were we going to encounter another anxious horse coming towards us? Was a silent bicyclist going to catapult from behind a blind curve and whiz past us? Was someone's loose dog going to burst out onto the trail from a skirmish in the brush? I had to have radar, sonar and x-ray vision to anticipate all the possible triggers that we might confront.

Knowing Emma as I did I managed a scary but continual progress toward home. I sighed a tiny breath when the gate that exited the open space was at last in sight. I debated whether I should try to dismount to negotiate the gate but thought better of it. If Emma broke loose she would be on the road. If I was lucky, I could swing it open and maneuver her through it on the first try. If I challenged her to stand still for too long, she might rear and come down on top of the gate, impaling herself on one of the posts. I asked my guardian angels for help. I reached for the lock, slid it out of the catch and snatched the gate open, despite Emma's agitated movements. I had the same problem on the other side to close the gate. I managed to teeter off to one side of the saddle, stretch and connect with the side of the gate by my fingertips, slamming it shut. I didn't want to be the one responsible for cattle loose on the road potentially getting hurt or causing an accident.

The asphalt road was ahead of us. Although there were equestrian crossing signs on this section of the pavement, motorists rarely slowed down. I had to listen for cars and time our crossing. If I tried to contain Emma for too long she would bolt. If she bolted down the road we could run right into an on-coming vehicle. Even with no cars, the surface of the asphalt was tricky. The roadway was slick and coated with oil. If Emma tried to move quickly she could lose her footing and fall. I called on my guardian angels again, who in their silent wisdom must have been what guided us to the barn's driveway without having to negotiate any traffic.

My stomach was in my mouth until we reached the parking lot of the barn. Sitting on a powder keg is exhausting. I gave a few quick half halts to slow Emma's jog and then vaulted off, negotiating an upright landing. Emma's shoulder kept bumping into me as I attempted to restrain her from dragging me down the aisle. I stayed with her as she plunged into her stall. As soon as she set foot inside, Emma lowered her anxiety level a notch. With each minute that passed Emma relaxed more. After ten minutes she looked her normal self. Only then could I release the tension I was holding. Taking off her tack I swore that I would never try a trail ride again. Thank God she felt safe here in her stall. At least she had that refuge.

On the drive home my heart slowed from its hard-thumping beat. A full half hour had to pass before it could resume a resting rhythm. I agonized over how hard it was for me to predict Emma's behavior. She had been fine on the roads and trails in Briones Park when we lived in Lafayette, so the expectation that she would be fine on a trail ride here in the Mt. Diablo and Shell Ridge Open space was reasonable. I wasn't going to beat myself up on that one. I wondered if maybe Emma had some form of agoraphobia. Was it possible for horses to be afflicted with it?

Once I was settled at home, my thoughts had the opportunity to range free. My skeptical mind wondered if I might have opened Pandora's box with that trail ride. I pleaded to the universe to keep my horse calm.

Chapter 18

The memory of the trail ride faded and the grasp it held on my worries dissipated as my work with Emma continued without incident. Once again, the sound of Emma's hooves landing softly on the fluffy sand of the indoor arena lulled me into a meditative state. One day after I had been riding for a good twenty minutes, I slipped into the zone of complete harmony with my horse. I traveled to that delicious space of unity with another being. Sweet.

"Hey Diana, sorry to intrude on your ride," a woman's voice assailed my ears, invaded my consciousness and broke my concentration. "I have something I want to tell you."

I looked over towards the side rail covered with a thick layer of dust and to the kind-faced woman hanging over the arena fence. The sunlight from the overhead skylights struggled through the weather-worn fiberglass to gently illuminate her face.

I communicated to Emma through my seat, brought her back to a walk and crossed the arena over to the woman, who I recognized as a fellow boarder. I wondered what she wanted. Stopping a person in the middle of a ride was unusual, considered a bit rude, and it usually irritated me.

"I heard what happened when you took Emma out for a trail ride," she said, putting her hand out to rub Emma's forehead. "You must have been scared."

"It's terrifying, frustrating, you name it," I said, dropping the reins to stroke Emma's neck. I looked down at the woman's sympathetic face. Her short brown hair framed brown eyes and softly tanned cheeks. The woman was probably in her early thirties. I looked up and over to the hills and sighed. "Arena riding can get really boring. I miss trail riding."

"I have an idea for you," she said, looking up at me with a steady, kind gaze. "I heard Denny Cook is giving a clinic down at Carters next week. He is one of the best horsemen around and is in this area for a little while."

"Great, I remember him from the barn where I first stabled Emma," I said, my mind conjuring up memories of his teaching methods. "He gave a weekend clinic and I was very intrigued by his techniques with the horses."

"I have nothing but respect for him," the woman said, handing Emma a piece of carrot. "If anyone can help your horse, it's him. He specializes in troubled horses. If you're interested, I'll leave the contact information on your stall door, so it will be there when you finish your ride."

"Yes, I'm willing to try just about anything," I said, hope springing alive in my heart. "It can't hurt and I might just learn something. Thanks." Although I picked up the reins and put Emma back to work, I couldn't help thinking about this opportunity. I liked the idea of getting help from a well-known trainer of difficult horses.

Denny was not a cowboy yahoo who used harsh bits and spurs, but rather, as a student of Ray Hunt, used methods that recognized the horse's psychology and intelligence. Instead of force, he figured out what would work with each horse to develop a willing, cooperative partnership. Denny was successful with both badly trained horses and untrained horses and had decades of experience. As part of his rehabilitation program, Denny would sometimes take the horses of his clients with him to work cattle. The horses were returned to their owners who swore their equines were reborn with excellent attitudes, manners and skills. I wondered whether he would be able to help Emma get over her anxiety attacks and apparent agoraphobia. When I got home, I made the call and nabbed the last opening in his clinic scheduled for the following week.

The day of the clinic the weather cooperated. The sun shone and there was no wind to frighten horses with swaying branches and scudding leaves that took flight in a gust. I managed to ride Emma down the half mile of road to where the clinic was being held. Once safely on the property and away from traffic, I took a deep breath. I felt even more relaxed when I closed the gate to the arena. Emma seemed to do better when she was confined.

Denny was sitting on the top rail of the wooden plank fence with his back rounded over his chest. His blue jeans, plaid snap-buttoned shirt and well-worn pointed-toe boots spelled cowboy. His dark blonde hair was slicked down and matched in color his thick handlebar mustache. Jumping down from the fence, he shuffled into the center of the arena. He exuded a quietness that commanded attention with an unspoken invitation. His bowed legs and slow gait were the perfect stereotype of someone who makes his living on the back of a horse. He squinted, shielding his sparkly blue eyes from the sun. His brow and the crinkled skin of his cheeks could not hide the vibrancy of the energy that poured out of his eyes.

The other horses that had shown up for the clinic were a motley assortment. I speculated that there was not one registered horse in the bunch. They looked of random breeding and moved rather plainly with short strides and little impulsion or suspension. Shaggy coats and unkempt manes spoke to their unpampered life. I was embarrassed by what a snob I was for a beautiful, well bred, well-groomed horse.

The first part of the clinic was held in an arena so small that Emma would have to collect to maintain her canter stride. Fortunately, we didn't have to do much cantering. It didn't take long to see that

Emma was much better trained than any of the other horses. The spectators around the arena ooh-ed and ah-ed when I asked Emma for an extended trot. There was a part of me that liked to show off. The other riders were mostly pleasure riders who had not yet made the acquaintance of a half pass or canter pirouette. I hoped I wasn't turning into a DQ – a dressage queen - with all the airs and attitudes of righteousness.

When the participants had trouble understanding the exercises Denny had asked them to perform, he decided to demonstrate. He ambled over to the side of the arena where a rather rangy, squat horse was dozing. I hadn't really noticed the little dun horse because he had hardly flicked an ear since we arrived. He could have been a wooden sculpture.

Without even the tiniest tug on the reins the little horse followed Denny to the center of the arena. As soon as Denny settled himself in the saddle, the horse came to life. It was if someone had put a quarter in the arcade game. From nothing to full energy in a split second. I wouldn't have recognized the pony-sized horse from a moment earlier. He grew in stature. Denny proceeded to show more than the exercises he wanted us to do. He did spins, Mach 1 backups, and flying changes. His horse responded with punctuality and animation. I couldn't see any cue or aid that Denny gave to the horse. They looked as if they were one being. When Denny had completed his ride, he retied the little horse to the fence where the horse promptly dropped his head, cocked one hip and went back to snoozing. That horse knew his job and knew how to economize his energy. He seemed to be content with his role in life. I mouthed a silent prayer. "Please do that for Emma."

Denny came back and addressed our little group. "Okay, it's your turn." When the other clinic participants attempted a simple turn on the forehand, I heard a lot of fussing and mild oaths exclaimed. Their horses looked confused and tossed their manes, mouths open in protest.

"He made it look so easy," I heard the young woman on the pinto say as she tried to budge her horse's hind quarters to the side, only to have her horse step into her leg instead of away from it.

"Why won't my horse do it?" an older man riding a buckskin asked, having thrown down his reins in disgust.

"I appreciate what he was able to do even more," a middle-aged woman astride a short bay gelding called out to her buddy.

I couldn't help but giggle at their frustration. While the other riders had difficulty in their attempts, I had no trouble. Emma parked her front end and took long, even steps with her hind end making a half circle around her front legs. When Denny asked for a turn on the haunches, Emma stepped in place behind, and swung her front end around in a half circle. Denny wanted us to continue doing that exercise down the length of the arena. Emma breezed through. Her dressage training made these exercises rudimentary. I felt a certain amount of satisfaction that we could demonstrate our well-earned competency.

"Nice work," Denny said, nodding at us. "I can see she's well-schooled." He turned his attention to the others and gave each a suggestion to improve their connection with their horses.

I glowed inside. Yes, Emma and I were connected and she responded to anything I asked brilliantly. Our partnership was characterized by her willingness to respond to the subtlest of cues. We could make our work look fluid and effortless.

The second half of the clinic was going to be conducted on the trail. That's where I needed the help, not with obedience or schooling in an arena. I wondered how long it would take for Emma to act out. I noticed that I didn't think "if" she would act out, but rather "when." I wondered if I was being overly pessimistic. If it were to happen, I hoped it would be close to home so I wouldn't have the chore of getting her back to the barn. Or better yet, maybe Denny could fix her on the spot.

When the participants were finished with the last of the arena exercises, we all lined up and followed Denny on his dun horse into the open space. About three blocks out into the hillside Emma didn't disappoint me. She seesawed her head left and right, scanning the surround for danger. Her eyes went wild, the whites showed and she started shaking. Denny's attention spun over to us. He studied us for a couple of minutes.

"Drop your reins and let her eat the spring grass," Denny called out, riding closer to me. "That should settle her down."

"I'll do as you ask, but I'll be surprised if it helps," I said and let the reins slip through my fingers.

With her head free Emma snatched a mouthful of grass, threw her head up, grass dangling from her mouth and began to jig in place. Her body shifted from jigging to shaking and back again. She had no interest in eating grass.

"You better take her home," Denny said, staring at Emma. "Let's make an appointment for a private lesson."

The next weekend Denny came back to Walnut Creek to work with Emma. He didn't need to ride her since he would be just as effective by working her from the ground. We took her across the road towards a flat space near the barn. As we neared our destination, Emma shook and tossed her head. This was great. Denny could work with her during one of her anxiety attacks. Using her lead rope to guide her, he asked her to roll over her hindquarters and change direction. Even though Emma's anxiety went rampant, she seemed to know what Denny wanted and responded quickly to the constant changes in direction. She didn't resist his requests or show any aggressive behavior. She did her best to comply, but her anxiety level didn't seem to diminish. Denny never took his eye off her and never let up on providing her direction. I kept saying to myself, "Emma, please give in." But I knew it wasn't in her control. No matter what Denny tried, Emma didn't show any signs of relaxation. She never dropped her head or softly chewed and extended her tongue in a licking gesture. At the end of an hour Denny was winded and exhausted.

"Let me try one more session," he managed to say between panting gasps. "At the very least I'll teach you some techniques to help stop her from bolting away. It won't solve your problem, but it will help get you safely home."

The next session Denny showed up on time and again worked her in the same manner. And with the same results. He asked me to get on and then taught me the one rein stop. I could do it, but it didn't diminish Emma's anxiety.

"I've worked a lot of horses," Denny said at the end of the second session. "What you have here is not a training problem, but a chemistry problem. I think you need to seek the assistance of a vet. There's nothing I can do to help."

"I've already taken her to the vet school at the University of California at Davis," I said, "a few years ago when this behavior first started. They had no idea how to help."

"That's too bad," he drawled, adjusting his Stetson, darkened with a sweat ring around the head band. "She's a highly intelligent and sensitive horse. What a shame she has this chemical imbalance. She's the kind of horse that every professional wants. She's one in a million."

"Denny, thank you for that evaluation," I said, stroking Emma's neck. "A lot of people think she's crazy and that I'm even crazier for keeping her. You've validated what I've always seen in her."

"She's not crazy. She's a fabulous horse. Best of luck," he said, nodding his head and slow-walking down the driveway, bowed legs spread wide.

In my car I took a moment to think about Emma's beginnings in this world. My anger at the injustice of her life oozed molten. The chemical imbalance probably had its origins in the way humans had treated her. Besides her early abuses, when she was an adult she had been shipped off to a hunter barn where she was punished for how she used her body over fences – she didn't pick up her knees. That Emma hadn't gone rogue was a credit to her resilience and generous heart. She was born to love.

As I drove home my disappointment in Denny's inability to help Emma took root. Yet another failed attempt to help Emma hammered my mood into depression. Denny had been known to work miracles with troubled horses. Why couldn't Emma be like other horses for once? Why couldn't I find something to give her relief? Working with Denny cost a couple of weekends and some money, but I was glad that I'd tried this approach. Denny confirmed that I hadn't been amiss in my training. I thought I knew how to communicate with a horse, but I had lost confidence in myself. Emma's problems were in her psychology and, as Denny suggested, probably brought on by some sort of physiological malfunction. From my own experience and early traumas, I knew that these issues took years to resolve. Would Emma live long enough to process all the insults that she had experienced in her early life? There would be no quick fix. My heart ached when I thought about what that meant.

I reminded myself that life had unpredictable turns. Finding out about the Denny clinic seemed to pop out of the blue, so who knew what other kind of help might be around the corner? Leading a spiritual life tended to lead one down the path of optimism. Skeptic that I was, I did my best to talk myself into traveling down that road. What were my choices?

Chapter 19

Nearly a year after Denny's clinic, I was feeling pretty good about the progress Emma and I had made in our work together in dressage. Her intelligence, ability to concentrate and desire to please made her a fabulous mount. Although I pined for a trail ride, sometimes aching for it, our ring work had its own compensations.

As I drove out to the barn I was excited about continuing our schooling on flying changes. As soon as I opened my car door in the barn's parking lot I was assaulted by a piercing, high-pitched neigh. It was a shriek, a screech, a sound that you would imagine emanating from the bowels of a torture chamber. The sound was all too familiar. I froze and had to force myself to keep moving towards Emma's stall and the vocalizations that made the hairs on the back of my neck quiver.

My heart, already pounding from the screams, went into overdrive when my eyes spotted Emma. She looked completely wild - head hung low, neck flailing, mouth open, pacing back and forth along one side of her paddock. Every few minutes she halted to dig furiously in the dirt. The soil in her paddock had been compressed from years of horses walking on the adobe and packing it down. Quarter by dust had been tamped down on top of the adobe and was nearly as hard as concrete. Still she had managed to excavate a hole almost eighteen inches deep.

Dogs dig, not horses. My heart jumped into and disappeared down that hole.

I unhooked Emma's halter from the rack on the front of her stall and slipped in, ensuring that the door was shut tight behind me. Emma didn't acknowledge me. I hesitated before entering her paddock. Her jerky, rapid movements provided no opening to approach her. I tried to sooth her with a low, modulated voice. My words had no effect. They were overpowered by her desperate screams. Her halter felt heavy in my hands. My feet dug deeper into the shavings while my body was immobilized by indecision.

I willed myself into her paddock thinking I might try a Hail Mary. I coiled the lead rope and launched it over her neck to snag her, but she ducked her head and accelerated the agitation of her movements.

I didn't know what to do. Her unearthly calls made me crazy inside. I retreated and stood frozen outside her stall door, afraid to watch, but watching. I prayed to all benevolent beings to relieve the suffering of my horse. When it was clear that the intensity of her emotions wasn't abating, I turned away and scuffed my way down the aisle. She had been doing so well for so long. What triggered this reaction? As with her previous episodes, I was clueless.

In my car I rested my head against the steering wheel. How long was she going to stay this miserable? I hated the feeling of powerlessness. My mind attempted to assuage my tightened stomach with an optimistic suggestion that this might be a one-time event.

The next day the sun served up light and warmth and I felt its generosity try to lift my mood as I headed out to the barn. The closer I got, the more my apprehension grew. I didn't know what I might find. My heart soared when I opened the car door and heard only the twittering chirps of the local birds flitting in the eucalyptus trees that flanked the barn property. When I started down the aisle, Emma sounded a soft nicker and her bobbing head signaled her joyful greeting that lured those who walked by to come visit her. I sighed, threw my arms around her neck and pushed my heart against her shoulder in the biggest hug I could manage. My horse was back.

The ride I had that day was magical. Everything clicked. Emma's four tempi flying changes were for the most part through and clean. Her extended gaits were fluid and elastic. My heart soared with a lightness that these rides gifted me.

Emma remained at peace for a couple of weeks. Her next attack presented just like the first, with screaming, running and pawing. Looking at her face was difficult. The whites of her eyes showed and the glazed expression confirmed that she was ensnared in another reality. My guts wrenched with her distress. I went home disappointed and saddened but managed to keep myself from falling into a depression with the hope that the next day would be better.

She again got over her attack, but once again, peace didn't last. Something else was happening that was particularly worrisome. Between her bouts of terror Emma showed a heightened level of anxiety. She didn't seem to be coming back to her usual, relaxed resting state. In the past whenever an attack was over, it was over and I could enjoy my horse. In general, she was a sensible horse, with confidence and a certain amount of boldness, rarely reacting with fright to the barn environment. Now when I rode her, she spooked - a behavior that had previously been a rare occurrence. These weren't gentle startles where she stopped and planted her feet to get a better look. Nor were they a typical shy where she might take a few quick steps away from whatever was scaring her. One minute we would be heading down the side of the arena and then with no warning she would pivot ninety degrees and jump ten feet. I needed to stay attentive or I would be darted into the ground.

Each week I rode Emma I could measure the increase in her level of anxiety by the number of times she spooked during a ride. The magnitude of her reactions seemed to increase with each week. One minute here, the next minute a lunge into the air and we were halfway across the arena. The burning in my stomach after each ride testified to the level of stress I was under. I couldn't relax. I didn't want to get an ulcer. Even though I tried to keep Emma focused and calm, I couldn't seem to get her to trot down one side of the arena without an incident. Soon she spooked so often that the enjoyment of my time in the saddle plummeted.

Even for the short periods of time when Emma wasn't reacting to some seen or imagined threat, her ability to do dressage had changed. The deterioration had been gradual. Her soft and yielding back, which had given me such a lovely place to sit, was morphing into a hardness often described by riders as balancing on a wooden plank. Even stretching exercises were ineffective in getting her to release the tension. The lack of flexibility in her back and body broke our communication link. We could no longer advance in our dressage work together.

No matter what I tried I couldn't get Emma to trust that she was safe. Dressage training doesn't work with a stressed horse. Riding was the best way to exercise her or I would have probably given it up. Round pens are boring and don't give the horse the relief of a straight line. Their joints would need to work harder to sustain the constant turning.

The defining day came when I couldn't get Emma to calm down after one of her spooks. One fright reaction cascaded into another and escalated into one of her panic attacks. I vaulted off her back as the speed of her trot increased. On the way down, I clutched the reins. I needed all my strength to keep Emma to a jig as we exited from the arena. Every few steps she plunged forward and threw her head up in defiant resistance to the bridle. This was the same behavior that had forced me to leave the last boarding stable and look for our own place. Her actions were unsafe and keeping her at a pleasure barn wasn't fair to the other boarders.

Once in her stall, I raised my eyes to look up at Emma's head, craned high on her stiff neck. "Emma, what are we going to do?"

After I untacked her in her stall and let her loose, she raced into her paddock. She searched for the horse next door who was in his stall and not outside. That seemed to worry her even more. The whites of her eyes flashed and she bolted back into her stall. She whisked in and out, stopping briefly to paw the ground. I threw Emma's saddle and bridle in my tack locker and hustled to my car.

Driving home I scoured my brain for ideas. I had been fortunate that my work life had sorted itself out, so I wasn't stressed on two fronts. My former employer had required that I sign a non-compete clause before they hired me and they proved to have a propensity to sue former employees who hired on at other financial institutions. Changing industries would solve that problem. I lucked out. Securing a new job hadn't proved as difficult as I had imagined. A manager I knew had several openings at a major telecommunications corporation. The hiring process proved easy. Getting a regular paycheck again felt good. Although the job was lower on the organization chart than I was used to, I could go home at 5:00 PM and didn't have any of the stresses of my previous jobs. And I was grateful that it paid well enough to manage my needs and more. Now I could focus completely on Emma.

Yes, Emma. What was I to do with my beautiful horse. The best I came up with was to get help from my friend Elaine. I'd connect with her at the barn where she was boarding her horse. She often had good ideas. Besides I wanted to console her. She was dealing with her own disappointments. Her horse, Jack, had come up lame. I called her and we set up a meet time.

The following week I pulled into the barn where I first had stabled Emma.

"So, how's Jack doing?" I asked as I walked up to Elaine, who was grooming Jack in the cross ties of the saddling area. "I'm so sorry he fell down with you. That's scary."

Elaine's red hair shone with copper highlights, no hint of grey for a woman in her mid-forties, and when her kind blue-green eyes met mine her lips curled up in an engaging smile. I always felt better when I visited Elaine.

"My vet thinks he has navicular," she said, her lips slumping into a frown. She tossed the curry comb into her tack box with a thud.

"I'd be worried if I believed that, but I don't," I said. "Please take him to the vet school at UC Davis. He doesn't show any of the classic signs of that disease. Besides he's talked to me and he says the discomfort isn't in his feet."

"You know I don't believe in telepathic animal communication," she said, avoiding my eyes. "But, I think you have a good point about the vet school. Meanwhile, how's Emma? You said you wanted to talk about her."

"I'm at my wits end with what to do with her," I said, running my fingers over Jack's soft muzzle.

"What does your vet say?" Elaine replied.

"Same old, same old," I said. "He doesn't know how to help. I asked him about giving Emma anti-depressants. He doesn't know anything about using those kinds of drugs with horses. I knew they worked for me when I was experiencing terror. You remember that awful time at the bank with that abusive boss. The pressure was so intense I was concerned that I'd become non-functional. The anti-depressants got me through the worst of it."

"How could I forget?" Elaine said. "That was a horrible job. I think you should've quit it long before you did. As I remember, you didn't have to stay on the meds very long."

"Just about eight months," I said, and followed her as she returned Jack to his stall. "I'm so distraught for Emma. I refused to read Black Beauty because I knew that the story was heart breaking. I never imagined that I would come to know that my own horse had experienced abuse that would affect her for years."

Elaine unbuckled Jack's halter, freeing him and latching his stall door behind her. She started to say something and then stopped.

"What?" I asked. "I'm looking to you for some help, a suggestion maybe."

Her hand lighted on my forearm as if to reassure me that her message was well intended. "Are you really sure that you can't afford another horse?"

"Emotionally I don't think I can pull it off," I said. "I'm grateful that my work life sorted itself out. Changing my profession to telecommunications has gone rather easily. Although that worry is behind me, Emma uses up my spare energy. What if the other horse had problems? I think I'd collapse from emotional exhaustion."

"Diana, I've seen what Emma does," Elaine said, softening her voice. "When it first started and now. I'm very concerned for your safety. I know you don't want to hear this, but it might be time to put her down. Have you considered it?"

I clenched my teeth and thought: *et tu Brute*? "No, Elaine I haven't. When we were at Sweet Mountain, for a short time I considered the option of giving her to the folks who run a blood bank for horses. Our lives would take different paths, but I couldn't part with her. I couldn't give up responsibility for her. Putting her down is not an option. I know that other people do that. I can't. I appreciate your honesty and you aren't the first to suggest that solution. No, I was wondering what you might recommend as a next step to help Emma."

"Let me think for a minute," she said, and hung Jack's halter on the hook on his stall door. "This is not an easy problem."

"I know," I said, looking first at Elaine and then out at the hills and the trails that crisscrossed the open space. Sometimes the urge to be on those trails was an almost unbearable longing. The vibrant green of Elaine's blouse reminded me of spring growth – the grass-covered slopes I hadn't been able to enjoy with my horse.

After a minute her eyes twinkled and she said, "Yup, I think I may have thought of something."

"Let's hear it," I said turning to face her. "And don't suggest I buy horse property. Been there, done that."

She leaned back against the stall door and looked up as if she were imagining something. "Do you remember the place that I told you about where Lily and Betty turned out their pregnant mares to have their foals? They are two fussy women about their horses and were very pleased with how they were treated. Apparently, their mares received excellent attention and the facility is set up with horses in mind. It's about a half hour from Davis. They breed the old-style Morgan horses."

"Yes, I remember," I said as I could feel a slight amount of hope returning. "They had nothing but praise. I think it's the Woodland Stallion Station."

"It might work for Emma," Elaine said, her body language getting more animated. "If she's turned out with a group of baby horses, she wouldn't be bullied and would have absolutely no pressure put on her. She could de-stress and re-group. The babies would be good company. There would be absolutely nothing out there to frighten her or to trigger an episode. She might be able to live there peacefully."

"Emma has said she likes teaching young horses," I said with more energy creeping into my voice. "She didn't have any panic attacks for the short time she was with Elizabeth in Gualala. Thank you, I'm going to sleep on that thought."

The next day I called my vet. No new scientific breakthroughs had come to his attention since the last time I'd spoken to him. No revelation had come to him that would help a horse with panic attacks. He thought the plan of turning her out was worth a try. He reminded me that if living there worked out, several stallions stood at the farm and I would have the option of breeding Emma myself, if I ever decided to pursue that course. He confessed that in all his years as a vet he hadn't ever seen behavior like Emma's.

With as much anxiety as Emma was experiencing, riding her was out of the question. I couldn't continue to keep her where she was. She was getting too dangerous. I didn't know what else to do.

The thought of trying to find another brood mare situation felt as if it would be another exercise in frustration. Finding a placement when Emma was younger was hard enough. She was 13 years old now and less likely to be of value as a brood mare. Horses' fertility like humans declined dramatically with age. Besides, Emma had been through so much emotionally that she had asked that we not try motherhood as a solution again. The memory of what she suffered kept me from trying to change her mind.

Maybe Elaine's idea would work. In a large pasture Emma could self-exercise. She would be handled only for the periodic vaccinations and hoof trims. At least Emma could live her life eating her fill of grass, exercising when she wanted and sharing wisdom with young horses. Without stress she might not have any more panic attacks. Maybe living in a boarding stable didn't work for Emma. Had I misread her? She had said she liked dressage because it engaged her mind and body. She had even offered once that dressage helped her with anxiety since it forced her to concentrate on something other than her fear. But was dressage at some deeper level too demanding for her? Did I unconsciously put too much pressure on her? No one who witnessed my riding thought that. I was confused and out of ideas.

I picked up the phone and called the Woodland Stallion Station.

Chapter 20

The drive to the Woodland Stallion Station would take about an hour and a half. Once in my car I couldn't help but think about a similar drive to Gualala. This drive could very well end in another separation from Emma. My skeptical mind, fervently at work, kept nattering away. Was I ever going to find the conditions that would allow Emma to be happy and free from terror?

During the trip, my sadness and frustration consumed me. I wanted my horse near me and in my daily life. I needed the peace and joy that horses brought me. But Emma couldn't live in peace. I was angry, disappointed, confused. I couldn't help but wonder what lesson God had for me that I wasn't getting.

My car eased into a flat gravel area next to the main house. The ranch owner, Jeannette, appeared immediately, offered a friendly greeting and proceeded with the expected tour. Her short, brown hair looked easy to keep and her clean, pressed clothes gave the impression that she was a competent businesswoman.

As we made the rounds of her ranch, we exchanged observations on a variety of horse topics from feeds to conformation flaws to the challenges of breeding horses. We paused at a vantage point. Fences divided the land into several pastures deep and rich with grass and each was at least several acres in size. The terrain was mostly flat to gently rolling. An abundant assortment of trees provided shade. Each pasture undulated with raised areas where the horses in winter could get out of the wet that accumulated in low areas. Emma's pasture mates would be two-year old Morgan babies who, in their joy of youth, were very cute. The old-style Morgan was typically small and Emma would dwarf them. Size tends to rule in the animal pecking order, so Emma should have a leg up, so to speak. The large size of the pastures meant that the horses should have grass to nibble on throughout the winter and with the daily hay supplement there should be no problem keeping up the calorie count. My observations of Jeannette led me to believe that she was capable and interested in providing for the special needs of her charges.

When Jeannette wasn't looking, I swooped down and scooped up a handful of dirt into a plastic bag. My pocket hid it from view and eliminated any questions that were not easily answered.

On the drive home, I replayed all I had seen. I was relieved that the ranch lived up to its reputation. I felt that Emma's needs would be well taken care of. The owner was able to describe the personality of each horse in her care and the actions she took to keep each happy. I liked that.

The next day I drove out to the barn. I greeted Emma and described my trip to her. I offered her the plastic bag of soil I had collected at the stallion station. She snatched it and smeared the dirt over her tongue. I cleared my mind and did my best to connect to what Emma was feeling. When I was sure that I had established the connection, I got the answer deep in my gut. I felt Emma's approval. Once again, I found myself making the arrangements to send Emma to another home. To let her continue to be so disconsolate was impossible. I had to try something.

Over the next few days my actions were guided by a list of the necessary preparations for her move. The blacksmith took off her rear shoes but left her front sneakers on. He wanted to ensure she didn't get sore feet and recommended removing them after a couple of weeks when there would be more hoof growth. My vet came out and gave her all the vaccinations required by her new home. When all checkmarks were applied to the boxes on my list, I made plans to trailer Emma to Woodland.

On the drive up, that horrible feeling of powerlessness descended and clasped its slimy fingers around my heart. I stared straight ahead out of the windshield of my truck as we sped over the highway. Emma stood quietly behind me in the trailer. I felt her heart was equally uneasy. I couldn't seem to get myself into a place where I could enjoy the landscape as we motored by.

Why didn't veterinary science offer a solution? Why couldn't I identify the resources to make this horse happy? Why did this horse have to suffer? The universe did not offer up any answers.

My brain continued to be cruelly active, despite my best efforts to silence its needling. I questioned whether I was doing the right thing. Emma was the most giving and kindest horse I'd ever known. She gave her food away to a horse that needed it more than she did. She connected me to my dog who had passed away and who had a message to give to me. She took care of me when I was sick ensuring that I stopped riding before I exhausted myself. She warned me about a peer at work who was scheming to do harm. She was my best friend and I felt as if I was letting her down. I was angry at God and the world for this cruelty. At best, I could hope that Emma would live the remainder of her life without panic attacks.

I sighed long and loud when I turned the truck onto the driveway and through the gates of the Woodland Stallion Station. I did my best to put on my happy face. Not sure I managed very well.

Jeannette came out of her home and greeted us. I guessed that I was one of many owners she had greeted who were worried about leaving their horse. She seemed comfortable in the situation and capable of handling the emotional side with some detachment.

Her eyes greeted mine and looked as if they were accustomed to dispensing compassion.

"Do you need help unloading your mare?' Jeannette asked as she walked towards the back of the trailer.

"Thanks, but no. She's fine," I said as I undid the latches on the doors. Whenever anyone referred to Emma as a "mare" or "horse," I was startled. Emma was Emma. It would be as if someone referred to your significant other as "that man" or "that woman" rather than by name.

Emma backed down the ramp slowly and stood while I grasped her lead rope. She raised her head and looked off to the distance. She seemed to be taking a moment to absorb the energy of the land.

"What a pretty mare," Jeannette exclaimed as she moved her eyes over Emma's body. "She's really quite beautiful and well-muscled. It's hard to understand why you're turning her out to pasture and why she can't be a riding horse."

Her comment hit me hard and I worked to dispel the pain of sadness it caused. "I agree she looks great standing here right now," I said as I took off Emma's shipping boots. "I'm hoping that you'll never see why I've had to do this, but as I explained she has severe anxiety attacks."

"I have a two-acre pasture ready for her where she will be alone," Jeannette said as she turned and headed down a path. "It borders the young horses I will put her with eventually. They can become friends over the fence. I'll turn her out with them in a couple of days."

"She may fret for a while," I said as I followed Jeannette down the path. "She doesn't always adapt to change well."

"Most horses quickly settle down here," she said as she opened the gate to the small pasture. "It's a low stress environment."

I unbuckled Emma's halter and let her loose. Her eyes opened wide and she took off at a huge extended trot to the other side of the pasture and halted at the fence line.

"She's not only beautiful to look at, she's a beautiful mover,"

Jeannette said as she watched Emma's floating, ground eating stride. "What a shame she can't be used."

"Yup," was all I could manage as my tears started to well.

Emma made a few more passes back and forth at top speed.

"She will continue fretting like this for maybe a day or two," I said as a reminder to Jeannette.

"I'll go grab some oat hay and put it in the manger," Jeannette said as she left the pasture. "Food has a way of calming down a nervous horse."

"I don't think it will do any good," I yelled after her.

She returned with a generous flake of oat hay and spread it in the manger. She clearly had the expectation that Emma was going to come over and eat it. Spotting the activity around the manger, Emma trotted over and buried her nose in the hay for at most a quarter of a second and then sped off again calling out to the other horses.

"Wow, that surprised me," Jeannette said as her gaze followed Emma to the far side of the field.

"She may not eat until she stops fretting," I said trying to reassure Jeannette that Emma's behavior was not surprising. "I imagine you're probably used to working with horses who are highly motivated by their food and relax as soon as they start eating. Emma has never shown much attachment to food. When she's stressed like this, she'll even refuse her favorite treat of Fuji apples."

"I've never seen anything like this," she said with concern in her voice as she watched Emma running back and forth. Worry spread across Jeannette's face.

"This is a typical behavior of hers when she's stressed. As I mentioned, she doesn't always cope very well. She'll be okay in a day or so," I said as I went out of the gate. "Thanks. I'm heading home."

My stride quickened the closer I got to the truck so that I was nearly running by the time I reached the door. I didn't need to stay and watch Emma's distress. I turned the key of the ignition and did my best not to feel. I would go home and wait to hear how Emma was settling into her new home.

True to her word, Jeannette called me a week later to provide an update on Emma.

"She's been turned out with the other horses," Jeannette's matter of fact voice reported, "and seems to be doing fine."

"Is she running the fence line?" I asked with a dry mouth.

"No, she stopped her pacing in about a day," Jeannette reassured me. "She's a beautiful horse and several people have approached me to find out if she was for sale."

"Thank, you," I responded. "No, not ever."

For the first couple of months, I went to visit Emma every other weekend. She dropped some weight, but her coat looked healthy and her ribs were covered. I comforted myself by saying at least she could hang out like a horse, have lots of room and wouldn't be digging a hole in her paddock. Maybe she could make some friends who would comfort her. Despite my attempts at a positive spin, my intuition was warning me that Emma might not be doing as well as she looked.

When three months had passed, I called Carol to talk to Emma. My feelings kept nagging me that all was not right with her. I couldn't dispel a generalized discomfort that had lodged in my gut whenever I thought of Emma. I needed to hear from her how she was doing.

"My anxiety is quite bad," Carol translated for Emma putting stress into her voice. "I'm sinking into a black hole."

"Emma, I'm so sorry to hear that," I said, my stomach tightening. "Do you know what's causing it?"

"I don't know," Carol translated with sadness in her voice.

"It always amazes me," I said, shaking my head, "that Emma can be feeling such strong emotions and the care givers around her don't suspect anything. This is not the first time it's happened."

"Maybe you see more because you feel more," Carol said.

"Perhaps," I said, finding it still hard to believe that others didn't register the same feelings.

"You and Emma are very in tune with each other," Carol said.

"I suppose what others are unable to understand will remain a puzzle to me," I said. "Hey Emma, are you getting enough to eat?" I asked, thinking that food was something I might have some control over. "Have you made any friends?"

"I have enough food," Carol translated. "I don't relate to the young horses here. They do silly stuff."

"I thought you liked teaching young horses," I said, thinking I may have misunderstood Emma.

"Yes, I like teaching them," Carol translated, "not living with them. I prefer horses with experience."

My heart ached. I didn't anticipate that complication. "Emma, I don't know what to do. Jeannette has a smaller pasture for older, retired horses. Would you want to live with them?

"No, I'm not old," Carol translated. "I don't relate to them either."

"Is there anything I can do to help you in your current situation?" I asked.

"I have a dream," Carol translated. "This is the best dream I've ever had. The sun is shining and it's warm. The grass is so tall it comes up to my knees. I have a foal next to my side. When I think that I can't possibly be any happier, I see you walking in the field towards me. Then I know bliss."

I sat there feeling sad and helpless, and then an overpowering rush of love came over me. "Emma, that's a beautiful dream. I'm a bit confused since you said that you didn't want to try for another baby. Meanwhile is there anything I can do to make you more comfortable?"

"No. There's nothing I know that can be done," Carol translated. "I know that you love me."

I hung up the phone and sank deeper in my chair. The daylight turned to dark and I didn't move to turn on the lights.

"Dearest God," I prayed. "Please help Emma."

Chapter 21

Several months after I moved Emma to her new home, the warm spring weather activated my yearnings to be close to a horse. Not just emotionally close, but physically close as well. The lush green hills only exacerbated the feeling. Giving up the belief that one day Emma would again be my riding horse had been hard for me. Having exhausted all my resources, I forced myself to accept that I had done everything that I could. I turned her future over to God and did my best to surrender to what was. And now the need to ride kept pressing me to action.

Boarders at the barn where I kept Emma knew of my riding skills and offered their mounts to ride a couple of times a week. They wanted their horses to benefit from dressage training. I tried it. The experience wasn't the same. The horses ended up getting confused between the different riding styles of the owner and me. I couldn't follow a training program. One owner offered her horse to me full time. That brought to light that the issue was more than just the horse's confusion. I missed the special bond of the unique relationship of a horse who connected at the heart level. I didn't just want a ride, I wanted a life partner.

One evening when I was beside myself for missing contact with a horse, I decided to do some arithmetic. Out came my calculator and scratch pad. After I added up the columns of numbers and did the appropriate subtractions and additions, I figured that I could afford the maintenance of another horse. I was living in a house with roommates and the cost of my room had diminished my living expenses. A room was a lot cheaper than the mortgage payment for a house, barn and acreage.

With Emma turned out, her daily care fell to Jeannette. Emma was going to stay put where she wasn't endangering anyone. That would free up the energy I had been using for her care giving. The sale of my house had padded my bank account, so I would have the funds for the purchase price of a new horse and still have the down payment on a condo should I want to move in the future. If I was lucky, I might be able to buy a young warmblood that was either a three or four-year-old and just started under saddle. Despite the joy that the results of my mathematical wizardry provided me, I didn't want to get too excited. I couldn't do it if it would hurt Emma's feelings. Before I did anything, I needed to know what she thought.

A couple of days later I opened the window of my bedroom and sniffed the sweet aroma of yet another gentle spring day. The pale pink blossoms of the fruit trees in the neighbor's yard were in the process of freeing their petals that then, like wispy snowflakes, glided on the air currents in fanciful sweeps. Settling down in my easy chair I fingered Emma's bridle, which I had taken out to clean. I drew in deep breaths of the mix of Murphy's Saddle Soap and leather. I looked at Emma's picture on the table and called Carol for the appointment I had made earlier in the week.

"I want to know what Emma thinks about my getting another horse," I asked when Carol answered the phone.

"Well, and hello to you too," Carol said with a mocking tone.

"Okay, okay," I said, "So, how are you? Fine? Great! Now answer the question."

"A little testy, are we?" Carol laughed.

"I'm sorry," I said, "This is a big deal and I'm anxious. I generally have better manners. I think."

"It would be fine to get another horse," Carol translated without any pause. "You need to ride and I can't be there for you. In my heart I know I will always be your number one horse. Our family will grow."

"Carol, Emma's generosity is touching and is so like her," I said as a warm wave of gratitude flushed through my body.

"She's never been otherwise," Carol replied.

"Emma, if I find a horse I like, may I ask your opinion?"

"Pshaw, of course." Carol translated adding a light laughter, "It's our family and I want a say."

"Emma, you're amazing," I said, once again humbled by Emma's generosity. "I'm so glad that I have you on my side. I hope with all of my heart that you'll feel better," I said, using a Kleenex from the table next to the phone to wipe away the tears that were forming. "I want you to be able to at least live out the rest of your life in peace."

"Diana, she thinks you're the most patient person in the whole world," Carol said. "And is grateful to have you in her life. She knows the only reason she's alive is because of you."

Emma's love was palpable. I choked with appreciation when I hung up the phone.

The next day I started a search for my new horse in earnest. No lead was too small to pursue. Horse magazines, circulars and equine newsletters replaced the novels I had been reading. Looking for the right horse became my single-focused passion. My new internet skills were put to good use. Despite a slow computer and the creeping speed of the dial-up connection, the best nineteen ninety-eight had to offer, I remained glued to the screen watching pictures of horses download. The thought of being able to ride again unleashed an exuberance of energy that left me feeling light-headed. Looking for another horse only made my ache to ride even stronger. Visions of my partnership with a horse and the rewards of being together spurred me to follow every lead.

A friend told me about a horse dealer in Germany who found and resold young horses at reasonable prices. She directed me to his website. The one horse that didn't have a price listed was the one I wanted to pursue. When I stared hard at the picture, something unusual happened. I felt the personality of the horse. I felt an energy surge leap off the computer screen and enter my body. The result was exhilarating. I fixed my eyes on the horse and opened my mind to whatever I would experience. The horse felt solidly grounded and honest. I couldn't call him kind or social, but rather work oriented and sincere. He had an open, wise expression. His chestnut coloring was a little on the light side, not that deep copper color that can be flashy. His body appeared well built for dressage and I liked all the angles of his joints. The dealer was going to be in Washington State for a few days, so I would have an opportunity to talk to him without international phone charges and time zone differences.

One night a couple of weeks later, I was able to connect by phone with the dealer from Germany.

"I like a four-year-old chestnut gelding I saw on your website," I said. "But there wasn't a price for him. He was the only horse shown without a price. I think it costs about $10,000 to fly a horse over here and with the quarantine charges and shipping charges from the point of entry I have to be a little careful with the purchase price."

"I haven't evaluated him yet," the horse dealer said with a voice that sounded straight forward, his words only slightly infused with a German accent. "I won't put a price on him until I get back. I need more time with him to see how well he responds to training."

Oops. That means if he trains well I probably can't afford him.

"Okay, when you settle on a price, please e-mail me." When I hung up, I checked in with my intuition. I didn't feel as if this lead would go anywhere.

The next time I called Carol to talk to Emma I reported on what progress I had made to expand our equine family. I settled into my chair facing a stack of clippings and video tapes on my desk. I mentioned the horse that I had seen on the website of the German trainer.

"The man can be trusted," Carol translated for Emma. "He has good horses."

"Wait a minute." I said, leaning forward in my chair. "How do you know the quality of his horses?"

"I talked to them." Carol translated.

"Remember Diana," Carol said. "Horses have a realistic view of their competencies. They are not ego involved the way people are. If a horse has a big head or pretty eyes they know it. They tend to be accepting of what is. They are aware of their attributes, so I would trust what they report."

"But Emma has never met these horses," I said, still trying to figure it out. "How can she know that?"

"When you talked to the German horse trainer," Carol translated for Emma, "I was connected to you. You were connected to him through the phone. Then I connected to him and through him to his horses."

I plopped back in my chair and stared at the ceiling as if that would make for a better understanding. "I'm sitting here dumbfounded."

"That's the way it works," Carol said. "Sounds reasonable to me."

"I wonder what my colleagues at the phone company would think about this method of communication," I said. "They would think that trans-Atlantic fiber optic cables would be needed."

"Oh, silly people," Carol said, laughing.

"But don't the other horses speak German?" I asked, still trying to understand Emma's communication abilities.

"It doesn't work that way." Carol said. "The message comes through the airwaves telepathically and registers in our filters in our own language. A specific language is immaterial to telepathic communication. Most communication is through pictures and feelings, but the words that are sent come through in the recipient's language."

"I've been talking to animals for how many years now? Five years," I said, "and I'm still a babe in the woods regarding how extensive their abilities are."

My mind started leaping around, sprouting ideas like a field bursting with so many springtime wild flowers.

"If we could talk to the German's horse in Germany, then can we talk to a horse that I recently saw here in California?" I asked.

"Sure," Carol translated for Emma.

Reaching over to find the clipping of the young horse, I said "Great. There's this young filly I saw in Galt. She was by far the best mover of any of the horses that I've visited although she was much younger than I want. Emma, can you help us get connected to that young horse?"

"Yes." After a moment's pause, Carol continued translating for Emma, "She's on-line now."

"You mean you can talk directly to her now?" I asked.

"Yup," Carol said. "I can feel her energy."

"Would you like to be my horse?" I blurted out, my impatience forcing me to ignore more polite pleasantries and get right to the point.

"Would you beat me?" Carol translated for the filly.

"Oh my God, no," I said sitting there with my mouth dropped open. Over the years several horses had observed how I took care of Emma and had asked if I would be their person. They wanted to leave their current owner and be with me. My heart broke to tell them no. This was a real switch.

"Would you work me too hard and make me sore?" Carol translated for the filly.

"No. I would do my best to exercise you sensibly," I responded to the filly, then asked Carol, "My God, what kind of experiences has this baby horse had? She hasn't even been ridden yet."

"Would you bring me treats?" Carol continued translating for the filly. "Would you make me move away from here? Would you whip me until I had welts?"

"Wow. she has a lot of concerns," I said, thinking that this probably was not my horse.

"She's a young baby," Carol translated for Emma, "and probably won't grow into a horse that would be powerful enough to do dressage. She's afraid of many things and is fearful in general."

"Thank you, Emma, for the heads up," I said. "She's probably not a good choice for our family. I need a horse who has the power to do dressage and won't be sidelined with emotional issues."

I was disappointed, but relieved because I didn't want to get a horse that I couldn't ride. This young horse was a couple of months shy of two years and had been turned out in a pasture to grow up. When I got on the back of a horse, I could tell a lot about how well the relationship would work. Without that knowledge I would be taking more of a risk than was already part of buying a horse. Besides, I couldn't evaluate her gaits. What if she had a jarring trot or canter?

How wonderful that Emma could help me assess the suitability of my next horse. What an incredible friend. I sat back and wondered what horse was in my future. Before I went to bed, to satisfy my curiosity I checked the website of the German horse dealer. Still no price on the chestnut I liked.

Chapter 22

My search for another horse seemed to be short on results. I never heard from the German horse dealer and the picture of the lovely chestnut gelding disappeared from his website without a price ever displaying. The horse probably was sold locally. No other horse on that website appealed to me so I let that avenue drop. I had the time and energy, so I kept at it with the same fervor I applied to any project assigned to me. After a few more months of phone calls, combing the internet, watching videos and reading through the classified ads in horse magazines, I saw a clip of a young horse that appealed to me.

The owner, who lived in Seattle, sent me a longer video tape of her filly running free in a field. The camera was hand held and the horse was at some distance, but she looked stunning and seemed to be a big mover. She was a 17.1 hand two-year-old Hanoverian filly that hadn't been started yet. She was halter broke and could be lunged but that was about it. I had been in the market long enough to know that if I was to afford a quality horse I would have to go younger than the three or four-year-old I wanted. I'd have to take the risk of not knowing what the young horse felt like under saddle and would have to be patient for the horse to grow up.

Before I made a trip to Seattle I wanted to talk to this horse and ask her if she was sound and try to get an idea of what her mind was like. Especially given the conversation I had with the filly in Galt.

Settling down, I looked out my bedroom window at the trees and noticed that the vibrant green leaves had lost their gloss. A few showed signs of color change. Fall was on its way.

When Carol picked up, I asked Emma to connect us to the horse.

"The baby horse is here now," Carol translated for Emma.

"Are you sound?" I had to ask, always wondering what made a person sell a horse.

"What do you mean?" Carol translated for the young horse.

"When you move, does it hurt anywhere?" I replied.

"Oh, no," Carol translated.

"Are you interested in a new home?" I asked, not wanting to start a relationship with a horse that would be traumatized by a move.

"Yes, I am," Carol translated for the young horse. "My person has let me know that she will be placing me in another home. She has prepared me for what comes next."

"Do you have any concerns?" I asked, my heart fluttering.

"No," Carol translated for the young horse and put emphasis in her voice.

"Wow," I said, letting out a sigh. "What a difference between this horse and the one in Galt."

I looked over to Emma's picture on my table. "Emma, what do you think?"

"I think you need to go visit her," Carol translated.

"Yes," I laughed. "I need to see her in person and feel her energy."

I thanked Carol and called the horse's owner. I decided to fly to Seattle the next weekend.

By the time Saturday rolled around the weather was perfect for flying and the trip went without a hitch. I rented a car at the Seattle airport and headed out to the home of the owner, Kelly. I would see the filly's mother first and then head out to the boarding stable where the filly was boarded. Kelly was waiting for me in her driveway and offered a hand in a warm greeting. She was a bitty thing - only about five foot two. Her strawberry blond hair harmonized with her green eyes and pixie-like face. Her expression of concern showed that she was probably sizing me up and wasn't going to send her filly home with just anybody.

"If you purchase my filly, when would you start riding her?" Kelly asked as she led me towards the barn.

Picking my way over the mud puddles I followed behind. "Not until she is two and a half years old," I said. "Then for a few minutes a couple of times a week so she gets used to the concept of riding. I won't really start any under saddle training until she's four years old."

"What do you have in mind in the meantime?" Kelly asked.

"There's a lot that I can do on the ground. I'm not in a hurry. I know that warm bloods take longer to develop. I also believe in starting horses with slow trail rides. Heading into the open spaces encourages a young horse to go forward and enjoy themselves."

The slow sweeping nods of Kelly's head seemed to show that she approved of my plan. She stopped to pry open a small, plank door on the side of the barn. The weathered door creaked on its hinges and opened slightly askew.

"I was really lucky to get my filly's mother," she said, glowing with pride. "I never thought I'd own such a beautiful mare, but I was in the right place at the right time. A divorce settlement required a quick sale of all the breeding stock. She has great conformation and is well bred. Her dam was imported from Germany after she had been confirmed pregnant. So, my horse was conceived in Germany but born here. You've come to see her first foal."

I stepped over the threshold of the door into a dark barn. The moisture, laden with hay and pine shavings scents, thickened the air. A doorway at the end of the aisle let in natural light. The mare was in the first stall. Her light chestnut coat was well groomed. Kelly was right - she had lovely conformation. Her expression seemed kind and her eye was soft. "Does your mare have any other foals?"

"I have a one-year old colt that is by the same stallion," Kelly said, turning to another stall and pointing to the chestnut colt. "Because my filly turned out so well and I liked the looks of this colt when he was born, I bred my mare back to the same stallion a third time. She's carrying that foal now. My mare and this colt will be the foundation of my breeding program. My husband is a contractor and we hope to have our own place in the next couple of years. I'm selling this first baby to help finance a down payment on our own place. I have my eye on one that has been for sale for a while. It's been my dream to breed dressage horses."

"That sounds like a great dream," I said, envisioning her future "I can't imagine a more satisfying way to use resources then to bring beautiful horses into the world."

Kelly smiled with a wistful expression. "I keep my filly at a nearby boarding stable, so I have the use of its facilities," Kelly said, heading for the door, "I'll drive you over there now."

We pulled up to an expansive, white washed barn perched on a hillock of gravel surrounded by an open field of thick, green grass. In the front was a small wood addition jutting out from the stone foundation of the larger barn. Kelly parked the car and headed for the sliding door that provided admittance to the addition. On entering the aisle, I shivered from the damp and cold. A slight odor of ammonia pricked my nose. I followed Kelly down the dark aisle to the last stall on the right. Kelly slid the stall door open and I walked in. Sunlight from a window high on my left poured warm yellow beams on the top line of the horse. My breath caught. The young horse loomed over me and looked down with a fully conscious eye and with recognition. She had big brown eyes that gleamed with life and knowing. She was stunning. Her coat was as deep a red as any chestnut I'd seen. She had a white blaze and three white socks - very showy. Her neck arched straight up and out of her withers making her 17.1 hands seem even bigger. She had a fabulous hind end with a long slope between the point of her hip bone and the point of her butt. Lots of power in there. Her back was perfectly coupled and promised to carry weight easily. The angles of her joints looked well put together. Her legs were straight. My appraisal of her conformation checked off my boxes for must or good go have. So far everything seemed promising. While my mind did its logical job of inspection, my heartbeat picked up its own rhythm. The energy that was being exchanged felt like a deep and all-encompassing love.

Kelly led the filly out of the barn and up the hill to the indoor arena. I followed behind, studying how the horse moved her legs. Her walk was a good clean four-beat. She tracked straight. None of her legs deviated from swinging back and forth on a straight line and showed no evidence of dishing or winging. Her walk was mechanically correct and with lots of overstep. Once the arena gate was secure Kelly turned the filly loose. She didn't bolt away, but rather eased into a trot and showed her exuberance when she stretched her legs into an energetic trot. Her strides didn't appear as free as what I'd seen in the video - the video that I must have watched fifty times. I wondered why. Was the ground different? In the video she had been out on a waterlogged pasture deep in grass. The footing in this arena seemed a bit hard packed in places. Perhaps the hardness and unevenness made the difference. She might not have confidence in the footing. Due to lack of experience, young horses were often sensitive to the footing.

"Her conformation is there to do the work," I said.

Kelly cracked the whip and the filly took off in big bound and cantered away. Again, when she settled into her gait, the stride was not as big as I thought it should be. My mind noted a concern, but my heart was pulling me in another direction.

Spotting a set of standards and rails on the ground in a corner of the arena, I asked, "Kelly would it be possible to ask her to pop over a low X?"

Kelly looked at me wrinkling her brow, "Why? I haven't started her over fences. She's too young."

"Perfect," I said, and walked over to Kelly. "I want something that she hasn't done before. It isn't about doing a jump. It's about seeing what she does to solve a problem. The X of the poles won't be any higher than a small log in the pasture."

"OK, I'll set it up." Kelly turned to get the rails.

We placed one end of the rails near the wall with the rails jutting out perpendicularly. Kelly stood on the inside and asked the filly to trot up to the cross rails. She would be between Kelly on one side and the wall on the other.

The horse trotted up to the rails and dropped her head for a better look. Kelly encouraged her with the whip. The filly hesitated and seemed confused. Up until now fences defined boundaries that weren't to be crossed. Then Kelly moved in behind her with more encouragement. The filly she picked up her front legs and leapt rather awkwardly over the fence. She looked like a typical green horse. I liked that she kept her head low and arched with a decent bascule. Although she didn't seem to be a natural jumper, she did well for a first attempt. More importantly, she was willing to try something new. I liked her attitude.

"Kelly, please ask her to do it again," I said. I studied the filly's expression as she trotted around the arena. "I want to see what she does now that she knows what we want."

The filly came around the end of the arena and approached the rails with more confidence. She jumped over them with a little more grace.

"Kelly, that's all I need to see," I said, smiling. "She didn't freak out. She was given a problem and figured out how to solve it. When she went over the second time, she did it better. She learns and isn't afraid of being presented with new things. That's great."

The filly trotted to the other end of the arena and then came back at the walk. She headed straight to me, stopped a stride away, stretched out her neck and nuzzled my hand. Her touch puddled my heart into mush. She liked her owner, but she came to me – the stranger. This had to be my horse. I sighed and stroked her cheek.

"Look how she focused right on you," Kelly said. "Wow. That makes me feel a lot better about letting her go."

After I had seen all I needed to see, I arranged to come back in two weeks and have the horse brought to a veterinary clinic for the pre-purchase examination.

The flight home was uneventful and as usual I was happy to ease my car into its parking space. As soon as I walked into my bedroom, I headed for the phone. I couldn't wait to talk to this horse again. Settling into my chair, I called Carol. With the phone ringing in my ear, I pictured the young horse and did my best to connect to her. In response I felt love spill over my body and bathe my heart with joy.

"She's online," Carol said right at the start of our conversation.

"Yes, I can feel her," I said. "Young lady, you are very beautiful."

"Thank you." Carol translated for the young horse. "I'm so happy that you're going to be my person. As soon as I saw you I knew. I love you."

My heart, pooled in joy, was immersed in golden puffs of love before my practical nature took over.

"Your stride seemed a bit shorter than what I saw in the video," I said. "Do you hurt anywhere?"

"No. I'm not hurt," Carol translated for the young horse.

"Are you sure?" I asked. "In your hooves, in your legs, your back?"

"No," Carol translated.

"Your way of moving seemed different from when you were in a field," I said, still needing to put this issue to rest.

"I like moving," Carol translated. "I like being outside."

"That could explain it," I said. "If the ability is there then it can be developed in other venues. Some horses don't feel as free in an indoor arena." I communicated to the filly, "You'll be moving to California. There'll be less rain here."

"I'm looking forward to my new life," Carol translated.

"Great." I beamed.

My eyes drifted to the blue sky framed by my bedroom window. What a high. I wondered how I could explain what I felt about the addition of a new horse to the family. Perhaps the joy is similar to bringing a new child into a family. Or a spouse. All the promise of a shared life, of potential, of love and relationship. This experience reminded me of when I first saw Emma and felt the electricity of love. That intensity of love kept me looking for ways to make Emma happy despite the anguish I felt whenever she had a panic attack and the hard times we suffered together. This young horse came with the same promise that Emma had for the growth that an intimate relationship provides.

Chapter 23

The Alaska Airlines plane taxied for takeoff from the tarmac of the Oakland airport. I pulled my mind back from its chatter, cleared my thoughts and focused my mind on my feelings. Getting a new horse is like being a bride all over again. The anticipation and bloom of new love is intoxicating. The prospects that lay ahead had my feelings whirring in a kaleidoscope of shared experiences. I conjectured what it would feel like to sit on this filly for the first time and view the world from the back of a 17+ hand horse. I imagined what it would feel like for our first trot or our first canter. Our first trail ride. Our first dressage show. I sighed with deep pleasure as the plane swept through puffy white clouds.

At the Seattle airport I picked up a rental car and headed out. The sky was overcast with low level foggy clouds. Although there was no rain and decent visibility, a spotty drizzle required the occasional use of the windshield wipers. Traffic was light and the directions from the office manager of the vet were spot on. I parked the rental car at the main entrance to the veterinary clinic and entered the building with a light and happy heart. In the past I had been lucky in my selection of horses. Each one had passed the pre-purchase examination. And this filly hadn't been put to work yet or sustained any injuries. It should be good.

Kelly said she would trailer her filly to the vet facility that I had chosen and would meet me there. I checked in at the office and waited for Kelly to arrive.

Right on time Kelly pulled her rig into the unloading area of the parking lot. The vet and her assistant greeted Kelly and showed her where to take the filly. Kelly led the filly out behind the offices to the barn area. The young horse was as beautiful as I remembered. Her winter coat gleamed despite this dull, drippy day. Her conformation appeared unflawed to my eye. What a jewel.

The vet asked Kelly to lead her horse back and forth on the hard-packed road. The assistant appeared to be taking notes. The walk looked great. The strides were long and the filly overstepped the imprint of her front hoof with her back hoof by about eighteen inches. That will make a great extended walk. Emma never overstepped more than about a hoof print at best, although you could get good scores with that limitation. Emma's free walk got my one and only nine of ten on a movement in a dressage test.

Next the vet asked Kelly to trot the filly out. Her strides were even shorter than when I had come to see her two weeks before. My ribs seized stopping my breath. The bottom of my stomach dropped. There didn't appear to be much suspension. My mind went on high alert. What's going on here? Was it the change in surface? I knew that an unyielding surface like asphalt will sometimes reveal problems that may be masked by softer footing.

"Wow, she's moving so differently than she was two weeks ago," I said, turning to. Kelly. "The harder surface really seems to be making a difference."

Kelly's eyes narrowed as she listened to me.

"In case she may be a bit sore footed," the vet said, "let's have her trot in the round pen where the footing is much better."

I followed the entourage and we all stepped inside to the center of the pen to get a good view of how the filly would move. Kelly unbuckled the lead rope from the halter and clucked her horse up to a trot. The filly thrust forward energetically with virtually no suspension and a short stride.

At the vet's request Kelly halted the filly. We all went back outside to the examination area. The vet strode up to the filly and faced her left haunch. She spread her fingers over the left stifle and pressed against the joint. She then walked around the horse to examine the right stifle. My heart pounded as I watched the vet with an intensity that was probably burning a hole in her back. She was spending a lot of time prodding those joints. I started to worry.

The vet stood up frowning. "She's short on both hind legs and I can palpate fluid on both stifles." She reached down and placed her palm on the left stifle indicating the area she had been examining.

The stifles, oh no. The stifles are the joints analogous to the human knees. One of the big load bearing joints of the horse's hind end. An important joint and one that is hard to treat.

The vet turned to me and looked me straight in the eye. I knew it wasn't good news.

"I won't be passing this horse as a dressage prospect at this time," the vet said. "She doesn't have the suspension you would want in a dressage horse, but that's not the issue. I'm suspicious of her stifles. If you want I can take x-rays and give you a definitive diagnosis, but I would guess that we're looking at osteochondritis dissecans - you may have heard it referenced as OCD. Besides being off in these joints she's also a tiny bit off in her left front foot."

Unable to take my eyes off the filly, I groaned and my heart split open, spurting disappointment and sadness with each heartbeat.

"No," I said, my mouth suddenly dry. "I don't need to see the x-rays. There's no need to pursue a horse that's showing up with problems before they're put to work or ridden."

My gaze jumped over to the filly. The skin above her eyes furrowed and white rings circled her lovely brown eyes. Her neck went stiff and her ears locked forward. I felt her shock and worry in my body as if it were my own. I turned to Kelly. Her face looked aghast. Her body looked rigid. I forced myself to form the words that I would need to say to her before I started crying.

"I'm sorry Kelly," I said, moving a step back, "but there's no need for me to continue with this pre-purchase examination. Your filly is showing up lame. That's enough reason to abandon the sale. Besides it sounds as if there is a good chance she has OCD."

Kelly's posture stiffened. I couldn't tell if she was still breathing.

"OCD is an unfortunate condition," I said. "I've watched a couple of my friends struggle with horses who were diagnosed with it. I know that you can remove bone lesions from the cartilage and surgery is sometimes a possible solution. One gal I know never got her young horse sound even after surgery. There just aren't any guarantees. The treatment is expensive and risky. It's worse because it seems as if both your filly's stifles may be involved. Thank you for your time and best of luck with this beautiful young horse."

Kelly's pallor grew whiter as the seconds ticked by. She looked as if she was trying to digest what the vet had said. She faced the vet. "I'm shattered," Kelly said. "If the x-rays confirm its OCD, I'm ruined. The condition is thought to be inherited and I have a colt on the ground and another on the way with the same breeding. I can't believe it. I need to know for sure. Take the x-rays. Might as well do it here and now."

"I'm so sorry, Kelly," I said.

"I understand your decision," Kelly said turning to face her horse. "Have a safe trip home."

Before I turned away, I took one last look at this stunning horse. Her beauty was breathtaking. The whites of her eyes were still showing. Her once relaxed posture of one hip cocked and head down was replaced with splayed feet as if she had just shied at something. Her neck was thrust up and her shoulder muscles quivered. I had no doubt she knew what was going on. I hurried to my car. The pain was not only my own. I was feeling the distress of both Kelly and her young horse.

A couple of days after I returned home and after my shock and disappointment had a chance to soften, I decided to check in with Emma through Carol.

I pulled my comforter up around my chin and let my weight sink down into my easy chair. A cup of hot tea steamed on the side table. I needed my comforts. I dialed the phone and Carol answered.

"What a sad outcome," I said feeling a tightening in my chest.

"Diana, what happened?" Carol asked, sounding startled.

"The filly didn't pass the pre-purchase vet examination," I replied.

"I'm so sorry," Carol said with a soothing voice.

I could feel her sympathy. She knew how long I had been looking and how emotionally invested I was in this young horse.

"When the baby horse saw you," Carol translated for Emma, "she knew that you were her person and she immediately fell in love with you. She was very pleased that you were the one to give her her new home. She was bewildered when you thought there was something wrong with her and went away. Your leaving left her confused. She didn't think that there was anything wrong with her."

"I felt her love from the first moment I saw her. It was strong," I said, picking up a tissue. "And I loved her in return. I don't usually fall for a horse at first meeting like this. It reminded me a lot of how I felt for you, Emma, when I first met you. This situation broke my heart. Why didn't she tell us that she had problems when we asked her?"

"She was telling you the truth," Carol translated for Emma, "She was that way from birth, so she didn't know any difference. Her stifles got slowly worse as she got older and grew taller. She just thought that was the way it was. Her discomfort was like a baseline. She had learned to live with it. From her perspective she wasn't injured and didn't have any pain from injury. You asked if she had pain. She didn't. She wasn't injured. She didn't know anything was wrong with her until that day at the vetting. That was when she realized that what they were talking about was always part of her."

"Unfortunately, her condition makes her sore," I said, putting the Kleenex to good use, "and working her would only make it worse."

"Emma says she's been talking to the young horse since you first visited her and likes her very much," Carol said.

"Oops. The young horse has just joined us," Carol said. "I can feel her. She is really worried now. She says after you left they took x-rays and it confirmed what the vet suspected."

"That doesn't surprise me," I said. 'The vet was pretty confident of her diagnosis. I felt she only wanted the x-rays as confirmation since it was such a career ending discovery."

"The young horse wants to say something," Carol said.

"I can feel her distress," I said, rocking back and forth in my chair trying to ease my tension.

"My owner plans to murder me," Carol translated for the filly, "and I'm not ready to die."

"Oh my God," I said and collapsed back against the cushions on my chair. My back gave way and I hunched over, clenching my jaw. My body ached. I tasted the metal taste of blood and realized I had been chewing on my lip.

"I can't believe that, I'm speechless," I squeaked. "Give me a minute to process this." I gasped for breath and tried to quiet the emotions that seemed to be ripping my body to shreds. I slowed my breathing and did my best to use my diaphragm to breathe instead of my chest. I had gone to visit this horse to adopt her into our family and instead I precipitated her death.

Breathe.

Mercifully my mind took over.

"I hurt for the horse, but I hurt for Kelly too," I finally managed to say. "I understand her point of view. Putting the horse down makes economic sense for Kelly. The horse isn't trained. She's lame. She isn't quite two years old yet and is already a tall 17.1 hands. Her future as a riding horse is questionable. The surgery, if surgery is even an option, can be quite expensive and may not give good results. Her problem seems to have a genetic component, so Kelly can't use the horse as a brood mare. What a really lousy situation."

"The baby horse wants you to do something," Carol translated for the young horse.

I sat back up and chattered my teeth as my mind spun for an answer. "What can I do? It's the owner's decision. I need a horse to ride. I don't have the money to set up a ranch for rescued horses." I looked at the ceiling hoping God would magically appear and take care of this horse.

"This young horse would benefit if you would win the lottery," Carol said.

"Wow, what I could do with a lottery-sized jackpot," I said with my mind leaping off into visions of ranches deep in grass.

"The young horse is pleading with you to save her," Carol said.

I groaned. My body churned with so much anguish that I felt like heaving. "I can't take this."

"Diana, I know you and I know the kind of things that you've accomplished," Carol said, "You can do what others can't."

"Stop it." I said. How could I resist the plea from this young horse? "Okay. I will try and think of something."

"Diana, if anyone can I know you will." Carol said, "Who else would intervene?"

Goodness gracious, why does Carol think I can do things? Feeling the weight of this problem I managed to choke out a reply. "Let me sleep on it." I promised myself that I would not take on another unrideable horse. I refused to do that. Yes, I refused to do that…I kept reminding myself.

The next day I woke up with pictures circulating in my brain. A clear image of the young horse being ridden by a small girl popped into my mind and settled as though it found a home. A course of action pushed through my body. After my computer warmed up, I wrote a letter to Kelly. My fingers sped over the keyboard. I wrote that I couldn't stop thinking about her horse and guessed that the final diagnosis might have confirmed the vet's initial thoughts. I couldn't say I knew what the diagnosis had been. Most people were freaked by telepathic animal communication. I went on to write that I knew she must be feeling awful and probably didn't know what to do with her young horse. I wanted to share with her that an idea had come to me and it left such an impression that I needed to share it with her. Might her horse find a home with a gifted young person who would ride her lightly? I wondered if an opportunity like that might present itself.

I sealed the letter in an envelope. The knowledge that I would plant an idea with Kelly and put some of my energy into bringing the result into form was the only consolation I could feel. After Kelly got the letter, I could ask Emma to connect us to the young horse again. But I wouldn't. I'd had enough emotional pain in my life and I couldn't bear knowing if there would be an unfavorable outcome.

I sat back in my desk chair and summoned Emma. I felt her join me. She probably was already with me, but I only sensed it when I tuned into her.

"Emma, if you continue your relationship with the filly," I said, "please don't share bad news with me."

"I understand," I heard Emma respond.

"Thank you for all of your help," I said, tears streaming down my face. "Each time we partner up and try to be of service to another being, I feel even closer to you."

"Aw, shucks," I felt Emma say.

"I'm so glad you're in my life," I said.

"Ditto," I heard back.

Chapter 24

The devastating news regarding what Kelly had planned for the future of her filly disturbed me to the core. I had no idea what affect my letter might have, if any, on her decision to end the filly's life. Continuing my search for another horse was unbearable so I gave myself permission to take a break. My need for a diversion was overwhelming. I pined for something to engage my mind and give my emotions an opportunity to calm down. It was an easy sell when a friend at work approached me with an intriguing proposal. His wife was looking for help with some of her projects. Her work efforts were focused on helping inner city youth and she needed someone else on her team. Who could resist that?

When I met my friend's wife, I liked her immediately. We shared our life histories and found we had much in common. We both had endured unspeakable childhood abuses, we both had attended the Massachusetts Institute of Technology and had other life events in common. Our conversation flowed naturally and I connected to her in a way that instilled trust. We seemed to share common goals.

After our initial meeting, I settled down in my bedroom chair to give her projects more thought. My job was mostly boring, a big step down from being a corporate officer. True I had reduced my stress, but the trade-off was a job with a lot less responsibility and a lot less to fully exercise my skill set. The adjustment made me hungry for something to do that was more meaningful. If not another horse, maybe a new project.

Working to directly improve the lives of children was quite appealing. My friend's wife had been collaborating with Stanley "Tookie" Williams, the co-founder of the Crips who was currently awaiting his execution on death row in San Quentin prison for several murders and robberies. He asserted he had experienced a spiritual awakening and was doing his best to steer children to a better life through his series of books titled *Do Not Follow in My Footsteps*. My friend's wife wanted to develop several programs that would extend the reach of these books and was wondering if I might want to come on board.

The first step in determining if this partnership might be a fit was to meet Stanley and obtain his approval. My friend's wife had taken several years to get Stanley's confidence and she, like Stanley, and unlike me, was African American. Stanley never had a visitor who was white, nor did he ever want help from a white person. And I was very white: blued eyed, blonde and pale skinned. And a middle-aged woman with a mediocre job – hardly a potent force in this society.

After reading my resume, Stanley agreed to meet me. A part of me was intrigued, but a part of me was unsure how to conduct myself with someone who had been convicted of murder and who had created a violent gang that had grown from its beginnings in South Central Los Angeles to several countries around the world. The one thing that had moved me to get involved was the progression that I had seen in Stanley's artwork of self-portraits. The first picture, when he was first put in solitary confinement showed a very angry person full of seething rage. His twenty-seven-inch biceps bulged under his prison garb. The next pencil drawing was of him in a much calmer state but with a look of uncertainty. The third, most recent, picture showed the face of a person who had been infused with spiritual yearnings. The light coming from his eyes was reminiscent of pictures I had seen of holy beings. It was remarkable. The series of pictures told a story. I believed in transformation and I believed in the power of God.

I had been warned about the process of visiting men on death row. I would be searched and scanned. The men would be strip searched going in and coming out of the visiting area. Unlike what you see on television, we would not be ensconced behind a thick glass window talking through a telephone. Nor would we be behind a metal grate talking to the prisoner on the other side of a table. We would meet with the other prisoners and their visitors in a large room with rows of folding chairs. Nothing would divide us from the inmates. When I was told that during the prior week a woman visitor had had her nose bitten off by one of the inmates, I shuddered. I wondered if I knew what I was doing.

I sought help from a friend of mine who was well on his way to getting his PhD in clinical psychology and organizational behavior. He had worked with criminals and filled my ears with reasons why getting involved with prisoners was a very bad idea. I listened and took to heart his admonitions. I hadn't yet had the benefit of the mobster TV show, *The Sopranos*, so I had a hard time picturing people who could willingly commit horrendous acts. I decided to go forward with the visit to explore my feelings and see what my intuition had to say. Besides I didn't want to pass up an opportunity to be of service to children. I knew what it was like to live with hopelessness.

The next evening, I cleared my mind and summoned Emma. When I felt her presence, I sat back in my chair and slowed my breath to fully absorb her energy.

"Emma, I need your help," I said.

"Yes, of course," I felt rather than heard her say.

"I'm going to visit someone who I don't know," I said, speaking into the air of my bedroom and hoping that none of my roommates were listening at the door. "I want you to be with me. Will you do that?"

"Of course," I felt her confirmation throughout my body and clearly got the message that I didn't need to ask. Emma reassured me that she did her best to be with me always. The next step was to visit Stanley.

The following week my friend's wife picked me up and we headed west to the San Rafael Bridge. As I looked out over the water towards Marin County, I tried to remember if I had ever been inside any form of jail. The closest I'd come to a lock-up was visiting a relative who had been held against her will using code 5150 (involuntary psychiatric hold). As we sped along the San Rafael Bridge towards San Quentin, I wondered what the prison environment would feel like.

My mind's wanderings to what might be the dark side of this visit were buoyed by the sunny day which sported the occasional billowy cloud zipping by. I enjoyed the warmth of the sun streaming through the car window until I stepped out of the car at our destination. The breeze coming off San Francisco Bay penetrated my jacket and invaded my bones with a chill. Sailboats darted across the bay fueled by the energy of powerful gusts. The brightly colored boats and their brisk thrusts back and forth spearing through the white caps seemed to represent a life free from encumbrance - a contrast to the drab, boxy prison anchored next to the water. The juxtaposition of the two lifestyles made me shiver. I had been told that Stanley didn't look out of his window because he didn't want to be reminded of a different life. His unpublished book on prison life, the manuscript that had been shared with me, described a horrible existence. No wonder so many inmates, the J-CATs, went insane.

I filled out the paperwork to verify my identity, submitted to the searches and entered the meeting room. The linoleum tiled floor was flanked with vending machines. Lines were drawn on the floor demarcating the areas off limits to prisoners. Coins had been brought so that Stanley could buy snacks from the vending machines to take back with him. The boredom of prison life was broken by a change in food offered by vending machine fare. How sad.

The next step in the process was to wait in line in front of the glass enclosed nook in one corner of the meeting room. I looked around the room at the other visitors who were here. My friend pointed out a woman who had married one of the convicts the week before. When we got to the front of the line, the attendant slipped us a piece of paper through a slit in the glass. I couldn't help but think, "Great that the workers were safe behind the thick glass, what about visitors? Where are the guards?"

My friend's wife filled out the form to "pull" Stanley from his cell. I did the same for another man who had been one of Stanley's lieutenants in the Crips. It should only take a few minutes before they would be released to this room. We sat down next to each other on the folding chairs.

Stanley came out first. He was not as tall as I expected. His black hair was combed back and snugged at the base of his neck. He walked slowly forward, each step a deliberate motion. His dark brown eyes were lovely and felt very present, unlike the spooky countenance of some of the other men in the room whose eyes were calculating, cold and sometimes vacant.

We shook hands and he seated himself next to me with both of us facing the same wall, sitting on metal folding chairs with our shoulders touching. I found the intimacy of the physical proximity a little unsettling. When he spoke, he turned his head to me and I scanned his eyes in search of the soul within. His deep brown eyes had a softness to them. They were round, open and seemed to emit gentleness. I was perplexed in trying to reconcile his violent history with the tender and placid quality I felt radiating from him.

I told him I had read some of his court transcripts and from the proof offered I believed he may not have committed the crimes he had been convicted of and for which he claimed his innocence. I knew enough to know that most prisoners claimed no wrongdoing.

He turned his torso to better face me and asserted that he did not commit those murders. He said with strong emotion that he didn't kill "white" people. He said it as though one would be stupid to think such a thing.

I added that I could accept his innocence for that crime, but I believed he had committed other heinous acts. He didn't respond to what I said, so I assured him I wasn't there to talk about what he had done in the past. He resumed his posture facing forward and equanimity once again engulfed him. I went on to say that this was an exploratory meeting to see if I might fit into his programs to help children. At this point his comrade came into the meeting room.

I stood up to greet him and shake his hand. In comparison to Stanley he was a young man, probably in his thirties. He looked energetic and presented himself as if he were a junior executive. Change his clothes from prison issue to a tailored suit and the picture would work. I couldn't understand how someone projecting that kind of energy ended up here.

Talking to Stanley was easy and flowed without hiccups, backtracks, misunderstandings or awkward pauses. In fact, his energy felt more like a grandfather ruminating from his rocking chair than someone who had spent so many years on death row including six years in solitary confinement.

We were well into our conversation when I felt a tap on my shoulder.

I turned to face my friend's wife who was sitting to my left lean over towards me. Her lips came within a few inches of my ear.

"There's Richard Ramirez," she whispered inclining her head toward a man sitting a few chairs away from us.

My eyes zoomed from Stanley's face to the direction of her head tilt. "Oh my God," was all I could think. The L.A. Night Stalker, the serial killer who raped and tortured. His face had a bizarre expression. What was I doing here breathing the same air as this person? What was I doing in a room of prisoners who were on death row? I turned my attention back to Stanley who in this company seemed so much more benign.

When our visiting time was over, I stood up to say goodbye. The energy that I felt from Stanley was gentle and paternal. I couldn't help myself as I accepted and returned a hug from this man. I think my friend's wife was shocked since Stanley had consistently shown an aversion to white people. I didn't know what to make of it. I accepted the gesture as an honest human emotion. On his way out, Stanley stopped at the vending machines and pocketed a bag of sunflower seeds.

When I got home, I told my psychology friend about the visit. He was extremely worried that I was getting into something that would be a slippery slope into disaster. He offered me his seminar time with Dr. Evanston, a PhD criminologist who grew up in South Central LA and who was familiar with the gang culture. I gladly accepted and was interested in his help to process what I had experienced. I had the hardest time resolving what I felt about Stanley when I visited him and what I knew about his past behaviors.

Within a week I met with Dr. Evanston in the home of my friend who had been meeting with him as a part of his independent study in psychology. Dr. Evanston made me feel at ease. He was a middle-aged man with greying temples, a round belly, and a laugh that emanated with a joy from deep within his body. He gave me his full attention, listening to my motivations and the purpose of my visit to Stanley and what I hoped to accomplish if I decided to support his programs.

"Don't forget they are cons," Dr. Evanston began, sitting up straight in his chair. "They will say anything and do anything they need to do to survive. Remember Ted Bundy and how his charisma fooled his victims."

"Isn't it possible for people to change?" I asked, thinking of Stanley's self-portraits. "If Stanley and his companion hadn't been raised in South Central LA, if had they been given different opportunities, might they be entirely different people?"

"Let's fast forward," Dr. Evanston said, leaning back in the upholstered chair to my friend's left. "Stanley gets out of prison. What next? He's a guest a couple of times on Oprah and then a couple of morning talk shows. How does he support himself? What skills and work habits does he have?"

"I see your point," I said.

"Let's assume that Stanley is 100% reformed and you are safe to help with his programs," Dr. Evanston said. "To be successful, you'd need to be a fund raiser. As a white person that won't fly." He went on to offer other reasons why my background would not speak to the constituents who would be those most likely to donate to Stanley's programs. "You're not in a position to be of much help."

"Okay, I get it," I said and looked over at my friend who was looking heavenward and nodding his head. "I wouldn't be effective in reaching the goals of the programs." Although I couldn't contribute much to Stanley's projects, I was delighted to learn years later that Stanley had been nominated four times for the Nobel Peace Prize for his work to stop gangs.

That night as I settled down in my bedroom with a book I had been enjoying, I found I couldn't concentrate on the printed page. My mind was at war with my feelings. Both my friend and Dr. Evanston were completely skeptical of Stanley's motivations. I had the hardest time believing that my read of Stanley's sincerity would be that far afield. Then it dawned on me. Ask Emma. She can read people's minds and observe their intentions. She had helped me with friends, in relationships and with people at work by clarifying what was really going on. I'd ask her about Stanley.

I called Carol, so I could get as much detail as possible.

"So how did your visit go?" Carol asked after I told her about my trip to San Quentin.

"Being at that prison was different from anything else I have experienced," I replied. "The physical intimacy took some getting used to. The energy of the place is hard for me to describe and is nothing like the psych ward I had visited. I'm not sure I can put it into words. My body had an adverse reaction. When I think of the place, I can still feel the unease. I accomplished what I wanted and had a long visit with Stanley. I've called to ask for Emma's help."

"I'm here," Carol translated for Emma.

"Wow, she's eager," I said.

"More and more she's always with you," Carol said.

"OK, so Emma tell me about Stanley," I said. "Is he really interested in helping children? Is he to be trusted? Is he sincere?"

"Your visit to that place was very interesting," Carol translated. "I was with you the whole time. The place you visited is most unusual. It was as if black gooey spider webs of tar infiltrated every inch of space. The webs were so dense that no light could come out. I could not see in, so I can't tell you about the people you visited."

"Wow, yes, it's a place of dark human misery," I said.

"Please know I was with you even though I couldn't see in," Carol translated for Emma. "And there were more entities besides me that were there protecting you. You weren't alone."

"Emma, I'm so glad you're on my side," I said. "All up it was a good experience. I learned something about this man and how he's trying to save children who are tempted to join gangs, but I've also learned more about you. Here you are struggling to maintain your mental balance, and yet you use your energy to look out for me. How blessed am I to have you as my best friend. I'm humbled."

"Oh pshaw," Carol translated.

"How many best friends can be with you every minute of your life," I said, feeling Emma's love wash over me, "and share your experiences and lend a helping hand when you need it? This closeness is profound."

"I love you," Carol translated.

"And I you," I replied into the air surrounding my chair.

After I hung up the phone, I flopped back against the pillows and rubbed my eyes. I took a deep breath. My restive mind inserted itself with a need to resolve unfinished processing. I tried to make sense of my emotions. I hadn't been frightened by the idea of a visit to San Quentin's death row. And when I was sharing a room with about twenty convicted murderers and rapists who had nothing to lose, I didn't feel particularly anxious. Yes, a little nervous since I was in an entirely new situation. I was familiar with that kind of edginess. And yet as an adult, just a couple of years before, when I spotted my father strolling through the perennial plants of Navlet's Garden Center, I scooted behind a row of hedge plants, crouched down behind the bushes, my heart pounding and body shaking, wondering how I could escape without being seen. Later I castigated myself for the reaction but allowed myself to own my reality. Just the thought alone of my mother, father, sister or the man she eventually married could send me into a full-blown PTSD episode of bone quaking terror. My family and the things they had done to me as a child were more frightening than sharing a space with unrestrained men who had been convicted of the worst crimes. That thought gave me a new perspective to understand the extent of the abuse I endured when I was a child.

My mind tossed and spun and agitated and gnawed on memories of my youth. I could feel the deep-cut wounds created by never being safe at the hands of the only people I knew. If I could survive that kind of abuse, what is left to fear?

I tried to shake off the negative feelings generated whenever I thought of my childhood. I pulled my gaze away from staring at the carpet and looked out the window of my bedroom. High flying clouds reflected pale pink light from the setting sun. Pink, an auspicious color. I wondered where life might lead me next. Perhaps I should resume my search for a riding horse.

Chapter 25

I was a bit disappointed that joining my friend's wife on her projects to help children hadn't worked out. I still felt the vacuum created by my uninspiring job and the lack of a riding horse. I needed something meaningful in my life.

The last days of autumn slipped by, deepening my gloom with the decrease in sunlight hours. As I sat in my bedroom chair one Sunday afternoon, I saw that winter was announcing itself with a day that couldn't be any darker. Despite the leaves having long departed from their willowy perches, the sunlight was blocked by clouds that roiled above and threatened rain. The darkness felt weird like what a partial eclipse of the sun might feel to the uninformed. The cold wind whipped branches of a nearby bush whose twigs pricked like nettles against the window panes.

My desk, once the home to a pile of happy clutter, was swept clean. The VHS cassettes of young horses had been returned and the newsletter clippings of sales ads had been recycled. I felt I had done all I could do. Despite the emotional exhaustion that resulted from my connection to the young filly in Seattle, I felt the stirrings of my need for closer contact with a horse. I dialed the phone. Carol picked up and was available to talk.

I fluffed a pillow and leaned back in my chair hoping to find comfort in the soft and familiar.

"Emma," I said, "Why is it much easier for me to talk to you and understand what you say? Some friends recently offered me help in one way or another and then disappeared."

"Humans are so complicated," Carol translated. "If another horse offered me help, I would know exactly what it would mean. Help. But when a human offers another human help I'm clueless what that means."

"Well, at least I have Elaine," I said. "She came right over to help when a dead, decayed rat fell from the ceiling into my bedroom. And me with a depressed immune system. Yuck."

"Elaine has been there for you many times," Carol translated. "She likes you."

"What I really miss is the day-to-day interaction with a horse," I said. "I've made a decision. When I resume my search, I'm going to look abroad. It's too hard to find a quality horse locally and this last try was heart breaking."

"Where are you headed?" Carol asked.

"Europe has been breeding great sport horses for decades," I said, "and is way ahead of us. What that means, though, is I'll have to go away for a while. I'll probably go to Germany first."

"You don't need to go to Germany to find your horse," Carol translated for Emma. "She's closer than you think."

"What?" I said and sprang upright in my chair. "How do you know?"

"That's all I know," Carol translated, saying each word with equal emphasis.

"Huh, what?" I said, pushing my hair behind my ear. "You know more than you're telling. How do you know the horse will be a 'she'?"

"Emma's not talking," Carol said, laughing. "She has a point, you know. You need a vacation. You've been doing an intense search for about, what, six months? Go lie on a beach in Hawaii and chill. Sounds as if Emma has a plan. You've been through too much emotional stress recently."

"Yes, that's a good idea," Carol translated for Emma. "Take a vacation for a while."

"I feel outnumbered," I said and plunked back into my chair. "Okay, I'll stop looking, but I don't feel like a trip to a beach."

"So, Emma, how are you?" I asked, hoping to hear she was doing better.

"Wow, I can hardly hear her," Carol said. "As soon as the topic changed to her, her voice went very weak. She seems very far away."

"Emma, what is it?" I asked, sitting up stiffly in my chair.

"I'm really miserable," Carol translated with deep sadness in her voice. "I'm in the blackest of holes and I don't want to live."

"Why?" I asked. "What's going on? I need to know." I waited for Carol to respond. The seconds ticked by.

"I'm sorry. She's not answering," Carol said.

I threw the comforter aside that I had pulled up over my legs and rose. "Emma, I can't get away until the weekend, but I'll be up there as soon as I can."

I hung up the phone and paced the floor. The Woodland Stallion Station hadn't brought her the peace I'd hoped for. I needed physical activity, but the day was too uninviting to go out. I wished I liked alcohol, so I might lighten my mood.

The storm had passed during the week and although the wind was cold, the sun shone with summer-like vigor as I headed out Saturday morning. I arrived at the Woodland Stallion Station without incident and headed out to the pasture where Emma was kept. I spotted her at the far end of a large green field. The grass looked good for the dead of winter. She had her head down and was eating. When I walked up to her, I gasped. Her eye was dull and lifeless.

"Emma?" I croaked. "Oh my God, Emma."

She didn't look up. I put her halter on and tried to lead her away. She pulled back and started fretting. She rocked back and forth on her front legs. The expression on her face revealed that no one was home.

Seeing her that way crushed me. Standing quietly, I cleared my mind and tried to connect to her telepathically. I heard nothing. She moved away from me, straining at the lead rope, so I took her halter off. She faced away from me, lowered her head and nosed the ground. With half-hearted nibbles at the tufts of grass, she plodded away dragging her hind feet through the dirt.

I turned away. With drooping shoulders and slumped spine I stumbled towards the gate. The cold wind whipped tears across my cheek. The feeling of powerlessness consumed me and fueled rage at my incapacity to alleviate her distress.

I sat in the car for a few minutes waiting for my emotions to settle. On the drive home my anguish mounted. This was not the happy, retired life I had pictured for Emma. Everything about her looked the worst I'd ever seen. No ideas of how to help her came to me. Now that I'd felt the full misery of Emma's existence I was compelled to do something. Yes, something, but what? Dearest God, what am I to do? I called Carol as soon as I got home.

"What's up?" Carol asked, interrupting my descent into the void.

"I went to visit Emma. I've never seen such a vacant look in all of my life," I said. I felt my head spin and I grabbed the armrests of my chair. "I need help, so I can help Emma."

"I'm in a deep agony," Carol translated with sadness in her voice. She continued, barely whispering, "I live in constant horrible terror. The world is a black, bleak place. There's nothing I can do to get myself out of this hole. I want to be put down. I don't want to live this way. This is no life. Please end it. Put me down."

"Diana," Carol said, lowering her voice, "I can barely hear her. She's never been this shattered before."

My entire body froze in panic. My heart fell to the floor and was barely pulsing against the carpet. I could imagine it there sputtering and flopping like a fish out of water. "Emma, I can feel your pain. I'm so sorry. I feel so helpless. Are you sure that there's no hope? Do you really want to end your life?"

"Yes, I'm sure," Carol translated with a strained voice. "I'm so deep into a black hole. There is no relief."

"Emma," I said. My voice cracked, the words catching in my throat. "I won't do anything like this in a hurry. I can't. I have to sleep on it," I said, struggling for air. "Let me see how I feel in the morning. I often get answers when I wake up. Things are clearer then. Are you able to hold on?"

"I don't want to," Carol translated in a low and hushed voice. "But I understand what you say and I'm okay with that."

I felt a tear streaming down my face, the heat of it searing my cheek. "Carol, I feel horrible. Why isn't there something that can be done to help my horse?"

I could feel gentle energy wash over me when Carol answered. "You know, I don't have any answers for you. This has been a long journey for the both of you. It will end as it's meant to end. Please let me know what you come up with. If you decide to put Emma down, I want to be there to support the both of you."

"Thank you, Carol," I said, whispering between the sobs. "I hope it doesn't come to that."

That night I went to bed feeling as if I was falling through space with no soft spot to land. Not one cell in my body could resist resonating with the exquisite pain I felt. This was not the pain of the body from an injury, but the pain of a heart that has been shredded into so many pieces that no amount of repair would make it whole. Despair, frustration, futility, rage, took their turns rampaging through my body. Finally, exhaustion won over and I fell into a deep sleep.

When I opened my eyes in the morning, I bolted upright. The sun shimmered through the eastern facing window. The soft light reminded me of the light in Venice, Italy. Soft, golden and comforting. I sat perfectly still and cleared my mind. I hadn't taken but one breath when I heard a resounding, "No." Goose bumps rose on my arms and although I was warm, my shoulders shivered. The voice was loud, strong and clear. Perhaps one can never be certain of the origin of that inner voice. Most people would say it came from my deepest knowing. I recognized the source and completely trusted the message. There would be no second guesses.

I was relieved that I wouldn't be putting Emma down, but I was distressed that she was living with so much psychological pain. I felt trapped. Once again all I could do was go on.

Two weeks later I received a phone call from Jeannette at the Woodland Stallion Station.

"Emma has been kicked by one of the baby horses," Jeannette said, her voice steady and businesslike, "and she needs treatment. The University of California, Davis vet school is only a half hour away and they make ranch calls. I recommend using them. Do I have your permission to have Emma treated?"

"Yes, of course," I replied as anxiety rose up my spine.

"Don't worry," Jeannette said. "The wound isn't bad, but it can't be left. It won't leave a scar, but I'm afraid of infection with this wet weather. I would feel better if she had a course of antibiotics."

"Thank you for seeing that she's properly cared for," I said. I sighed and crumpled deeper into my chair. "Next time please go ahead and secure treatment. You don't need to contact me."

Two days later Jeannette called me again and asked that I call UC Davis. She explained that one of the vets who had come out to the ranch wanted to talk to me. She reassured me that Emma's injury was doing fine and not to be worried. She gave me the number and I dialed it as soon as our conversation ended.

The vet who picked up the phone identified himself as the person who treated Emma's leg wound. With a distinctive Spanish accent, he introduced himself and explained he was doing a rotation at UC Davis to improve his skill set to take back to his veterinary medicine practice in Argentina. With a melodious, soft, voice he said, "Your mare is really quite beautiful."

"Thank you," I said, wondering why this vet wanted to talk to me. Surely not about Emma's looks.

"How old is she?" he asked.

"Fourteen years old," I said as my foot tapped out a vigorous beat. I had no idea where this was going and was almost afraid of what he might say.

"I thought so," he said, his voice sounded more like purring than English words. "Jeannette was telling me about her. She mentioned that you were having difficulties with her moods and that's why she's been turned out. She's too young to be retired. When we worked on her leg she was cooperative and easy to treat. Her temperament is very sweet. She looks as if she is quite the athlete."

"Yes, she's what I have always wanted in a horse," I said. "The problem is that she has panic attacks and heightened levels of anxiety that make riding her dangerous. She's even dangerous for anyone on the ground during one of her attacks."

"I may be able to help," he said, his words spoken with a calming cadence.

"I feel as if I've tried everything," I said, attempting to beat down my skepticism. Six years of following every lead I had encountered had left me jaded. "I've taken her to UC Davis before and we saw Dr. Madigan. He wasn't able to provide any assistance."

"Let me explain," he said with a reassuring voice. "I have two theories."

"Okay?" I managed to get out despite my doubts.

"One theory," he said, his voice now a bit stronger and shaded with authority, "is that she has a tumor on her ovaries and it is causing an over-production of hormones. If she has a tumor we can remove it."

"I don't think she has a tumor," I countered, fully knowing that he wouldn't believe me. Sometimes I wondered why I bothered.

"The other theory is related to an imbalance in her reproductive cycle," he said. "In Argentina we've been successful in treating show horses with progesterone. Mares can get unruly during their cycle and competitors want a reliable mount. We implant progesterone pellets into their necks and it lasts for six weeks. It seems to be a big help. Some mares become more manageable and some return to their normal personality. Although your mare may not be cured, it may be possible to let her live out her life a little more comfortably."

I wondered if he could hear the springs as I bounced up and down on my chair.

"What you are saying makes sense," I said, my mind reeling through the archival pictures of my life with Emma. "Her bouts seem to get worse seasonally though not in alignment with her estrous cycle. I know that the estrous cycle in some mares shuts down for the winter and then starts up again in the spring. Recently, though, even seasonality doesn't seem to ease her emotional distress."

"I understand what you're saying," he said, "Because we've experienced success I believe this treatment may be effective for your horse even though she doesn't exactly fit the pattern."

"Anything that might help is welcome," I said, my heart racing. Hope once again sparked and fluttered in an effort to take hold. "What's the next step?"

"We can set up an appointment to check for the tumor," he said. "If she doesn't have one then we can arrange to come back and implant her with progesterone."

"Excellent," I said. "Bring out the progesterone pellets when you check her for a tumor. I don't think she has one and I want to get started with the treatment right away. How soon after the implant will she experience a difference?"

"It takes about six weeks for the full effect, but you should start seeing something in about four weeks." The roundness of his vowels and the softness of his consonants seemed to calm an internal excitement I was feeling throughout my body. Each of my cells seemed to be vibrating at an elevated frequency, making me heady.

As he spoke, I marked my calendar for two weeks from the scheduled appointment. After a few more questions, I hung up the phone. At first, I sat staring out the window at the sky ornamented with high flying clouds. Then like a kid let out at recess I ran around my bedroom leaping into the air and grinning from ear to ear with joy. I squealed and squeaked. Oh, my God, after all these years, Emma may get better. Now I know why my question about putting her down was answered with a "no." Emma was going to get help. Thank you, dearest God.

Two days later, I wasn't surprised when I got a call from the vet telling me that Emma didn't have a tumor. I knew that the way I know when truth is being spoken. Scientists must do their thing. The vet reported that the progesterone implant went well. Now all I had to do was wait. But this waiting would be accompanied with renewed hope for a happy outcome.

The night that two weeks were up I called Carol. I eased down into my chair feeling the soft cushion rise to support my weight. I breathed out a huge sigh as hope frolicked in my mind and skittered into my heart with the tapping joy of tiny padded feet.

"Diana, her voice is stronger," Carol said with a sigh. "I can hear her so much better."

I noticed a couple of specks of dust on Emma's picture frame and wiped them off with the cuff of my sweatshirt. "Emma can you feel any difference since the implant was put in?"

"Yes," Carol translated.

"She feels so much lighter," Carol said with more energy in her voice, "You have no idea how hard it was to talk to her before. Her mood is not nearly so heavy."

"I'm happy to hear that," I said, replacing Emma's picture in its prominent place on my side table.

"I'm feeling better," Carol translated. "The world isn't so terrifying or so dark."

"I'm coming up to see you in another two weeks," I said, my heart doing back flips and somersaults after what felt like an incarceration of decades.

"I'll be waiting," Carol translated.

"And I'll be bringing the Fuji's."

Time seemed to drag as if I was hitched to a wagonload of sandbags. I pulled and huffed with every stride as if I had been weighted into slow motion. Each day I willed the earth to move faster in its orbit. On the Saturday that the two weeks were up, I headed out. Although it was against my belief system to speed, I perhaps went faster than the posted speed limit on the highways leading me to Emma.

When I unfastened the gate at Emma's pasture, she looked up at me but didn't come over. I walked towards her, moving with precision and deliberation and keeping my attention focused on the expression of her face. When I got closer, I saw her eye seemed clearer. I slipped the halter on her head and she raised it. My breath caught. I had a close view of her head. No missing it. Despite her eye looking a little wild, she was present. That horrible vacant look of the tortured soul was gone.

We left her pasture and headed for the barns. Near the parking lot at the entrance to the ranch was a round pen with decent footing. I led her there, closed the gate and unsnapped the lead rope. She spun away and trotted in an animated, bold, long stride around the circle. The expression on her face faded into being present and alive and then faded back to a vacant expression. The transformation was eerie to watch as she slipped away and then came back into being herself. She did it several times during the five minutes she trotted around the pen. But in that place where truth resides, I knew she would be whole and sound in her mind before long. When I returned her to the pasture, I let her know that I would be back in two weeks and would be bringing her home to the boarding stable that we had just left. I had already called the owner and reserved a stall that would be available at the end of the month. That's how confident I was in her recovery.

I brought Emma back to her pasture. "See you soon," I said as I watched her head off to join the other horses.

I hopped into my Mustang 5.0 and although it was a cold day, I put the top down and let the wind blow through my hair.

Chapter 26

The beams from the late winter sun, strong and warm, sparkled off the gravel that welcomed me as I drove down the long winding driveway of the Woodland Stallion Station. I hastened to park the rig and headed out on foot. As soon as I spotted Emma at the far end of her pasture, I felt a magnetic urge to rush to her. Because I didn't want to spook the other horses, I restrained my pace. As soon as I was within a couple of feet of Emma, I could see the bright shiny eye that I so dearly loved. Her ears were pointed at me and she stared at me with recognition. When I slipped her halter on, Emma jigged in place with what appeared to be the joy of anticipation. What a contrast to her anxious pacing, her wild eye and desperate vocalizations. I joined her exuberance. The closer we got to the horse trailer, the more animated Emma's gestures became and the more light-hearted I felt. My horse, my best friend, was coming home to me.

Jeannette popped out from the stallion barn and strode towards me. "Do you need some help?" she called out as her eyes followed Emma's leaps to the left and then the right.

I had to admit Emma did look a bit out of control. For someone who didn't know her, the rearing and four-footed capers into the air were impressive and might suggest that Emma wouldn't be easily loaded into my trailer.

"Don't worry - she'll be fine," I replied, fully confident in my familiarity with my horse, despite the fact I was nearly being jerked off my feet with the vigor of Emma's escapades. I knew the source of Emma's behavior was a frolic and not a frenetic release of tension. "Thank you for taking such good care of her," I yelled out over my shoulder as I was whiplashed into facing yet another direction. "I appreciate all you've done. Having her back is a huge gift."

"She's a lovely horse," Jeannette called out and watched with an air of suspicion and a wrinkled brow that suggested she didn't believe that I knew what I was doing. "I'm glad it worked out." The intensity of her stare showed her growing concern.

More like a jack rabbit than a horse, Emma bounded over to the trailer and as soon as I turned her to face the back opening, she hurled in with perhaps only one foot bothering to touch the loading ramp. She then stood quietly which she would probably continue to do for the two-hour drive to Walnut Creek. I waved goodbye to Jeannette and started the engine. Out of the corner of my eye I saw Jeannette shake her head in what appeared to be disbelief.

Coasting down the highway in my truck with the trailer towing smoothly behind, I thought about where we were heading and the last time Emma had been at this boarding stable. The year before, her behaviors had forced me to seek another home for her. I prayed that this time would be different. Last time her stall had been across from the indoor arena. This time her stall was in a corner far away from the hubbub. She was between a young chestnut thoroughbred mare and a bay Arabian gelding and more importantly two full rows away from the stallion. I liked the quiet of this stall - next to a creek and backed up to the eastern hillside, which was grazing land. This setting felt close to nature with all the wildlife that populated the creek and the cattle that roamed the open space.

Emma took even steps down the ramp and I led her to her new stall. Once there, I felt an emotional release. Emma was home and back in my life. I took my time and carefully inspected her from ears to tail. I sighed. Not a happy picture for a loved one. I reminded myself that pasture horses who spend the winter outside with a group of other horses don't usually look like well-cared for show horses. Her coat was unkempt and sun-bleached. She had evidence of several nicks and bites – raw skin revealed the fresh ones. A couple of bald spots on her back revealed rain rot. A wash with Betadine would get those spots under control. Now that the sun was shining she would stay dry and the skin infection would clear up in no time. I was lucky it wasn't worse, since this had been a particularly wet winter. I knew that to most people at the stable Emma looked sad. The scientist in me knew how to care for her body. It wasn't her physical state that was driving my emotions. She may have lost her condition and there were now sunken places where muscles had been, but every time I looked at her face, her eye was bright and present. My joy purred. A little exercise, more groceries, some ointments and when she shed out in spring she'd look like the athlete I knew.

When I got home, I called my blacksmith, Robert, and asked him to put sneakers back on Emma as soon as he could fit her in. He took the opportunity to educate me on a development in shoeing.

"I've been using a new shoe with good success," he explained. "They're called natural balance shoes and have been developed by a blacksmith who spent time in the high desert studying how wild horses move and how their feet wear. From that experience he designed a shoe that mimicked the way wild horse's hooves land on the dirt and break over their toe."

"What are they made of?" I asked knowing how Emma appreciated her sneakers.

"That's not the point," he shot back. "They improve the mechanics of the horse's movement."

A little annoyed at his evasion I said as sweetly as I could, "That sounds great. What are they made of?"

"Steel," he replied, clearly annoyed.

My back bristled. I was determined to take care of Emma. She had pretty much stayed sound with her rubber sneakers and while the shoe looked clumsy, it was much softer than metal. She only came up sore when her anxiety attacks forced her to pound her feet in endless pacing.

"What you say makes sense, but Emma has told me that she likes her sneakers," I said, risking his ire with my reference to Emma's voice. I knew that few people believed in the ability of animals to speak telepathically. "They help cushion the concussion of her feet. Let's just stay with the sneakers for a while. She stayed sound when she was here before. She says she got a little sore out in pasture, so I would like to recreate the situation we had when she was sound."

I assumed the silence on the phone represented concurrence.

On the day Emma was to be shod I left work early and arrived at the barn just as Robert was leading Emma back to her stall. The first thing I did was glance down at her feet. I gasped. Metal shoes. I felt a furious burn of anger rip up my back. He must have seen my face change and stopped up short.

"I know you wanted sneakers," he said as he turned to face me. "Hear me out." He steadied his vibrant blue eyes on mine and ran his fingers through his sandy blonde hair. I may have been angry, but my love of beauty interrupted my thoughts. I couldn't help but notice that for a middle-aged man Robert had a great head of thick, wavy hair, a ruggedly handsome face and one heck of a body. I sighed.

"Trust me," he said in a soothing tone. He looked at me and an easy smile softened his face. "If these shoes don't work out, if they are not clearly better, I'll put the sneakers back on for no charge. These shoes are designed to improve the health of the foot and I believe in them."

If it hadn't been for a long history of appreciation for Robert's intelligence, intuition and the competence of his shoeing, I would have insisted on an immediate change. "Okay," I acquiesced and silently made a mental note to call him within a couple of weeks to change the shoes.

One night after work two weeks later, I decided to call Carol, so I could hear how Emma weighed in on the new shoe design. After all it was her body and she had the strongest vote. To my surprise they hadn't seemed to make her sore, so I was curious to hear what she felt. I turned the light on in my bedroom and headed for my chair and the telephone. I dialed Carol's number.

"The only negative thing I can sense about the new shoes is that they seem to make Emma uncertain," I said, opening the conversation.

After a pause Carol said, "You're right. Emma says it's taking some time to get used to them, but she likes the way they feel. She says that anytime the design of her shoes changes she must figure out how to move in them. She says that the first time she wore the rubber sneakers she felt like she was walking on stilts. You heard her right that she hasn't totally adjusted yet to these shoes, but she doesn't want you to change them. She says that these seem to feel more natural."

"OK Emma, if you change your mind let me know," I said, thinking that Robert would be pleased with this result.

"Emma, while we have Carol on the line is there anything else you want me to know?"

"I'm having a hard time making friends," Carol translated. "The other horses make fun of me. They say only old horses are turned out to pasture. They say that something must be wrong with me."

"Emma, forgive them," I blurted out. "That's what their persons are saying. They don't understand. Ignore them. You're beautiful and it won't be long before you look as great as you always have. Better yet, tell them you were treated to a very special vacation at a spa and ask them what their person is doing for them."

"Diana, you're a trouble maker," Carol said, laughing.

To get Emma back in shape was going to take about three months of slow work. Because I wanted to train at the upper levels of dressage, these weeks of measured conditioning were needed, yet boring. First, I would introduce the trot, then I'd bring back the canter and in the third month I would introduce the lateral movements in preparation for collection. She needed to get her weight and muscle tone back before I could ask her to consistently shift her weight from her front end to her hind end. Skipping steps would be easy if it didn't risk joint injury and other problems. I had to be slow and methodical. Given my lack of patience, this was an agonizing process. When we could at last start doing some collected work, I felt in my element and even more content with my riding. Another month or so would be needed to get us to our highest level of accomplishment.

Even though it took a while to get Emma's muscles in shape, I was exquisitely happy to have Emma back in my life. Spending time with her every day helped center me emotionally. The physical exercise with a horse, breathing the smell of horses and just hanging out with Emma nurtured me on a deep level.

Every six weeks like clockwork I called the vet to have him inject Emma with the progesterone pellets in her neck. She wasn't at all anxious like she had been. I even took her on short trail rides. She sometimes got nervous and sometimes was just fine. Trail riding always put my head back on straight. No therapist could match what a trail ride could accomplish.

The summer seemed to go by quickly. Emma was grateful that I hadn't pushed her back into work and instead took time to let her muscles fully develop. To be back riding again was glorious. Not just riding but riding my horse. The horse that I loved and who knew me so well. Our bodies blended and melded together.

By the end of summer Emma was in the groove. Her lateral work was brilliant. She could canter sidewise across the arena with ease. I even attempted some zig zag patterns where we put in flying changes before doing a half-pass in the other direction. Her precision and responsiveness felt marvelous. I was stoked.

Now that I was riding consistently, my emotions seemed to be better balanced. Getting through each day at work was easier knowing that my horse and a good ride was waiting for me at the end of the day. So many of the programs I worked on at my job never got implemented for reasons out of my control. It felt good to be able to have a measurable impact on something. Our progress in dressage was continual and demonstrable. Happy days.

On one of those clear, sunny days in September I came out to the barn and saw that Emma was looking a little listless. I saddled her up and went to lead her to the indoor arena. She dragged her feet leaving tracks in the dirt. Her eyes were bright, she had eaten her breakfast. I asked her to try a jog. She hesitated and then gave a halfhearted attempt to move faster. She didn't seem to have any energy. I took her back to her stall and got out the thermometer. Her temperature was normal and her eye was clear. I couldn't help but worry. What would it be this time? I felt as if every time we got it together one of us was sidelined. I'd call the vet as soon as I got home and get a scientific opinion before I imagined what horrific disease Emma might have.

A couple of days later the vet made it out to the barn. After what appeared to be a thorough examination, the vet didn't have any idea what was causing Emma's malaise. Emma was exhausted. She was sound, no limping and other than her lack of energy had no symptoms. When two weeks went by and there hadn't been any improvement, I called the vet again. If Emma stayed out of work much longer we would be doing a lot of back tracking and reconditioning. My vet examined Emma again and took a blood sample. All indicators came back normal.

Four weeks later Emma was still too tired to be ridden. My body was bursting with the energy that is only released from riding. Emma's symptoms were unchanged. Her eye was bright, she was eating and had no desire to move. She wasn't in pain. Each day that she stood in her stall was another day her condition slipped. I questioned everyone I knew who had horses to ask them if they ever had a similar experience. I heard all kinds of stories. Not one fit Emma's symptoms. Emma had no idea what was causing her condition. She was dumbfounded as well.

One day at work I bumped into a friend who kept a couple of horses at her house. When I mentioned Emma's lethargy, she suggested Emma might have been infected by a tick. She had an excellent point – ticks were abundant this time of year. I called my vet who confirmed he hadn't made that test since those infections were rare. I asked him to go ahead and check for tick-borne diseases.

My vet called me at work when the results came back. He seemed embarrassed when he told me that the diagnosis was Ehrlichia, a bacterial disease carried by ticks.

"The treatment is ten consecutive days of antibiotics administered IV," he said. "Given how long Emma has been infected, I think you're better off letting her recover naturally."

"But she's been sick for so long," I pleaded. "She's lost some of her conditioning."

"There's no way that I'm going out there to administer a shot for the next ten days," he said, "and you'll have trouble finding someone to do it. Emma's own system will knock this out in a couple more weeks. I'm sure of it. You'll save yourself the expense as well. It wouldn't be cheap."

I hung up the phone with a bit too much energy.

That night I settled in my chair and felt antsy about not being able to ride. I dialed Carol's number. Talking to Emma always made me feel better.

"Emma, I'm so sorry you aren't feeling well," I said when Carol picked up and we completed the opening pleasantries. "At least we know now what the problem is. The good news is that you'll be feeling better soon. You'll need to be stall bound and rested for the next couple of weeks just like you've been doing. What can I do to help keep you entertained?"

"I like Oprah," Carol translated without a moment of pause and with notable nonchalance.

"Wh-wh-what?" I said, taken by surprise.

"I like watching Oprah," Carol translated emphasizing the word 'like.'

I couldn't imagine where this was coming from. "So, Emma, how do you know about Oprah?" I asked. "I work during the day and don't watch daytime TV. Even when I've been home sick I haven't watched TV during the day. There aren't any TV's out at the barn. I don't get it."

"I watch Oprah through Carol's eyes," Carol translated amid her giggling.

"Emma's right," Carol said. "My shift ends in time for me to get home and watch Oprah. I really like her program. I had no idea that Emma was watching too."

"This is incredible," I said, shaking my head in disbelief. "My horse watches television through your eyes."

"Yup," Carol said. "That's how it works."

"Give me a minute to digest this," I said, letting out a deep breath. I rearranged the pillows behind my back. "Okay, Emma, what do you like about Oprah?"

"I especially like the way she treats horses," Carol translated. "She lets them run free."

"I remember an episode," Carol said, "that showed Oprah's farm and her horses in a field."

Not knowing how I could do it, I decided to ask anyway, "Since you are sick and can't do much, do you want me to put a TV in your stall?"

"No, that won't work." Carol said laughing. She went on to translate, "My eyes don't see that well. I have to watch it through human eyes."

"I remember you telling me that you could see better through human eyes," I said, "but I didn't realize that you dropped in on others unannounced. I can't help you with Oprah," I replied joining in the laughter, "but it seems as if Carol is a good bet."

I slipped into my bed that night content that Emma was on a path to recovery and that I had done everything I could to make her happy. I couldn't help but wonder what other TV programs might appeal to her and decided to connect to her whenever I watched something that might be of interest.

Before I dozed off, I thought about my life and the communications I had with Emma. No wonder people thought me strange whenever I tried to explain the richness of my life. Better to keep it to myself. Finding human friends who understood me was hard, never mind finding someone who lived in the world I did. The best I could hope for was toleration. I was grateful that Emma was back in my life. I could be myself with my best friend. I couldn't imagine a greater gift than being authentic with another being. So much of my life I was forced into being something I wasn't. Thank you, God, for sending Emma into my life.

Chapter 27

I had marked on my calendar the exact day the vet said Emma should be fully recovered from her tick disease. When that day came, Emma greeted me with vigorous head bobbing and kicked her stall door with an eagerness to get things going. Her coat was shiny, her eyes sparkled and her body language said, "get me out of here." I tried to zone in on her internal sensations. What I felt was a healthy horse bursting with the need to move.

Emma's immune system had taken a hit and her muscles had had plenty of time to get soft. The joy of getting back on her was dampened by the need to go slow with both her muscle development and her time to fully heal. All up she had been on stall rest for over two months. That was about the same amount of time that would be needed to get back to where we were. I reminded myself to be thankful that I had a horse to ride.

I set about my program of strengthening Emma. Not long after the two months of reconditioning were over, I had a day that could best be described as one with mixed reviews. Emma was strong, healthy and totally focused on her training. Riding again was a blissful event. I would have gone home ecstatic if it hadn't been for her spooking a couple of times with nothing discernable in the area. I squirmed in the saddle and used self-talk to quell the burgeoning knots in my stomach. I counseled myself to wait for a trend before I engaged in a major fret. My ride continued with no other incidents and I surrendered to the sheer joy of riding.

Our canter pirouettes were getting stronger. Emma's lateral work was fabulous. Her legs stretched sideways with such scope that we seemed to be moving more sideways than forward. She seemed to spend more time in the air than on the ground. We floated across the arena. Some days the schooling went so well and Emma and I were so connected that everything we did was smooth and effortless. The transitions were immediate and flowed with an ease that only an elastic and responsive horse can offer.

Within the next couple of weeks I couldn't help but notice that the number of times that Emma reacted with fright during a ride increased and she manifested a generalized edginess. Her uneasiness permeated my body. Why was this happening? All I wanted was a happy horse and one who I could ride and partner with in my sport. It seemed as if we had just gotten into the groove after her illness. And now this. Arghh.

A vet consultation was the next step with the hope that it could potentially ward off my descent into emotional hysteria. When I described the situation, my vet reassured me that he could deal with Emma's behavior change by increasing the number of pellets in her neck. He felt strongly that the increased amount of hormone would control her anxiety. I let out a sigh of relief. And he was right. Within days of treatment Emma's anxiety level diminished.

After a few months passed Emma's shying returned and she seemed easily irritated. I called my vet immediately. Over the next several months, my vet had to increase the number of pellets twice. When Emma's anxious behavior reappeared the fourth time, I made another appointment to have her pellets increased.

My vet came to the barn his usual one to two hours late. The crown of his hair, freed from the confines of a hat, had been lightened by the sun to a dark brown. His naturally tanned skin gave him a look of health. When he spotted me, a darling smile crept across his lips. His warmth and easy-going manner worked wonders with my personality that had a hair trigger for stress.

"Emma is spooking again," I said, my voice perhaps emitting a little too much screech. As I approached him, I expected my message to be treated as it had in the past with his suggestion to increase the dosage.

He looked at me with a hesitant gaze as his brow furrowed. "I don't know what you want me to do."

"What do you mean?' I asked, my back stiffening. "Put more pellets in her neck."

"I've been doing that already," he said, removing the stethoscope from around his shoulders. "There comes a time when you run out of space in the neck for more pellets." He coiled his fingers around the end of his stethoscope and then imitated a jack hammer injecting all up and down a horse's neck. I wish that I could have laughed at his gesture. Instead my breath shortened and I rocked back and forth. I wondered if I had come to the end of another road with Emma.

My vet must have guessed what I was thinking. "Wait, don't panic, there is something we can do," he said, inching closer to me. "We can move her up to Regu-Mate which lets us administer a higher dose of progestin since it's given orally. I've been avoiding that for as long as possible because it's absorbed through the skin and caretakers must be especially careful. There are other complications."

"What?" I asked. "If it offers a solution, I want to know."

"It costs over $250 a liter," he said, wincing, "and has to be administered daily. And it needs to be kept cool."

"Not a problem," I said, nearly shouting with the exuberance reflected by my mood change.

The next day I bought an ice chest and a dozen blue ice packets. During warm weather I would have to go out to the barn every day and replace the blue ice, so the Regu-Mate would not heat up. The medicine was expensive and required more work for me to prepare Emma's food for administration. If it meant I had my upper level dressage horse back, it was a small price to pay.

Sure enough, after Emma was put on the Regu-Mate her anxiety lowered. No more spooking when I rode her. Our dressage work was nearly brilliant all the time. Emma's half passes were gorgeous and she was carrying herself in more and more of a collected frame. I couldn't have been happier with our progress.

Once again I was in a state of bliss when I rode. I could feel our consciousnesses join. We eased from one transition to another as if there was no change in speed, gait or direction. Canter, walk, canter. Half pass left into half pass right. I couldn't always feel Emma's footfalls land on the ground. We moved forward, the air parting as if curtains were swept aside to let us pass into rarified realms. The experience of floating from one movement to another lifted me into a space without dimension. What a divine unity.

My addiction to this euphoria lasted week after week. This was why I rode. This was why I needed a horse in my life. My heart sang. I could more easily deal with the challenges life presented.

Emma did well on the Regu-Mate for almost eight months. The first time she shied I conveniently ignored it. Over the next few weeks the trend couldn't be missed. When I could no longer deny that this new course of treatment had lost its efficacy, I called my vet with a dry mouth and cold palms.

When we finally connected, I shared the dreaded development.

"I'm sorry," he said. "I don't have any other ideas for you in terms of medications. This is my only thought. Why not try taking her to UC Davis again? After all, the idea of using hormones came from a visiting resident and science might have more to offer now."

"OK," I said, feeling only a pittance of relief. "Please, go ahead and make the referral."

Two weeks later I pulled my rig into the parking lot of the large animal veterinary clinic of the University of California at Davis. The weather was warm and sunny and the lack of rain meant we wouldn't have to scurry for cover. I unloaded Emma onto the dirt walkway and headed towards the main building.

My appointment was with the same head vet, John Madigan, whom I had seen when I first brought Emma to UC Davis several years before. Dr. Madigan and his gaggle of vet students joined Emma and me in the courtyard between buildings. His kind expression, steady gaze and air of authority exuded confidence. This time he seemed to listen with a better sense of understanding. No eyes rolled from the students in attendance. I felt relieved that he wasn't viewing me as a hysterical middle-aged woman with tendencies to exaggeration.

"Not too long ago I was donated two horses that supposedly suffered from panic attacks," Madigan explained, "just like what you describe your mare having. It was the darndest thing. I was at my kitchen sink looking out the window at their paddock. They had just been fed and were peacefully eating their dinner. Then out of nowhere one of them reacted. His head shot up into the air and I saw the whites of his eyes. He bolted into a flat run as if he'd seen a bear. I've never seen anything like that. He wouldn't settle down. He kept running the fence line as if that bear wouldn't leave him alone."

"I'm grateful you've experienced what I've been struggling with," I said.

"Being at a university teaching hospital gives me a lot of advantages," Dr. Madigan said, directing his comments to the vet students who were surrounding us. "I have virtual laboratories around the globe. At this time, I'm treating a few horses in New Zealand with the same diagnosis."

My jaw dropped open. "So, more people are running into this problem. I'm sorry to hear that, but I'm grateful for the research it promotes."

Pulling out his pen, Dr. Madigan jotted notes on his clipboard that held Emma's file. "I'll write a prescription that solved the problem for a couple of the horses that are being treated. There are pharmacies that make up prescriptions for animals and will charge you a lot less than drugs that are intended for humans. Do a little hunting and you'll save yourself quite a bit of money."

The medication, cyproheptadine, that Dr. Madigan prescribed stopped Emma's anxiety attacks but made her muscles and joints so stiff and sore that she didn't want to move. She was physically miserable. I emailed Madigan about the side effects and he prescribed propranolol.

This drug irritated Emma's stomach so badly that with each dose I had to add a cup of kaolin (the chalky tasting pink stuff) to her bucket of grain. To get her to eat the mixture, I held the bucket while petting her and encouraging her to take a bite. Her lips curled back and she grimaced with each mouthful. She chewed slowly and it took about twenty minutes for her to finish all of it. If horses could gag, she would have been doing it. But God bless her, she ate her medicine every night. Emma said she actively participated in her health care and didn't like living in fear.

Emma's disgust at having to eat her meds with a cup of pink stuff every day made me think about another solution. I called Madigan and asked him if he would prescribe Paxil for Emma (knowing it worked for me when I had excessive anxiety). He wouldn't. He didn't have any experience with antidepressants in horses. The dreaded nightly routine continued.

The nuisance of eating the medicine proved worthwhile. Within a couple of weeks the propranolol controlled Emma's anxiety enough so that I could continue to ride her in the arena. I soon learned though that the control of the medication didn't extend to the trail. Thankfully her dressage work was again top notch. Emma loved her work and put her energy into learning what I was asking. I was approaching a level of dressage that was new to me and I lucked out when I was invited to join a monthly clinic in Woodside. The clinician, Gerhard Politz, whom I had taken lessons from when he still lived in Germany, would fly up from his home in Southern California. I was thrilled. Getting instruction with someone who shared my vision of dressage was rare. I trusted his methods and his respect for the horse. He believed in rewarding the horse and any mistakes weren't the horse's fault but rather attributed to a lack of proper preparation on the rider's side. His masterful instruction guided my training of Emma.

Our progress in dressage was stunning. I received a deep satisfaction from the beauty we created. Then after several months on propranolol, Emma started showing her signs of increased unease. Her pattern of habituating to her treatment provoked a cry of anguish from deep within me. I chastised myself for being so naïve to expect a different outcome.

When Emma's anxiety increased to a level I couldn't tolerate, I called Dr. Madigan. I explained that her anxiety was increasing and her panic attacks were sure to follow given her pattern of behavior. He didn't have any other suggestions and wished me well. His voice sounded abrupt and final.

I felt abandoned. Once again, I was on my own with Emma's escalating fears. It wouldn't be long before her panic attacks returned. I felt exhausted. I only knew to dig deep and ask God for another door to open.

When I shared my situation with a couple of boarders at the barn, they told me about a vet who kept her horses at our stable. Although Walnut Creek was out of her service territory, she made an exception for the horses at this barn. She was known to be an out-of-the-box thinker who had worked miracles with some horses. I had been warned that she was notorious for ignoring phone calls, so I planned to approach her as soon as I saw her at the barn.

Within a few days I got my opportunity. When Dr. Clare was between clients, I scooted up to her and asked if I could talk to her.

She smiled at me and patted back the loose hairs that had escaped from her pony tail tied at the back of her neck. Her gingham blouse, tucked loosely into faded blue jeans, suggested a casual approach might work with her. In as few words as I could manage, I explained my challenges with Emma. I felt an anomaly between her soft brown eyes and the intensity with which she followed my explanation. I could tell her mind must be engaged when light flashed from her eyes as they whisked back and forth.

"I like challenges," she said. "I have an idea. I'll be right back." She turned and went to her truck and came back with a syringe and then proceeded up to Emma's stall.

"The first thing that I'd like to do is test Emma for allergies," she said as she stuck the needle into Emma's jugular vein to draw blood. "The behaviors you describe are so extreme that I wouldn't be surprised if there might be a component that was allergen related. I'll get the results back in a week."

The thought of an allergen causing Emma's anxiety was a new concept for me. I was very interested where this investigation might lead. Waiting for the results made the daily grind go even slower. The following week I spotted Dr. Clare's truck when she drove into the parking lot. She stopped the engine and motioned me over to the cab.

Her big brown eyes sparkled as I approached her truck. She opened her door and pulled out several sheets of paper.

"The results of the test stunned me," she said, flipping pages back and forth of a lab report filled with columns of numbers. "I've never seen anything even close to this. She's allergic to almost everything that horses eat or come in contact with."

"Nothing about Emma has been particularly normal," I said. "Given all of the stress that she's experienced when she was younger it's no wonder she has a depressed immune system. That could explain why she has so many sensitivities."

I couldn't help but notice that this was another way Emma and I were similar. I had many sensitivities, not just food related. I found it easier to list the foods I could eat than the ones I should avoid. And my Chronic Fatigue syndrome was associated with an impaired immune system.

I always felt closer to Emma whenever I discovered yet another way our lives were alike. No wonder she understood me so well. We were mirror images of each other, residing in the bodies of different species. My sense is that other animal owners have felt what I did – being blessed to have a soul mate.

The vet looked up from the lab results and stared at the horizon for a few moments as if she was searching for an answer. "The only thing she isn't allergic to is timothy hay and almost no stable provides that feed. It's unbelievable. She's allergic to flies, pine shavings - which of course almost all stables use for bedding. Oat, wheat, alfalfa, rye, corn and barley. What are you going to feed her?" She laughed and looked at me sheepishly. "I'm sorry to laugh, but this doesn't leave us a lot of room to try and treat her for allergic reactions. I had hoped to eliminate from her environment those items she was allergic to. I'll need to zone in on treating the anxiety in another way. Let me think about this for a while."

I didn't feel hopeless. I knew deep inside this vet would find something to try. She didn't have the personality to give up with the first try.

The next time I saw Dr. Clare she pulled me to one side and looked at the ground. I wondered why she wouldn't look me in the eye.

With her head inclined towards the dirt in front of her feet, she said, "I have an idea."

"What is it?" I asked, concerned that her lack of eye contact signaled an unpleasant message might be coming. I struggled to hold on to the belief that she had a plan.

She spun her head around looking as if she was checking out who might be within earshot. She leaned away from me a couple of inches and lowered her voice to just above a whisper.

"I've been giving this a lot of thought and consulted some articles," she said, and rocked back a step.

That was odd. When people lower their voice, they usually step closer. I hoped she wasn't concerned about my reaction.

"What would you think of giving Emma..." she paused and tilted her body back even further, "Anti-depressants?"

I couldn't believe my ears. "Are you kidding? That's exactly what I've been thinking she needs for some time. I even asked Dr. Madigan to prescribe them because propranolol irritated Emma's stomach."

She let out her breath and raised her face. "I did some research and think that we might get some help from that kind of treatment."

"At last - Paxil or Prozac for my horse," I said working hard not to jump up and down with glee.

"No, not Prozac," she shot back. "Dogs are getting it, but you couldn't afford the amount you would need for your horse. It's costing a client I know about $1000 a month for her Great Dane. I was thinking about an old antidepressant – doxepin. You'll be able to afford it since it's been on the market for a long time."

"That's great," I said. "How long after we start administering the pills will I see a change?"

"Just like any of the anti-depressants, it takes about six weeks to ramp up the medication," she said. "By the sixth week you should see the difference. You can stop the propranolol immediately."

When I returned to Emma's stall, I paused to stare out at the hills. Three years had passed since Emma had returned from the Woodland Stallion Station. Each time she habituated to a drug, my inner life was thrown into turmoil. She was now seventeen years old and starting to reach the end of her prime. If we were going to make it to the highest levels of dressage, this was the time. If the medication steadied her enough, we might even be able to go a show now and then. I didn't care if I had to declare her medication and ride hors concours. Competing wasn't the goal. Putting a test together to demonstrate our accomplishments and getting the judge's comments would be satisfying enough. I didn't need the ribbons.

People had been successfully treated with anti-depressants for years. There was no reason Emma shouldn't have the same experience. I was thrilled that at last we might have a permanent solution to Emma's anxiety. When I spoke to Emma, she was elated that she didn't have to eat the pink chalky stuff anymore. Doxepin here we come.

My mind couldn't help but wonder whether Emma would be well in six weeks. And if she got well, how long would it last? I forbade any consideration to either of those questions. Emma would be at peace and happy and I would enjoy each of those days as a gift. I wondered if I could really talk myself into believing that.

Chapter 28

On the second week of treatment with doxepin, Emma's panic attacks ceased, and her generalized anxiety subsided. Her shying stopped and with its absence, I could once again concentrate on our work in dressage, our connection and our ability to move as one. I was in my element, in the zone.

Emma was also staying physically sound despite the increased workload. She was so sound that I asked my vet about her front feet. He said it was possible that Emma's feet had regenerated bone. He had seen evidence in several X-rays that natural balance shoes improved the bone structure of horses. At last we seemed to have everything together. I wondered what God had in store for us next.

I didn't have to wonder long. I received a call from my friend, Cherie, to come take pictures of Emma for her photo library. Cherie generated images on her computer and needed pictures of horses to use in artwork she wanted to create. Emma was to be the model for the horse ridden by the Kalki Avatar, Meher Baba. I was delighted. Emma, in her relaxed state, had a soft, doe-like eye that exuded the gentleness of her personality. She would make a great model with her classic thoroughbred looks of long limbs and an elegant, refined head with a symmetrical white star in the middle of her forehead. Getting her picture taken would be a fun activity.

When Cherie came out to the barn, I let Emma loose in the arena. I chased her around while Cherie clicked away. Dust from the footing floated on the air, catching sunbeams meandering through the skylights. When the last photo was taken, Cherie shared how much she had loved riding horses in the past and how much she wanted to ride. I asked her if she would like to ride Emma, and with delight, she accepted. Emma's anxiety was controlled so it was safe to let others ride her. Emma had taken care of beginners before and did a credible job of babysitting the newbies. We made a date for the following week.

The day Cherie came out was one of those early summer days when the flies seemed to emerge from every crevice with an insatiable need to assuage a voracious appetite. They spied their prey, dive bombed, lit, chomped and made their getaway. The atomizer I had installed on an upper board in Emma's stall hissed and spritzed bug repellant into the air. I reminded myself that I had done everything I could to make Emma comfortable when I wasn't around. To give Emma relief when she was being ridden, I misted fly spray all over her body. This would keep her mostly fly free while Cherie rode her.

I put on Emma's bridle and we headed for the indoor arena. Cherie hopped up on the mounting block and eased her weight onto the saddle. She picked up the reins and gently guided Emma around the ring. Seeing Emma's neck stretched out horizontal and relaxed warmed my heart. Even though she may have been relaxed, she wasn't dozing. Every time Cherie spaced out from her joy of riding, Emma would initiate an action that wasn't requested. She would change her direction, increase her pace or just stop. The way Emma teased Cherie made for good comedy. Cherie laughed whenever Emma surprised her. She had to pull her thoughts back to her riding and pay attention to her communications with Emma. Over time, Cherie did better with Emma, simply by staying present.

On one of her visits to the barn Cherie mentioned she was thinking of sending DeeDee, her daughter, to a horseback riding camp. I suggested she bring DeeDee out with her before she made such a big commitment. Cherie could determine if DeeDee had any interest in riding that could be sustained for the several weeks that the camp would last.

Emma had met DeeDee several years before when she was a girl of about twelve. Cherie had wondered whether her mentally disabled daughter who didn't use spoken words had any capacity for language that was waiting for a means of expression. The idea had come to me to use Emma's capability to read minds to help evaluate DeeDee's communication abilities. DeeDee was slow to feed herself and didn't have the motor skills to manage buttons on her clothes.

Because DeeDee was shy and easily frightened in new circumstances, Cherie had thought for her first visit we should ease her into an introduction with Emma. Cherie was convinced it would take several visits to get DeeDee to go anywhere near Emma. We would first get DeeDee acclimatized to the barn, then to Emma's size and hopefully to feeling safe in this entirely new environment. At a later meeting when DeeDee was more relaxed, we would invite Carol, the animal communicator, out to the barn so that she could translate what Emma had to say about DeeDee.

When the day arrived, I went out to the barn ahead of our meeting. I groomed Emma in preparation her for visitors. Every inch of her coat gleamed and with satisfaction I sat on a tack trunk in the barn aisle listening for the sound of a car driving up. The barn aisle, recently wetted with a sprinkling of water, smelled of fresh dirt. The damp coolness of the air soothed my skin. The horses, letting out the occasional snort to clear their nostrils from dust, were preoccupied with chewing away on their breakfast. They used their noses to spread open the flakes of hay looking for the choicest tidbits. All the stirring up of the hay filled the air with the sweet perfume of the rich, green alfalfa that many of them were enjoying. The full-bodied scent of the alfalfa was so delicious that it was no wonder Emma believed this hay was a favor bestowed on horses by a benevolent God. Birds flitted in and out of the stalls landing in the horses' feed troughs pecking about for a few missed grains of oats or corn. Their joyful twittering seemed to announce another great day.

The slam of a car door was followed by the crunch of footsteps on gravel. I was surprised when DeeDee entered the barn first. She stepped into the aisle and then halted and made gentle gurgling sounds. She looked around seeming very pleased. She showed no fear at all. I was surprised when she strode with confidence down the aisle and stopped only a few feet from Emma. Newcomers to horses usually kept their distance and assessed the situation before approaching an animal who overshadowed them.

Apparently intrigued by Emma, DeeDee stretched out her hand with a tentative gesture in Emma's direction and then snatched it back. Each time she offered her hand, she was able to straighten her elbow a little bit more before withdrawing it. After a few attempts, she was able to briefly touch Emma on the shoulder with her fingertips. When she made contact, she giggled and pulled away.

Something caught DeeDee's attention and she looked away, stepping back closer to Emma. Wow, she was standing next to Emma's shoulder. That was a sure sign she wasn't feeling afraid or she wouldn't lose visual contact with Emma while in Emma's space.

With the introduction having gone so well, I put Emma away and offered a tour of the barn. DeeDee seemed to enjoy her walk about and when the tour was over, our guests headed home sporting smiles.

Cherie and I weren't sure how much had transpired between Emma and DeeDee and whether Emma had had the opportunity to evaluate DeeDee's communication competencies. DeeDee's acceptance of Emma seemed complete, so we planned to invite Carol out when DeeDee visited next time.

A few days later I had the opportunity to chat with Carol. I explained the success of DeeDee's visit with Emma and I was curious to learn what Emma had to say.

"I like the child very much," Carol translated for Emma. "It was an unusual experience."

"How was it unusual?" I asked.

"I've never known anyone who didn't have language," Carol translated.

"What do you mean doesn't have language," I asked. "Is DeeDee able to communicate her thoughts to you?"

"Yes, DeeDee can communicate," Carol translated, "She just doesn't use words. She doesn't think in words. She communicates through feelings and pictures. She is clear and expresses herself with lots of emotion. I understand her. She communicates well."

"Are you able to communicate back to DeeDee?" I asked.

"Yes, duh." Carol translated.

"Does she hear you as well as you hear her?" I asked.

"Yes, of course." Carol translated.

When I hung up with Carol, I called Cherie and let her know what Emma had said. While it wasn't quite the result she had hoped for, it did answer the question Cherie had asked. At this stage of her development DeeDee didn't have an internal use of words.

And so, it was a happy reunion when DeeDee at age sixteen came to visit Emma. She bounded out of the car as soon as soon as it stopped. She looked around and spotted the pyramid of pine shavings piled seven feet high in a narrow, corrugated iron barn near the entrance of the ranch. She dove in and tried to climb to the top but was foiled as her footing gave way. Giggling with glee she slid back down to the bottom and tried again. Her play in the shavings sent fine particulates spewing into the air tickling our noses and sending us into rounds of sneezing.

Next DeeDee spotted a mound of soft, fluffy Angel Island sand near the indoor arena that would be used to amend the footing. She sprinted over to the mound and ascended to the peak with three bounces. The sun had baked the top layer dry leaving the sand underneath slightly damp. For a moment I closed my eyes and let the scent of the beach whisk me to the sea.

While DeeDee was cavorting in the sand, I could feel myself growing more and more uneasy. I wondered if Emma was sending me her feelings. The discomfort grew. Because I knew Emma's patience was about as ill-formed as mine, I identified the pull in my gut as coming from her. I suggested we go on up the hill to greet her. As soon as we approached her, I could hear her high-pitched neigh trumpet an enthusiastic hello. On the way I grabbed my grooming brushes out of the tiny tack room that was constructed from a converted stall. My uneasiness vanished.

With Emma securely tied up in her stall, I invited Cherie and DeeDee to join me. I picked up two body brushes and started energetically giving Emma a vigorous once over. Even though my back was to her, I could feel that DeeDee wanted to help. I handed her a brush and she patted Emma a couple of times rather than using sweeping strokes. Smiling with her impish grin, she handed back the brush. That simply was not her idea of play. Then while Cherie and I were fully engaged in brushing Emma's coat, DeeDee ducked down and somersaulted in a neat roll under Emma's belly to get to the other side. Although this is something that would normally make me gasp and cringe, I knew that Emma would take extraordinary care not to move. I had a hard time imagining another way DeeDee could express her complete trust in Emma. After I saddled Emma up, we took her down to the mounting block in the indoor arena.

Cherie would ride first with the intention of demonstrating to DeeDee that riding was fun. DeeDee seemed interested in the process and watched Cherie intently as she guided Emma around the arena. Her display of interest was encouraging. When Cherie finished her ride, I asked DeeDee, "Would you like to ride Emma?" At the same time as I spoke the words I was careful to send pictures of what I was asking.

DeeDee's face lit up and she shook her fist as her symbol for "Yes."

Before we got started, I thought that Cherie and I had better discuss how we were going to get DeeDee on Emma. Emma was 16.1 hands and DeeDee was a little over five feet. I took Emma over to the mounting block and asked her to stand. Next, I demonstrated what to do. I picked up my left leg and put the toe of my boot in the stirrup hoping DeeDee might learn through imitation. When I motioned to DeeDee to try it, she stood there without moving. I tried picking up DeeDee's leg and maneuvering her foot near the stirrup. She resisted my guidance of her leg, whisking it back.

"Let's get basic here," I said.

"What do you mean?" Cherie asked.

"Let's try and do it the way I get on a bareback horse," I said. "Let's move DeeDee next to the saddle and have her lay across Emma's back. Then we can rotate her body and swing her right leg over. That way we don't need the stirrups."

DeeDee was able to mimic that movement and got her stomach inched up and leaned over the middle of the saddle. As soon as she straddled Emma crosswise, I eased her hip away from me to rotate her body and have her right leg swing over Emma's back. The moment I started the rotation, DeeDee reacted by wriggling forward with surprising vigor. She did it with such speed and unpredictable gyrations that I was unable to grab hold of her. Cherie grabbed at her shoulders but was unable to push her back. DeeDee squirmed forward with a couple of choppy thrusts, lost her balance, tumbled off the other side and thumped to the ground. I gasped and scrambled around Emma. DeeDee looked up from the ground giggling and smiling. Thank goodness for the soft sand providing a cushy landing and the flexibility of young people. Deedee popped up unfazed and bounded back up the mounting block. She faced Emma and motioned that she wanted to get on. My heart pounded. She could have been hurt.

Given DeeDee's eagerness, Cherie thought we should try it again. This time I had a firm hold of DeeDee's belt and Cherie was better prepared to stop a wriggling DeeDee from suddenly advancing.

DeeDee inched across the saddle. I centered her torso while clasping her belt. I then eased her right hip towards Cherie. Cherie then pulled DeeDee's right leg over to Emma's other side. Then with great relief I saw DeeDee sit up erect with what seemed like a mixture of pleasure and pride. I guided her feet into the stirrups, making sure to send her pictures of keeping them there.

I felt something boring into my back and turned my head to spot one of my fellow boarders glaring at me. Her dark brown eyes seared a hole through me. The lines of her forehead and mouth were hard and the curly, black hair that surrounded her face did not soften her expression. I suspected that this boarder questioned my sanity in allowing a disabled child to ride Emma. Over the previous three years when Emma's anxiety was not being controlled by drugs, the boarders had witnessed on too many occasions my difficulty in controlling her. They had observed her bouts of anxiety that would sometimes suddenly intensify, to be followed by my need to vault off her in haste. They would watch Emma spin and careen around me as I tried to maneuver her back to her stall without hurting her, me or others. I remembered those days as well. This was a different day.

With DeeDee settled on Emma's back, I asked if she was ready for me to walk Emma. She signed "yes." She gulped and tensed when Emma started to move but then a tentative smile crept across her face. I led Emma down the long side of the arena. When we finished the first lap around the edges of the arena, DeeDee's smile sprouted into a grin from ear to ear. I felt this was the first of what was going to be many happy visits.

My intuition was right. DeeDee wanted more trips to the barn. The next time DeeDee came out to ride, several boarders at the barn approached me and let me know that they had serious concerns about DeeDee's association with Emma. No amount of assurances assuaged their worry. Fortunately, the barn manager had been content with Cherie's signing a liability release form.

Despite Emma's previous challenges, I had faith that her anxiety was being controlled by the doxepin, and if not, she would let us know. I was sure that if Emma thought that she couldn't control herself she would clearly indicate that DeeDee should not ride that day.

Unfortunately, the boarders were not content with my assurances and went to the barn manager with their worries. He responded by requiring DeeDee to wear a hard hat. That was a fair request and I was relieved that he would allow DeeDee's visits to continue. On the next trip out Cherie solved that problem by bringing out a bicycle helmet that belonged to DeeDee's brother.

Cherie had to insist that DeeDee put the bicycle helmet on when it became clear that she didn't want it on her head. Apparently wearing something on top was a new experience for her. The hat did look a little silly. It was a bit too big and sat cockeyed on top of her head. Once DeeDee settled down and accepted the need to wear the hat, we got her to mount Emma the usual way - lie across the saddle, swing the right leg over, find the stirrups.

We had just finished one lap around the arena when DeeDee turned in the saddle and pointed at Cherie, wriggling her fingers. I signaled Emma to stop by sending a wave down the lead rope. She came to a halt behind me. Cherie and I looked at each other and shrugged, not knowing what DeeDee was trying to communicate with that gesture. Then before we could say anything, DeeDee unbuckled the chin strap of the helmet, whisked it off her head and flung it high up into the air. My eyes tracked the helmet's path as it rose and rose and rose. In horror I watched the hard hat spin in the air. With each revolution I prayed it would deviate to one side, falling harmlessly to the ground instead of coming straight down on top of DeeDee's head. My body finally responded and I scrambled to reach Emma's bridle. I was about half way to closing the gap between Emma and me when the helmet slammed down with a wrenching thwack in the middle of Emma's rump. My heart stopped. I had visions of Emma bolting and hurling DeeDee to the ground. The boarders' predictions were about to come true.

Emma grunted. Her eyes popped out, whites showing. Her haunches dropped a foot, her hind legs splayed. She tensed her thrusting muscles as if she was preparing to catapult forward. All I could think was, DeeDee is going to be hurt. Her confidence in herself is going to be shattered. I froze and stared at Emma with her coiled hindquarters ready to rocket off just like a race horse breaking from the starting gate. Then I saw a flash across Emma's face. Her body shuddered. She released the tension in her back and sighed. Not a foot moved forward. She straightened her hind legs into a resting posture.

"Oh my God," I said, letting out my breath. "Did you see what just happened?"

Cherie's eyes were wide and she sputtered, "Em… Emma didn't move."

I closed the gap between us and grabbed the reins in case there were any delayed reactions. "Do you have any idea how much self-control it took to stay motionless?"

"I think I do," Cherie said. "Emma knew what she had to do to protect DeeDee."

"Horses don't have the control we do over instinctual responses," I said. "Horses are preyed upon and when startled, flee."

My heart was still pounding against my chest wall, so I suggested we end the session at that point. I didn't want to put the helmet back on DeeDee and risk another unscheduled departure of either the hat from DeeDee's head or DeeDee from Emma's back.

When next I spoke to Carol, we noticed that Emma had started referring to DeeDee as her child. Emma had decided to invite this young woman into our family and under her watchful eye. Emma asked if it might be possible to bring DeeDee out at least once a week. I let her know I didn't see any reason why we couldn't continue the visits.

At home, Cherie worked with DeeDee and the helmet, asking her to wear it for periods of time that extended up to several minutes. The desensitization to having something on her head only took a week, so DeeDee didn't miss a riding session with Emma.

Watching DeeDee ride was a joy. She was a natural rider. Her center of gravity remained stable. She didn't need to flail her arms or make sudden movements with her body to stay balanced as the horse shifted weight through different speeds at the walk and during turns. While DeeDee seemed to possess the balance to free up her legs, her own body control wasn't that sophisticated. She gripped Emma's sides with her thighs and calves with all the strength she could. My sensitive thoroughbred who responded to the slightest tension in my calf was able to ignore the death grip of DeeDee's heels.

DeeDee became a regular at the barn and seemed to blossom before my eyes. Her confidence improved as she worked around Emma both on the ground and in the saddle. Cherie's appreciation for her daughter seemed to expand and she took pride in her competency. DeeDee could excel at something.

I wondered how Emma's and DeeDee's friendship might develop.

Chapter 29

Over the summer and into fall DeeDee came out to visit Emma almost every week. When they weren't physically together, Cherie reported that DeeDee and Emma spoke or rather sent messages back and forth telepathically. Watching the relationship grow warmed my heart. DeeDee didn't seem to come with the prejudgment that Emma was only a horse.

DeeDee had ways of naming her associates. She named Emma with a clicking sound, probably her version of giddy up. When she would make that sound for no apparent reason, Cherie would ask DeeDee if she was talking to Emma and DeeDee would shake the fist of her hand as her signal for "yes." Because so many people came to think of Emma and me as inseparable, I wasn't surprised when Cherie told me that that the clicking sound that DeeDee had used to name Emma was also the name she had chosen for me. My dog had told me once that the first time she saw me she had seen that I had horse written all over me. DeeDee must have received that wavelength.

After a visit with Emma and as a special treat for DeeDee, all three of us humans would sometimes go to a fast food restaurant for lunch. DeeDee was particularly fond of Burger King. Once, over a hamburger and fries, DeeDee suddenly burst out laughing - a full belly laugh with clear joy and delight. Cherie and I spun our heads around checking out the other occupants in the nearby booths to see what might have intrigued DeeDee enough to catch her attention and entice her to respond in such a boisterous way. We looked at each other and shook our heads. An idea seemed to register with Cherie and she asked DeeDee if Emma had just made a joke. DeeDee signed an emphatic "yes."

I thought about what I had witnessed. DeeDee, who was limited in her communication skills with humans, had at last found a unique friend. Here was a companion with whom she could easily relate. She and Emma could communicate with each other in real time telepathically through pictures and emotions and without the struggle that words imposed.

On one of their visits out to see Emma, Cherie related a touching story. As we walked up to Emma's stall, Cherie recounted that the previous morning when DeeDee woke up and saw Cherie, she had made the clicking sound that was her representation for Emma. When asked if she had been dreaming, DeeDee signed "yes." DeeDee then moved her hands up and down in a scissors motion as her sign for Emma trotting. Cherie asked if she had been riding Emma during the night and again DeeDee signed "yes." When Cherie told me about DeeDee's nighttime adventure, I let her know that Emma often purposefully entered the dreams of people to be with them and to help them heal.

After saddling up Emma, we walked down to the arena. I couldn't help but notice that the other boarders not only cleared the riding ring but also the general vicinity. Once mounted, DeeDee couldn't go any more than once around before her impatience manifested. She scissored her arms in the air indicating that she wanted Emma to trot. I tried to ignore her request, but her insistence won out. I learned that persistence was one of DeeDee's more developed attributes. Each time I would lead Emma into a trot, DeeDee would screech with an energy that seemed to erupt from the depths of her innermost being.

The sound was ear splitting and the hairs on the back of my neck quivered to attention. I could easily think mayhem was at play until I soaked up the beauty in DeeDee's face. The happiness and delight she exuded made it clear that the sound was an expression of sheer joy. Her pleasure gave me the courage to ignore the stares and barbs of the onlookers. I couldn't blame them. Her high-pitched screams trumpeted and echoed off the walls of the barn.

As DeeDee grew older she expressed a need for more independence and a need to have friends outside of the home. Cherie grew to realize that DeeDee might benefit from life in a group home. The search started and Cherie identified what might be a workable placement. When it came time to send DeeDee to the group home for a weekend trial, Cherie was anxious and concerned about DeeDee's well-being. DeeDee had never been away from home for an overnight and Cherie wasn't sure what kinds of coping mechanisms DeeDee might use in situations where she wasn't under the protective and watchful eye of her mother.

Knowing how Carol's dog Bailey had stayed up all night to guide Emma home when she was lost in the Sierra foot hills, I reasoned that Emma could do something similar with DeeDee. Emma could stay connected to DeeDee throughout her weekend trial visit. I decided to ask Emma about it.

I called Carol to chat with Emma about what I was thinking. When Carol answered the phone, I explained what we had in mind.

"So, Emma," I said, "DeeDee is going to spend a weekend with people she's never met. Five caregivers and about fifteen residents."

"Yes, my child is excited about it," Carol translated for Emma.

"DeeDee doesn't have a means to communicate with the residents or the caregivers with her limited use of gestures," I said. "Only her family understands the meaning of the body language she has developed in her attempts to communicate with them."

"DeeDee expresses herself very well," Carol translated.

"For you Emma," I responded, "but not for most humans. Would you be willing to look after DeeDee?"

"What do you mean?" Carol translated.

"Would you stay connected to DeeDee for the entire two days she's away from home?"

"Yes, of course I can do that," Carol translated.

"If you have any suspicions that anything is troubling DeeDee." I said, "or if she's miserable, would you contact either Carol or me? We would then alert Cherie that DeeDee needed to be brought home."

"Of course," Carol translated.

"Super," I said, "Cherie will feel more comfortable knowing that you would monitor DeeDee's activities. This experience has the potential to be frightening for DeeDee. She may be disoriented or worse."

I alerted Emma as to when her vigil should begin. Throughout the weekend of DeeDee's visit, I checked in with Emma. Each time Emma reassured me that DeeDee wasn't being harmed and hadn't asked to go home.

Sunday afternoon, at the end of her visit, Cherie headed out to pick up DeeDee. I breathed more freely. When I got to the barn, Emma seemed nonplussed. That was a good sign since she could read DeeDee's emotions and be tuned to her experiences. She had first-hand knowledge.

The next day Cherie called me. She wasn't sure how to assess what DeeDee had experienced in this group home. Cherie said that DeeDee appeared unharmed and not overly emotional. Although she was sure nothing bad had happened to DeeDee, she suspected that DeeDee had not enjoyed the experience. When Cherie asked her if she wanted to go back she shook her head with an emphatic "no." Cherie couldn't get any more information to generate light on the reasons behind her daughter's "no."

That night I called Carol to get Emma's input on what happened with DeeDee.

"Emma," I said, "DeeDee did not appear to like her weekend stay. Do you know why?"

"My child liked the other residents and she felt as if she was treated with respect by the caregivers," Carol translated.

"That's all good," I said. "So, what happened to make her not want to go back?"

"She felt embarrassed," Carol translated.

"Why?" I asked.

"The other residents could dress themselves and do more of their own self-care," Carol translated. "My child felt embarrassed because she needed additional help with the daily activities. She felt bad when a couple of the other residents in the home made fun of her."

"Ouch," I said. "That wasn't the way to start a new living situation."

DeeDee's experience helped Cherie to better assess DeeDee's capabilities. She wanted the best for DeeDee and probably at some unconscious level hoped DeeDee might function at a higher level when living with peers who could do more for themselves. Cherie began her search for a facility with a different rating. Eventually a suitable situation was identified for DeeDee.

When DeeDee's future home was settled and her new life began, I thought about how we could use Emma's skills to help other children. Perhaps she could communicate with severely autistic children, to help understand what they were thinking and open a dialog that might not be possible otherwise. Or perhaps we could ask her to let us know what was going on in the minds of those in comas or who were unconscious. And it didn't have to be Emma. Other animals could be used. My mind was full of possibilities, but no clear actionable path to make them happen.

I couldn't help but be frustrated by the reluctance of people to accept the sentience of animals and their extraordinary abilities to communicate. Although animals might be less complicated than humans, they offered up wisdom and the ability to love with their entire being. We could learn so much from them.

That night when I turned out the light, I thought of Emma.

"Emma, you make an exceptional partner," I said. "I wish that I could feel this close to humans. I feel we have come together to try to be of service to the world."

"Oh, pshaw," I heard Emma reply.

Chapter 30

Nearly a year had passed by without Emma showing any signs of habituating to Doxepin. I had begun to believe that we had at last found a permanent solution to her anxiety. People had been on anti-depressants and anti-anxiety medications for years without needing a change in prescription either in dosage or formula. With that assurance of hard-earned peace, I was free to fully enjoy my horse and not be so focused on her every misstep. My health was a bit stronger, so I was able to spend more time being social at the barn. Barns offered more than a boarding facility for horses. They offered a gathering place for humans. The small community of boarders was a mini-society. We were all connected at some level. We all had a need to have horses in our lives and were willing to make emotional and monetary commitments and sacrifices.

Taking time to study the resident Peruvian Paso trainer ride his mounts provided an opportunity to learn more about this breed. The small, fiery horses with abundant energy glided around the arena with all the frenetic activity below their bellies. Their front legs swung out wide with each stride and flipped back and forth like a pendulum on steroids. The fastest gait was a flurry of flaying limbs for a small gain in distance. Containing their energy took tact from their riders lest they explode into a blur of forward motion.

Then in contrast were the serious Western pleasure riders with their ultra-calm horses. I could never understand why they made a perfectly good three beat canter into a sluggish four beat lope with the horses' noses nearly on the ground. The logic evaded me.

A couple of the boarders knew I talked to Emma and would sometimes ask me what I heard from their horses. Practicing my telepathic animal communication skills was fun. According to Emma, when talking to her I always got the concepts right but didn't always hear the details. With other people's animals it was much easier. I didn't have as many built in filters or expectations.

One night a boarder who had wanted a filly for the longest time asked me to talk to her pregnant mare to see if I could find out the sex of the unborn foal. When I asked the horse, I heard in my mind as clearly as if sound waves had landed on my ears, "It's what my person wants." Immediately after hearing the horse I heard in my mind the high-pitched voice of a tiny child: "I'm a girl." I giggled and told the owner what I had heard. My confidence in what animals were telling me was growing and months later when the filly was born I appreciated the validation.

Although most of these experiences were enjoyable, there were a couple of situations that I could not wrap my head around. The one that puzzled me the most was why Jill who loved her horses and was dedicated to their well-being should keep her horse, Sabina, alive for so long. The horse had suffered from a severe case of laminitis in her front feet and was in such excruciating pain that she lay down for almost the entire day.

Laminitis of this degree is unbelievably painful. I wondered what it would be analogous to in humans. A vet explained to me that the lamina connects the hard-outer layer of the hoof to the soft tissue of the foot – like our fingernails. Having laminitis was equivalent to separating the nails of our toes or fingers from the underlying pink tissue and then trying to make a living by walking around on fingertips and toe tips. I shuddered when my body gauged the impact of that kind of pain.

When Sabina stood she parked her hind feet way under her belly, humping her back in an arc that I didn't think was possible for a horse to make. She did whatever she could to relieve the weight on her front feet. Watching her try to stand was even more agonizing. Whenever Jill tried to take her for short walks out of her stall, I had to look the other way. With this severe condition, the horse is usually put down since it is most likely a life sentence of unbearable pain. Horses are animals that are meant to stand on four legs and move around. Their digestion and health are all related to standing and moving. The pressure sores on Sabina's hip bones and other joint areas made her even more miserable when fly season hit. Several of the boarders who had to pass by her stall quickened their pace and often turned their heads away.

Jill had enlisted the help of a very capable vet who was experimenting with a style of shoe to see if it would improve the condition of horses with severe laminitis. A couple of boarders told me that they had observed the two horses at our barn that were in this trial since the test began. They felt that neither horse appeared to show any improvement. They were angered by the condition of the horses and questioned why the owners were allowing them to suffer. Some hard feelings had been created. On more than one occasion I had heard the boarders question Jill's decision to let her horse live.

I suspected that Jill was in tune with her horses and heard them perfectly well, but perhaps unconsciously. She often made changes in their regimen that were identical to what I had heard them request. Jill knew that I communicated telepathically with animals and she would sometimes ask Emma's opinion on different subjects. Before she would invest in equipment for her riding horses, she would ask which bit was more comfortable or which saddle blanket would fit the best. She never asked me to talk to Sabina and I never broached the subject. I gave up trying to make sense of why Jill had chosen to keep Sabina alive. I accepted that this mystery was one I would observe in silence.

Despite my Chronic Fatigue, which if it had its way, would totally sideline me, I rode Emma after work in the evening. I would take Emma down to the indoor arena where there were generous banks of light. I rode late enough that I hoped few riders would be there and I would be able to concentrate on my training. I didn't want to worry about the novice riders who seemed to forget that one passes left shoulder to left shoulder around the ring. Unfortunately, we also had our share of Yahoos who would race their barely-in-control horses around the arena and be so absorbed in their love of speed that they were oblivious to the mayhem that followed in their wake. I could feel in my stomach the fear generated in each of the other horses by the careening riders. Horses seem to sense when a rider was not in control and it could frighten them. Community life in a barn stretched my patience, which I was all too aware was easily tested.

These annoyances were nothing compared to what I heard and felt from Sabina, stabled in a stall along one side of the indoor arena. I would hear her just as I was zoning out with a relaxed mind clear of any thoughts. After my ride, I would slacken the reins and let Emma lengthen her neck and walk forward in an easy, poky rhythm. She would wander around the arena cooling herself out and I was content to let her pick her own way. This was a delicious interlude to take deep breaths, smell the honeysuckle and feel the cool night air on my face. The time was perfect to contemplate the day's activities and let my mind drift into whatever realm enticed its attention. The silence of the night and the steady, even beat of my horse's foot falls lulled me into a welcome meditation.

At times like these I was most vulnerable to the communications of other animals. If I'm distracted I usually don't hear what an animal may have been trying to tell me. With my mind in neutral, I would sometimes be snapped back from my reverie. During these zoned-out moments I would hear the screams of agony that Sabina and her stable-mate made in response to their excruciating pain as vividly as if the sound came to my ears. These were telepathic so no one else in the arena knew what I was experiencing. That it did not come directly by way of my ear did not mean the sensations had been muted or the impact lessened. Earplugs wouldn't block the sound. I felt as if a silent wave form penetrated my body and set up a reverberation that blasted straight to my brain. The screams were a haunting reminder of their pain. My body would cringe in sympathy and my muscles silently strained for relief. Internal communication is wonderful, but not when you feel another's agony so strongly and are helpless to do anything.

In exasperation I would look over at Sabina and the horse two doors down. If no one was around I would speak out loud, "I'm so sorry. There's nothing I can do except say that I hear you and I feel for you." I wondered if this was why Carol was careful about screening new clients – to avoid unnecessary pain for herself. No, probably not, she had better boundaries than I did.

Despite how hard I tried to block the silent screams they usually continued to land in my body. The noise in my head and the feelings in my muscles created a discomfort so severe a "flight" response was generated. As hard as I tried to distract myself, once these horses got my attention, I was powerless to shut them out until I retreated. Any parent who has been unable to console a child screaming in pain has an idea of the impotence I felt. When I couldn't tolerate the sensations any longer, I would spring off Emma and hurry her away from the arena, trying to focus my mind on my footsteps as they led us down the dark pathways to Emma's stall.

On one occasion the cries of pain started at the beginning of my ride and I couldn't focus or concentrate enough to suppress the impact. I rushed Emma back to her stall, ripped her tack off and sped my car away. Distance and diverting my attention were the only cures I knew. I found it interesting that I could talk to animals hundreds of miles away, even continents away, but driving just a few hundred yards broke the connection that I didn't want. The properties of animal communication continued to intrigue me.

One day in the middle of the week when I was riding Emma in the arena, I clearly heard Sabina say, "Please put me down. I can't stand it any longer. Now is the time."

I was distraught. I had enough trouble trying to manage her communications of pain, and now the wattage had just gone up. Although Jill and I had never talked about Sabina's condition, I somehow knew that I needed to tell her what I heard from her horse. How I would do that perplexed me. How do you tell someone that it is time to kill their companion animal, a being loved as dearly as a child? Especially one that had been kept alive for so long, despite peer group pressure and criticism. If Sabina's message hadn't been as clear and my escalating discomfort so profound I would have dismissed the idea and not had the courage to risk telling Jill. I decided that the next time I saw Jill I would test her receptivity and do my best to share her horse's request. Since Jill rode during the day, I probably wouldn't see her until the weekend. The dread of that moment colored my waking hours.

On Saturday I arrived at the barn before the usual opening time so that I could get Emma cleaned up and ready to ride in the indoor arena before anyone else got there. I would look for Jill at her usual arrival time of midmorning. I parked the car near the entrance. The parking area was empty except for a vet's truck. That was unusual. I wondered who was sick or injured.

When I got to the front of the main barn, I saw splayed across the gravel road a blue tarp smothered in sawdust with a foot-high peak in the center. I wondered what was happening. I sensed movement at the entrance to the barn. My body responded first. My knees buckled as I slammed to a halt. The vet emerged from the aisle and led Sabina slowly and painfully over to the tarp. My breath hitched when I gasped for air. Sabina's mane was artfully braided as if she was going to a beauty pageant. In each braid was woven a fresh pink rose bud tied with a deep pink satin ribbon bow. Tears welled and then drenched my cheeks. I choked and froze.

Once the vet managed to get Sabina in the middle of the sawdust pile, she petted the horse and drew her syringe. She administered the first shot. The one to relax her. This was a private moment and I wanted to leave. I managed to get my muscles to act and I rose on my tiptoes to be as noiseless as possible. I knew that the next shot would be lethal. I had witnessed a pony put down a few years before.

The moment I inched by the mare, she crumpled to the ground. Her dead weight thudded into the sawdust. I was stunned and forced myself to move past. Then a tremendous blast of love enveloped me. A big, billowy golden cloud of joy encircled my entire body. I felt warm. A peaceful sense of well-being permeated every cell. The love I felt was so overpowering that I nearly lost my balance. Sabina sent me a picture from her viewpoint of Jill walking down the barn aisle to her stall and the tremendous joy and love she felt in Jill's presence. In the instant she breathed her last, Sabina was telling me why she had chosen to live and why Jill braved the critics of the barn to keep her horse alive. I realized that Sabina was sending me the feeling she experienced every time Jill came out to the barn to see her. She told me that Jill was in tune with her and heard her correctly. Sabina knew Jill loved her completely and this love sustained her. The pleasure and love of their time together was why she had chosen to live and endure the pain. She was sending me all those feelings and pictures.

Reverberating with the joy I had been gifted, I managed to move my feet down the aisle towards Emma's stall. I would need time to process the gift I had just been given and to honor the passing of this soul.

I didn't run into Jill for a week. The next Saturday I spotted her cleaning out Sabina's tack from her locker. I didn't want to cause her any more grief but felt compelled to approach her.

"Jill, I'm so sorry about Sabina," I said. "What happened?"

Jill stood up and brushed the dust off her sleeves. Her eyes were red and her cheeks were puffy. "I can't explain it. Something changed during the week. It was time to put Sabina down. I just knew that it had to be done. I couldn't face being there when it happened. The vet said she would take care of it."

I reached down to help her load grooming brushes into the canvas bag at her feet. "Jill, one night during the week while I was riding Emma, I clearly heard Sabina say she was ready to go. I've always believed that you hear your horses. This is more proof."

She traced her fingers over the letters of Sabina's name engraved on the brass nameplate adorning the side of the leather halter. She nestled the halter in the bag amongst the winter blankets. "I had no doubt about what I had to do. It was so hard. I loved her so much. She was a really great horse."

"Yes, she was a very special being," I said and helped her zipper the bag shut. I stood up and faced her. "As fate would have it, I was here when the vet put her down. Sabina answered a question for me that I had wondered about for a long time. I couldn't understand why she was kept alive. She gifted me that understanding. She let me feel what she felt whenever you came to visit her and the love you both exchanged. It was a profound experience."

"That sounds exactly like Sabina," Jill said. She dropped her eyes and fought back the tears that were collecting in the corners of her eyes. "Always thinking of others."

I gave Jill a hug and helped her finish cleaning out her locker.

As I headed up to Emma's stall I tried to absorb and integrate all I had learned. I felt I had been given another of life's lesson in the power of love. Trust in love.

When I got to Emma's stall, her head was bobbing up and down to greet me. She stopped her activity and her gaze locked on my eyes. Then I heard Emma say, "You know how Sabina felt whenever Jill came to her. That's how I feel when I see you."

Tears came to my eyes as I buried my head against her neck.

Chapter 31

Although I hadn't known Sabina at her best, Jill had shown me pictures of her when she was young and sound. With Sabina's passing, Jill spent more time with her other horse. Jill loved Arabians and she particularly loved perfectly conformed horses. Her other horse was also a well-bred Arabian. Cordelia was a stunningly gorgeous pure black mare. She was a horse straight out of one of Walter Farley's books. Her head was pure Arabian with dished nose, small ears whose points curved in towards each other, large wide-set expressive eyes and a small delicate muzzle. Her long elegant neck was adorned with a flowing mane and her hindquarters were blessed with a long and generous tail. Her conformation was flawless. Straight legs, good angles in her joints and a spectacular way of moving. Before Jill had gotten Cordelia, she was a successful show horse who had consistently won in the conformation and performance classes. Jill had kept her eye on Cordelia and waited for an opportunity to get this beautiful horse.

Her wait lasted a few years. When Cordelia started coming up lame from sore legs, her performance in the show ring suffered. With fewer blue ribbons being awarded, her owners lost interest. In consequence, her show career ended and Cordelia was put up for sale at an affordable price. Somewhere along this extended show career Cordelia's disposition turned from cooperative to sour. Jill conjectured that it was probably due to too many demands to perform or too many times her needs were subjugated to the cause of winning. She once explained, "Show horses often are blanketed year-round to keep their coats from bleaching. Tight wraps are put around their neck and tail to keep the hairs from matting or breaking. Their lives are controlled by the needs of the show ring."

The things humans did to horses simply to win a class troubled me. Looking marvelous came with a price. Supermodels had a choice, horses didn't.

By the time Jill got Cordelia, the mare's disposition had been ruined. Her attitude to the world was "I don't like you - don't bother me." Despite the loving care and kindnesses that Jill lavished on Cordelia, her progress towards a relationship of partnership seemed to be slow to emerge. It's testimony to Jill's indefatigable love that she invested the highest level of care for Cordelia who seemed to be able to give back so little. Even with light riding, Cordelia's legs would sometimes come up sore. Jill would wrap them and hand walk Cordelia, doing everything she knew to make the horse comfortable.

On several occasions Jill had asked me to talk to Cordelia to see if there wasn't something that could be done to make her happier. On one such occasion I was just finishing up with Emma when Jill came sauntering up to Emma's stall. Her long blonde hair was pulled back by a clip at the base of her neck. A blue checked blouse was tucked into well-worn blue jeans.

Stopping at Emma's stall door, Jill handed Emma a carrot and said, "Hey Diana, do you have a minute to talk to Cordelia for me?"

Slipping Emma's halter off I said, "Sure, what's it about?"

"I've been having a hard time blanketing Cordelia," she said pulling out another carrot. "It's so cold she needs the extra warmth."

I stepped out of Emma's stall and secured the door. "What does she do?"

Pushing her baseball cap higher up on her forehead Jill said, "She drops her head, so I can't slip it over her neck and puts her ears flat back in annoyance. Then she turns and puts her head into the corner where I can't reach her."

I walked over to the tack room and put Emma's grooming brushes away. "Okay, let me go down there and talk to her."

Once in Cordelia's stall, I cleared my mind. Turning to Cordelia I said, "Jill says you don't want your blanket on, but she thinks you need it."

I shivered and said to Jill, "Yes, Cordelia is cold. She says she doesn't like being cold."

Jill looked over to the mare, "Well, why do you resist then?"

I translated for Cordelia, "I can't help it. As soon as I see the blanket I have an automatic revulsion towards it. My previous owners kept it on me in the summer. I was so hot. I suffered for too long. I tried to let them know not to put it on me, but they always forced me."

I looked over to Jill, "I know you told me she had an unhappy past but that sounds abusive."

Jill's eyes squinted almost shut and I could feel her anger welling up inside. "Just before I bought her, I saw that her sides were raw from where she had been spurred repeatedly. Her sore legs probably made her reluctant to move."

My eyes moistened and I said, "Her reluctance to be blanketed is something that you're going to have to work with. Try giving her treats when you blanket her. Maybe you can soften the old memories with new pleasant ones." What I didn't tell Jill was that whenever I spoke to Cordelia her responses came through a filter that seemed to shade every response with a sneer. Her unhappiness with her condition and her ill temper came through her communications.

Knowing that Cordelia was cold gave Jill the answer she needed to insist that the mare wear the blanket. The use of treats changed Cordelia's negative response over time. I was happy that the problem was solved.

One Saturday when I returned from the grocery store, I picked up a message on my voice mail from Jill. Her voice was stressed, and she sounded almost hysterical. She told me that Cordelia was very ill and to call her as soon as possible. My stomach took a major wrench. It hadn't been that long since Sabina had been put down. I felt for Jill. Too much trauma with her horses in too short a time frame. Because I wanted to have some information for her before I returned the call, I decided to talk to Cordelia first to find out what was going on. When I concentrated on the image of the horse, she quickly joined me. I was surprised that her energy felt like a fresh and gentle spring breeze on my cheek. She said that she was fine and in no pain. I was relieved that whatever the crisis had been was now passed.

I called Jill but didn't get an answer. After leaving her a message that I had called, I went about the rest of my daily chores.

The next day at the barn I immediately went to Cordelia's stall but found it empty. One of the boarders saw me staring at the stall and joined me. She told me that Cordelia had been rushed to UC Davis vet school for treatment for severe intestinal pain. Before any treatment could be administered, she died a violent death. Apparently, she started thrashing, wildly throwing her body against the walls of her stall and so badly injured her face and body that it made it impossible to try and save her. Jill had no choice but to make the hard decision to have her put down.

I thanked the boarder for letting me know what happened. I walked up the hill drawn ever more intensely by the soft nicker I heard. When I got to Emma's stall, I buried my face on her shoulder and she wrapped her head and neck around me. I felt so much love that I rested there until my tears stopped.

Later that day when I had a quiet moment, I called Carol to find out why I had heard from Cordelia that she was fine. I explained the situation to Carol and then waited until she had connected to Cordelia.

"You spoke to her after she had died," Carol said. "That's why she reported no pain."

"Why did she have to die such a horrible death?" I asked.

"Throughout my life," Carol translated for Cordelia, "people valued me because of my looks. Early on no one saw me for who I was or cared about my feelings. My body and how it performed got tremendous amounts of attention. My physical form was highly prized and it made me special. Over time I started to identify with my body. I lost who I was in the process. When it came time to leave this life, I was so attached to my body that it had to be destroyed for my spirit to leave it and move on."

By the time Carol finished her translation, my cheeks were washed in a cascade of tears.

"Thank you, Cordelia," I managed to whisper, "for sharing your story. I am so sorry for your early life experiences. People need to see beyond physical beauty." My sorrow for this poor soul was profound.

The next day I spotted Jill at the barn. Despite her sadness she wanted to tell me what happened. She related how she had found Cordelia in her stall in pain and rushed her to UC Davis vet school for the surgery she thought the horse would need to relieve the abdominal distress. She described the difficulty she had in watching Cordelia's final struggles. I told her what Cordelia had said about the need for it. Jill immediately understood. When I started to explain the difference in Cordelia's energy after she'd died, Jill interrupted me. She gestured a soft sweep across her cheek as she said, "She was like a soft, spring breeze."

Chapter 32

Life at the barn evolved into a happier harmony when Jill invited another Arabian into her life. A new being helps fill the hole that a loss creates. I was grateful that Emma was well and I could concentrate on my riding. I welcomed this period of peace.

When I rode Emma, we blended into a union so complete that the other boarders at the stable would sometimes stop and watch us while we were practicing the more difficult dressage movements. They sang out their compliments, which warmed my heart. Validation was a sweet reward.

"It looks like magic," an upper level dressage rider said, "the way you float across the arena." One of the western riders leaned over the fence when we walked near. "You two look in perfect harmony." "Breathtakingly beautiful," one of the trail riders exclaimed. "Let me know when you show her. I want to watch."

That last comment left me with a pang. Even though the doxepin had reduced Emma's anxiety and eliminated her panic attacks while on the barn property, she still wasn't able to venture away with any assurance of a stable emotional state. The uncertainty of her ability to maintain her emotions kept me from entering any shows. Only these few boarders would ever see what we had accomplished. I knew that the goal of this sport was ephemeral. But in a hidden cubby hole in my heart I had hoped for a wider audience.

For now, I would be content that Emma's accomplishments created beauty. She could carry more of her weight on her hind end. She was so light on her feet she seemed to only touch the earth long enough to spring off airborne again. My trophy was the good ride. They happened often enough. Each glorious ride was another blue ribbon displayed in the chambers of my heart.

Each day that I rode Emma I said my prayers to the gods of pharmaceutical chemistry and thanked them for doxepin. Emma's anxiety no longer escalated into a full-fledged panic attack. She almost never spooked and her ability to concentrate and her willingness to learn ensured a steady progression in our dressage work.

This respite lasted about two years.

When Emma's attacks resumed, I called my vet.

"They're back," I told her. "I'm frustrated. Each time she habituates to a drug I never know whether I'll find something else to help her."

I worried that no resource would appear that could ease her emotional pain. What made the situation worse was my emotional connection to her. Emma's distress was mine.

"We don't have good answers," my vet replied, "for the plasticity of the body's systems."

"Is there anything we can do?" I asked. "She needs something to stop the attack when it starts."

"Yes," she replied. "Perhaps we can use a stopgap measure. Try injecting her with ace (acepromazine). It's a good tranquilizer. On my next trip to the barn I'll drop off a bottle and some syringes."

Whenever Emma started having one of her attacks, I sprinted to the tack room and grabbed the tranquilizer bottle and syringe. With as many years as I'd owned horses I had gotten proficient in injecting drugs intramuscularly. But that was on horses that stood quietly in their stalls. I had to run alongside Emma as she wildly raced the fence line and try and get the needle into her neck without getting run over. Once the contents of the syringe were emptied into

Emma's neck the results showed within ten minutes. Emma's pacing slowed, her head drooped and her expression noticeably softened. Eventually her appearance took on a serenity that seemed to emanate from heaven.

One night when I was settled in at home, I called Carol to find out how Emma was experiencing the administration of tranquilizers.

"I love my drugs," Carol translated putting pleasure into her voice. "At first they make me not care about my terror. Then after a little while I start to relax. Over time I relax more and then the terror goes away and I'm myself."

"Emma, that's great," I said feeling relief spread throughout my body. "The ace seems to stop the panic attack and resets your biology somehow. I will leave a filled syringe at the barn so one of the boarders can inject you if you start to have an anxiety attack when I'm at work."

"Thank you so much," Carol translated, putting gratitude into her voice. "I love you."

"Nah," I teased. "You love your drugs."

Although the tranquilizer did its job to break the cycle of a panic attack, Emma's episodes were coming more and more frequently. Between bouts her anxiety level was increasing and riding her became difficult. When I told my vet about the increased number of attacks, she expressed her concern that I couldn't keep giving Emma the tranquilizer on such a continual basis. I was distraught. I wondered if something else might be done for Emma or had I run out of options.

While Emma's anxiety was getting worse, I was having my own difficulties. I suffered a great deal of loss in a short period of time. Elaine, my good friend who supported me throughout many of my ordeals with Emma, was the first to leave this world. She had a miserable bout with colon cancer. Chemo and the advancing cancer ravaged her body. She wouldn't let anyone except her immediate family see her. I reasoned her reluctance to be seen was driven by her work life as a model, which had valued her appearance. She didn't apprehend the irony of her behavior. Tom hadn't wanted a visit from Elaine for similar reasons when he was wasting from AIDS.

While Elaine was fighting her battle with cancer, another friend of mine who had been one who understood me and who could offer emotional support and guidance was also sick. She had been afflicted with lung cancer and had been diagnosed one month after Elaine had been diagnosed. She died one week after Elaine's celebration of life service.

A short few months after losing my two best friends, my emotional stability was getting harder to maintain. Each day my anxiety seemed to ratchet up another notch. I was so distressed that I spent my free time nestled in my bed looking for comfort. I wondered how I would even be able to function. Each morning I struggled by sheer determination to make it to work. And work was no blessing. I reported to a manager who seemed to take pleasure in creating pain in others.

I had a hard time processing the loss of my two closest friends. The days seemed to be interminably long and the weeks a test of endurance. Three months after my friends' passing my spiritual advisor of twenty years passed. He was also Emma's spiritual advisor and it put both of us into a state of shock. My actions became robotic and I would sometimes find myself in a place and not know how I got there. I felt as if the props that helped keep me upright had been yanked from me. I was laid out flat on a bed of quicksand. I had to remember to breathe. As each week passed I was dismayed by my inability to pull myself out of this debilitating state of emotional trauma.

My therapist recommended that I see a psycho-pharmacologist to prescribe drugs to keep me from retreating into a space that would render me nonfunctional. I didn't like taking any form of medication, but the emotional pain I was in was more than I could bear. The psychiatrist prescribed heavy doses of anti-anxiety drugs to get me through each day.

Just when I thought it couldn't get any worse, my sister called me to tell me that my mother had been brought to the emergency room of Kaiser Hospital and it was up to me to sort out the issues. My eighty-seven-year-old mother had fallen and my father at the age of ninety-four could no longer help her to her feet. He told the ambulance driver not to bring her back. By stepping up to my responsibilities I was zapped back into the family system, which had a way of making me instantly crazy. Up until that time I had separated from my parents and my sister, a condition insisted on by my therapist because of the toxicity of the family dynamics.

After Kaiser Hospital evaluated my mother's condition, the doctors transferred her to a skilled nursing facility for strengthening and rehabilitation. They advised me that they were skeptical of her ability to improve since her weakness was created by spinal stenosis. They explained that they had recommended surgery to correct the condition several years before, but she had refused treatment. They shook their heads baffled at how she could endure the pain caused by her pinched spinal cord as well as the loss of function of the lower half of her body.

My mother did her best to regain capacity in her lower limbs. A few weeks prior to her discharge date, the social workers at the skilled nursing facility informed me that when my mother exited the facility contracted by Kaiser, she would need to be transferred to another skilled nursing facility. Kaiser would no longer be responsible for her. According to their assessment, the social workers advised me that despite my mother's physical therapy and occupational therapy sessions she had not improved enough to live independently. Additionally, they advised me that my father, being legally blind, couldn't live on his own and would need assisted living, neither of which my parents had planned for or were in a financial position to fund. Before my mother was released from the skilled nursing facility, she contracted an infection that was eating away at her leg. The diagnosis was MRSA (commonly known as the flesh-eating bacteria which is resistant to antibiotics). She was transferred back to Kaiser Hospital and put in an isolation room.

Over the course of a few weeks, I watched as a small dime-sized wound on my mother's calf ate her leg away and revealed her tendons and bone. Eventually nothing could be done except amputate her leg. For as long as I knew her my mother was afraid of being dependent on others. She had witnessed her older sister's challenges after a leg had been amputated due to a malignant tumor high up on her thigh. At my gut level I knew my mother was going to die soon. The vision of her ensuing dependency when she would leave the hospital was her worst nightmare.

A couple of days after my mother's surgery, I went to visit her. This would be my opportunity to tell her that I knew she had done the best she could in raising me. Despite the abuse I had endured, I wanted to reassure her that I loved her and that she should be at peace in our relationship. I wanted to say all those things I had never been able to. I wanted her to feel my love and concern. I had worked hard to resolve the maltreatment and wanted her to pass over in peace.

I entered her room and saw her visiting with my father. I sidled up to her bed. She was fully awake and appeared to be comfortable. Her face seemed relaxed and free from signs of pain. I leaned over so she could see me without having to turn her neck. Before I could speak and as soon as she looked at my face she screamed in horror and called out for my father.

"It's me," I said, my fingers resting lightly on her forearm.

She screamed even louder for my father. I was confused and stepped back yielding my place next to the bed.

Her bulging eyes followed my retreat and spasms of her body broadcast her panic. I looked at my father and said, "I'm leaving."

That I could create such terror in my mother took me by surprise and shattered me. This was not the deathbed scene I had imagined. My need to express forgiveness and understanding wasn't going to happen. I felt robbed. With my heart pounding, my eyes filmy with tears, I stumbled towards Kaiser's parking lot. I ripped open my car door and slumped into the driver's seat. I took a deep breath and dug deep into myself for a soft-landing spot. The best I could do was assuage my shock by reminding myself what my spiritual advisor had told me about my parents – in their own way they did love me, but they viewed me as a whirlwind, awed by a force that they couldn't comprehend.

About a week after the surgery and a couple of days after the aborted visit with my mother, she went into a decline. Unknown to me, my sister decided to pull the plug on my mother's life support. Even though my sister had my pager and work numbers she left the message on my home phone voice mail. When I got home from work, I retrieved the first message informing me that my sister planned to pull the life support systems on my mother in the mid-afternoon should I choose to be there. Then I retrieved the next message that simply said, "Your mother is dead." I wondered why my sister hadn't called me at work. Later I would reason that perhaps my guardian angels were sparing me another hurtful family encounter.

That day was September 10, 2001. The next morning, I headed to work hoping to find solace and support from friends there. I didn't play the news that morning either at home or in the car. I tried to take comfort in my usual commute route and listened to the calming music from my collection of CDs. I wanted to be surrounded by things I knew and could feel sure of. When I entered the freeway, I felt as if I had entered a time warp of some kind. No one changed lanes on this busy section of road. No one was weaving in and out of traffic. No passenger cars with only a single occupant were cheating in the carpool lane. The behavior was peculiar. I attributed my distressed state as the cause of my perception. I shook my head and thought perhaps the morning commute had been sent into the same unbalance that I was in.

When I got to work, I spotted groups huddled together listening to radios throughout the building. Only a couple of people were at their desks working. I was puzzled by the strange energy I was feeling. I stopped by one of the offices to ask what was going on. Although my ears registered sound, I had a hard time comprehending the words. When I did, I had no room for the shocking news of September 11th. I had no emotional reaction. I would have to process the collapse of the two towers of the World Trade Center on another day.

I shuffled back to my office and fell into my chair. I turned on my computer and stared at the blinking screen. I decided that my work friends were in enough shock, so I wouldn't ask for help in processing my own grief of my mother's passing and her final painful rejection of me.

I managed to stay functional throughout the day. When I got home, I watched the planes, the towers and the aftermath. I went to bed early and curled up into a fetal ball.

The next morning, on September 12, 2001 I was awakened by the phone. My father called me to tell me that he was dying. I shook my head to clear my mind and to absorb his message. I told him I would be right over. I called 911, didn't bother to dress and sped to his home in time to see the EMTs load the gurney and drive the ambulance away. The firemen who were the first responders had cautioned me that it was serious. They shook their heads, indicating that this time the outcome of their visit would be different.

I drove over to the emergency entrance of Kaiser. The staff led me into a treatment room where I found my father connected to several machines. In a few minutes a doctor joined me by my father's bedside. He informed me that he had two possible diagnoses. Either a heart attack in which case they were doing everything they could or his aortic aneurism was leaking. If the latter, surgery would be the only recourse. It was the same surgery that my father had been offered when he was eighty-five and the doctors advised against it then. He was now ninety-four and even less likely to survive the operation. I faced my father and asked if he wanted the surgery. He voiced a vehement, "no," shaking his head back and forth to punctuate his meaning.

I sat with my father stroking his brow. I asked him if he wanted me to call my sister. He was again emphatic, "No. She frightens me."

My father on a previous occasion had told me that after my mother had been rushed to the emergency room, my sister had begun removing items from my parents' house. This behavior and others of hers had troubled and saddened my father. I don't believe that he ever quite trusted my sister.

When the emergency staff discovered in their records that my mother had passed away two days earlier, they called for a social worker to come to the Emergency Room to support me. A nurse informed me that the social worker was on her way. A few minutes later a stately, tall woman with glistening brown hair entered the room. We spoke briefly. She seemed to get that I had a spiritual perspective on the recent events of my family. Her friendly, calm manner soothed my raw nerves.

"I don't want you to be afraid," the woman said, as she stared at the back of the room.

I followed her gaze over the beeping machines, tubes and IV's. I didn't see anything. I looked back to her for an explanation.

She pointed with her hand. "There's a big brown horse standing in the corner."

"Oh," I laughed. "Don't be concerned. That's my horse, Emma. She's here to help me."

"You mentioned that your father is afraid of your sister," she said. "As soon as a bed becomes available in the hospital wing, we won't be able to conceal his identity. Here in the emergency room it's different. We're going to station a guard at the door for now."

"I understand," I said. "The doctor who spoke to me about my father's condition had suggested that his passing may take three to four days."

"I'll stop by later to see you," she said and retreated from the room with a soft close on the door.

It took about another hour for a room to be prepared for my father. When the nurse entered the room to move him out of the emergency ward, the machines sounded an alarm and the telltale flat line appeared on the monitor. He passed away apparently in peace and safety.

I would remember September 11, 2001, or more commonly referred to as 9/11, for far different reasons than the rest of the world.

Chapter 33

My therapist had warned me that I would take the loss of my parents hard. She predicted that it would force me to give up the hope of ever being loved by them in a way that didn't damage me. She was right. I became a zombie. As if my grieving wasn't enough of a challenge, my distress seemed to up the need of my boss to be difficult.

Waking up in the morning was the worst. I didn't want to face another day. I had always lived my life waiting for the other shoe to drop and now a closet full had. I felt so much anxiety all I wanted to do was stay in bed and grieve. The world was dishing out more pain than I could bear. This was all more trauma to add to my post-traumatic stress syndrome. I was highly reactive. The slightest irritant made me want to run for cover with my heart pounding and a sweat breaking out. If I didn't have a mortgage and a horse I wouldn't have managed to get through a day at work. I was barely functioning. I needed Emma more than ever and this time she couldn't be there for me. Her anxiety continued to escalate.

Each evening after work, I went to the barn to try and calm Emma. Her level of anxiety was so high I didn't want to risk riding her while I was in such a fragile state. On one of my strolls around the barn property I chanced to meet my vet who was out visiting her horse. She motioned me aside.

"I'm going to be direct," she said. "You're not in good shape emotionally. Emma's anxiety attacks aren't helping you."

She stepped a little closer and lowered her voice. "What would you think about turning Emma out? I know of a lovely place up in Sonoma. The owners are knowledgeable about horses and the board is affordable. I'm not sure that Emma will ever be able to work out her emotional issues."

"You've been my last resort to help her," I said, tears welling in the corners of my eyes.

"Turned out in a big pasture, Emma can settle down and just be a horse," she said, lowering her eyes and giving my forearm a comforting touch. "Her anxiety attacks are coming with more frequency. It'll be whatever it is. You need a break. I'm not sure you can make a difference for her. For once you have to think about yourself."

I felt my stomach knot as she spoke. I knew Emma and knew how to take care of her. The conflict in my emotions was torment. My heart screamed out for the nurturing that I desperately needed. I couldn't be the strong one right now. Emma's anxiety only made me feel worse. The rapture and escape that I used to get from riding had vanished when her anxiety returned.

I looked at my vet. She was waiting patiently. Her eyes were a liquid brown and her face couldn't have displayed more empathy. I looked down and picked a strand of hay off my shirt. Caked dirt on my sleeve caught my attention. I brushed it off. I noticed I didn't hear the usually twittering of birds but instead a thundering roar blasted through my head temporarily deafening me.

"What you say makes sense," I said, when I recovered. "Most days I dread driving out here. I'm feeling so much anxiety myself I'm not sure I'm helping ground Emma. You have a point."

My throat turned dry. I snugged my shirt into my breeches.

"Emma might do better away from me," I said. "Her attacks are worse. I'm having a hard time forcing myself to go to a job where I feel the environment is dysfunctional. I'm not a good support system for her."

"Please think of yourself," the vet said.

"I wonder," I said, "if Emma's habituating to the drug could be worsened by my mental state. She may have been mirroring the growth of my own internal distress. She's emotionally sensitive and in many ways, we are inseparable."

The vet rested her hand on my shoulder and lowered her head. She raised her eyes. The tips of her eyelashes brushed her upper eyelids.

"Just think about it," she said lowering her head even further. "I'm out here watching what's going on. I had to say something."

I was in too much shock with my grief to feel much. All I could say was, "Thanks. I need to sleep on it."

The next morning when I woke up I felt a clear message. An astrologer had told me that he had clearly read in my chart that in this life I was to learn self-care. My therapist had concurred with his message. I really didn't want to ride Emma anymore. Her anxiety attacks stressed me. They left me even more exhausted. My vet's words resonated in my head. Putting me first was totally against how I was built. I rolled over and pulled the covers over my head. The warmth felt comforting, but didn't give relief for long. I sat up and tried to clear my mind. I did my best to imagine how I would feel if I didn't have to go out to the barn to take care of Emma. My muscles released some tension and I let out a deep breath. I sank deeper into the welcoming mattress of my bed. Those signs spoke volumes.

The first step would be to call the ranch in Sonoma for an appointment to visit their facilities. After a brief interview on the phone with the owner/manager, I made arrangements to make the trip the following weekend.

Stress and immune system diseases are best buddies. My Chronic Fatigue syndrome came back to sit on my shoulder like a homunculus jeering in my ear, reminding me that I had no energy. For sure I didn't need the added complexity of a body that was giving out. Once again, I had to think ahead and manage my activities, so I could perform the basic needs of life. Thanks to modern medicine my grief and anxiety were kept in check by the prescription drugs I was taking. I could get out of the fetal position in bed. I may not have bounced up to face the day, but I managed to drag myself to work and perform.

Despite my own issues, Emma was my responsibility and she was dependent upon me for her happiness and the conditions of her life. If I couldn't take care of her properly then I needed to find a situation that could meet her needs. On Saturday morning I crawled out of bed by noon to keep the appointment I had made to inspect the possible retirement home that my vet had recommended. I concentrated on focusing on the road, so I would stay awake for the three-hour drive to Sonoma. To the place that Emma might be able to call home.

Fortunately, what was waiting for me sparked hope. From the lovely wrought iron gate at the entrance to the winding driveway flanked by gently rolling pastures to the horses lazily grazing in the field, each direction of the compass looked as if it were out of an idyllic countryside picture book. Unlike the hills of the East Bay I had left behind with their grasses bleached to a palomino gold, these hills were green. The owner explained that there was only a small herd of retired horses that couldn't possibly reduce the supply of native grasses kept green by the occasional rain cloud. In the summer they had to keep some of their horses in the barn for much of the day to keep them from getting too fat.

The energy from the land melted away my fatigue and I accepted an offer to ride one of their mustangs around the property to get a better view of the landscape. The over four hundred acres seemed huge and met my vision of a comfortable retirement home for a horse – enough room to get up a good gallop and kick up your heels. Plenty of forage of different grasses, clusters of mature trees to take shelter and several ponds fed by clear, cool streams completed the picture.

The owners were kind and appeared to want to do a good job of caretaking. The horses had shiny coats and were in good flesh. It was summer, so I expected them to be well filled out. Some might even be called roly-poly. I thought this place might work.

At home I started weaning Emma off her doxepin. The drug didn't seem to be doing much anyway. My vet thought in a turn out situation Emma would learn to adjust and be okay. I knew from my experience with the Woodland Stallion Station that what other horses might consider a healing and restful environment would not necessarily be that for Emma. She tended to bring her demons with her.

My emotional and physical exhaustion was driving my decision to retire Emma. I had to embrace the idea that Emma would have to fend for herself. The anguish I felt from that decision had made me rethink turning Emma out several times. Putting my needs ahead of hers was not something I had mastered. Acting towards that end catapulted me out of my comfort zone. I think I had a lot in common with other adults who had been raised in an abusive home and hadn't learned good self-care behaviors.

Arrangements were made for a driver to come and trailer Emma to his ranch. Three hours away meant I wouldn't be seeing much of her. I had to trust this separation would be helpful for me to regain emotional stability and that being away from my horse wouldn't propel me into a tailspin. We had been separated before – when she was at Gualala and then again when she went to the Woodland Stallion Station. She would make new friends and hopefully adjust to a new way of life. At nineteen years of age she was much wiser and perhaps had better coping skills. Or so I wished.

The day came to send Emma away. I drove out to meet the owner at the barn. With mechanical steps I led Emma to his stock trailer. My stomach churned as if it were kneading bread. My heart walloped against my chest wall and my tongue was so dry it stuck against the roof of my mouth. Emma's face was taut and the hollows above her eyes seemed more sunken. She threw her head high as I buckled her halter on. Her eyes bulged from her head. I held my breath and led her to the trailer. She dragged her feet but stepped in without resistance. I tied her to the side and she craned her neck towards me with what seemed a pleading expression. I spun around and popped out. The driver secured the door behind her.

He knew enough about fidgety horses to get moving. He hopped in his rig, started the engine and slipped down the driveway. I headed for my car and followed the rig to the freeway entrance. I could hear Emma calling. Her high-pitched neighs screamed through my brain. She must be really frightened. She usually stayed calm while trailering. With each of her whinnies, my insides convulsed. I had to put myself on autopilot so that I could go through with this separation. I was feeling Emma's pain. I simply had no room for any more pain. At last I was granted some relief when the rig turned towards Sonoma and I turned towards home.

I knew that at her age Emma would not be able to develop into a dressage horse at the FEI or international level. The time to school passage or piaffe had passed. That dream was over. Our relationship had evolved to one of deep friendship and I was sending my best friend away. I couldn't think about it. I expected that this move would be Emma's last. She would permanently retire and I would leave horses until I sorted out the next stage of my life.

The following week I cleared out my tack locker and gave away my tack except Emma's bridle, my two saddles and a few brushes. Giving everything away would be too much like going cold turkey. I did my best to simplify my life and my responsibilities. I sold my horse trailer and donated the pickup truck to a local high school. With each de-cluttering step, strong emotions ripped through my body requiring me to act with forced precision. I was gripped in terror so profound that the slightest discordant note ripped at my sanity. Emma and I were connected and were an integral part of each other's lives. I felt as if I had been broken into pieces. Anyone who faced the loss of a soul mate would have some idea of how I felt.

With Emma gone, I assessed how I felt about her absence from my daily life. As close as we were, I felt ashamed that her absence made me feel as if a burden had been removed. I didn't have the daily responsibility of meeting Emma's needs – needs I couldn't seem to fill. I prayed she would do well in her new home.

Several months had passed since my parents' death. I had a lot of work to do to take care of their possessions. They hadn't done any estate planning and my mother didn't have a will. The original of my father's last will couldn't be found and my nephew was irate that he might not get his share that a later will promised. The last words I heard from him was his screaming at me. My sister didn't seem to be coping well and threatened me with a criminal complaint, insisting that I had purposely killed my father by withholding surgery from him. Despite my efforts to move things along, I seemed to be stymied. I had trouble finding an estate lawyer who would deal with my sister. Between what felt like a hostile work environment and my family issues I was barely coping.

As promised, I received a phone call from the owner providing me an update on how Emma was doing after two weeks in her new home. "The first couple of days Emma stayed by herself," he said. "But now one of the sweeter tempered horses has adopted her and has been hanging out with her. Whenever I see her, she's eating grass. I think she's going to be fine."

"I'm glad that she isn't running the fence line or doing anything hysterical," I said feeling relieved that I wouldn't have to do a quick about face with Emma. "I'll go ahead and release her stall here."

"I'll take some pictures of her and send them to you," he said.

A couple of months later, despite how exhausting the trip would be, I thought that I'd better see what Emma looked like. Fall was nearing its end and the cold of winter would follow. When I arrived at the entrance to the ranch, I saw Emma in the front pasture. I gasped. She looked noticeably thinner. The expression of her eye looked far away. The owner had said that he had nicknamed Emma "Super Model" because of her long slender legs and thin body shape. I told him that I thought Emma had dropped weight and needed to pick up before winter or she wouldn't be able to stay warm. He clearly had a different concept of acceptable body weight than I did.

I groomed Emma briefly, reminding her how important it was for her to eat and to put on weight. Her unsettled expression broke my heart. Thankfully she ate the grain I had brought for her. I said goodbye and drove down the driveway to face the long ride home.

Seeing Emma in poor condition sucked the last remnants of energy from my body. The entirety of my concentration was needed to be on my driving, so I would be safe for myself and others. As soon as I got home, I slid into bed, pulled up the covers to my chin and dialed Carol's number.

"Emma, how are you doing?" I asked half not wanting to hear.

"I'm doing my best," Carol translated in a voice that was more of a lamentation than a statement.

"You need to eat more," I said as an order and not as a recommendation.

"I'm trying," Carol translated, putting a whining tone in her voice.

"Winter is coming soon," I warned.

"I'm trying to survive today," Carol translated with exasperation.

"I know how that feels," I managed to squeak despite the spasm in my throat. "Do your best to eat. How are you doing with the other horses?"

"They are mean," Carol translated in a matter of fact tone.

My chest tightened and I thought how similar our lives were. I often had a hard time relating to my peers at work. I replied, "I understand and I'm sorry to hear that."

"I keep getting kicked," Carol translated with emphasis on each word.

My legs involuntarily jerked back and forth to get rid of the beasts that were hurting my horse. "Can't you get away from the mean horses?"

"I mind my own business and just don't see them coming," Carol translated with sadness in her voice. "I don't think that way."

"I understand," I said. Silent tears streamed down my face in empathy with Emma.

After I hung up the phone, I pulled the covers over my face and froze in a catatonic state of hopelessness.

Chapter 34

Two weeks after I had made the trip to visit Emma, I received a call from the owner of the ranch who called me to let me know that Emma had gotten cornered by a couple of horses. In stepping back to avoid them, she put her leg through a wire fence. They had to have the vet out. A scar would remain, but she would be okay.

The thought that Emma was being bullied angered me. I knew what that felt like. I decided to make the trip to Sonoma the following weekend to see for myself what was going on. When I spotted Emma in the field, my heart sank. She was just too thin. She had bite and kick marks all over her neck, shoulders, flanks and rear end. Some of them were old but some of them were quite fresh and showed through her hide. What troubled me most was her weight. Her condition had deteriorated since my last trip and at this rate she wouldn't make it through the winter. Skin alone doesn't do much to protect internal organs and bones from cold. I let the owner know that I was very concerned about Emma's weight.

As soon as I got home, I went on the internet and started looking for another turn out situation - one where Emma would have her food supply better controlled and could be placed with gentle horses. Grass alone didn't seem to be enough to keep Emma at a good weight. She would need additional calories from grain or some form of concentrated feed like LMF Primetime. I also wanted her closer to home where it would be easier for me to check up on her.

The first dozen facilities I checked out wouldn't work. Emma couldn't eat alfalfa hay and most facilities supplemented pasture grass with alfalfa. That meant Emma would need to be isolated. No one wanted to be in the position of offering special care for a retired horse. Not one of the facilities that I called was interested in offering her supplemental feed if the hay wasn't enough.

When I was about to give up, I spotted a website advertising retirement and hospice care for the older horse. The pictures were of contented horses munching on green grass against rolling hills. And – bingo! - it was in Morgan Hill, only an hour and a half from where I lived. I couldn't help but think that if they were willing to care for horses in the final stages of life then they should be able to provide the additional care-giving that Emma needed.

I called the number on the screen and Sue, a pleasant-sounding woman with an energetic voice, answered the phone. Sue and her veterinarian husband owned the facility and she had just recently started a small business to take care of aged horses. I liked that. Sue seemed intelligent and very knowledgeable. She researched the best feeds, was willing to provide each horse with the supplements they required, administered proper worming programs and instead of poisons used fly predators to manage the fly population. Right on, I thought. We arranged for a visit the following weekend.

On Saturday when I arrived, Sue was waiting for me at the lower end of her property. She explained that they had subdivided the gently rolling hillside of their fourteen acres to accommodate small groups of horses. Matching harmonious personalities was her objective. A small barn with an overhang sat at the bottom of the slope and the lower pastures bordered a creek. The surrounding hills were far enough away to provide pleasing vistas and an open feeling of space yet were close enough to feel as they were protecting this little valley.

The pasture wouldn't be enough to feed the horses throughout the year and Sue said that she provided oat or grass hay year-round. The grass was considered a fresh treat rather than the main source of nutrition.

The horses had their own buckets so that each could be fed whatever grain, supplements or medications were required. Sue put only two or three horses in each pasture and would watch them carefully to make sure that they got along. Sue pointed out a twenty-eight-year-old quarter horse named Breezy who would be Emma's pasture mate. She described him as a very sweet horse with the manners of a southern gentleman. I checked in with my intuition and got a strong hit that Emma would like it here and would get the TLC she needed.

Sue called a friend who did trailering and helped arrange to have Emma picked up in Sonoma. Unfortunately, her person was only available for the next couple of days, so I couldn't give the ranch owner in Sonoma much notice.

I called him to let him know that I had underestimated Emma's retirement needs. Not wanting to offend him, I likened Emma to a human retiree. I said I had thought Emma was capable of independent living but with her weight loss it was clear that she wasn't. While she wasn't in need of a skilled nursing facility, she clearly needed an assisted living arrangement. He laughed and agreed. Emma needed more support than their retirement program was prepared to provide.

Within two days Emma would be living in Morgan Hill. I felt relieved she was closer to home and with someone who could attend to her physical and emotional requirements. She would be given her own allotment of hay and grain. Having a vet on the property also gave me a feeling of security regarding Emma's health.

I sighed. If Emma were happy, maybe I could attend to my own healing.

Chapter 35

A meeting I had to chair conflicted with Emma's arrival in Morgan Hill or I would have greeted her on the workday she was scheduled to be trailered to her new home. Besides, facing Silicon Valley and San Jose traffic during the work week would more than exhaust my patience and physical stamina. I made sure that I was free to go and see her on the weekend.

On Saturday morning the drive down was a mercifully short hour and fifteen minutes. The sun was shining and the temperature was unseasonably warm. I had no trouble finding Sue's place again. My sense of direction was reliable which meant, once traveled, well-remembered. I unlocked the metal gate along the road and drove my car onto the dirt driveway leading to the area designated for boarders. Emma was hanging out in one of the small pastures adjoining the barn. Attached to her halter was a black cloth that covered her left eye. She was painfully thin and her coat appeared dull. My heart dropped in my chest.

Sue must have seen my car. She came down the path leading from her house to the barn. With a broad, cheery smile she gave me a welcoming greeting. Beneath her floppy, wide-brimmed hat, brown eyes twinkled when she talked. Her small frame fit easily into her tight jeans and her loose-fitting peasant blouse billowed slightly in the breeze. With a quick sweep she captured her long brown hair back behind her ears.

"Your horse has been doing a lot of sleeping," she said. "She has a beautiful, kind face."

"I'm glad you can see her personality," I said and headed out to get Emma.

Sue quickened her pace and caught up with me.

"I had my husband look at Emma's eye," she said. "It's a nasty injury. We've been treating it. Even though the wound seems to be a couple of weeks old, it needs attention. I've been coming down twice a day to put medicine in her eye. I rigged up this old tee shirt to her halter to keep her eye protected from dirt and the sun. She's been great about being treated."

"Thank you for taking care of her," I said, turning to face Sue. "I'm very appreciative."

"Her leg wound is continuing to heal," Sue said, kneeling and swishing the dust off the area surrounding the injury on Emma's hind leg. "I'm afraid she'll have a scar on her cannon bone. My husband said not much can be done for the scar. I know you're concerned about her weight. I've added corn oil to her grain to get additional calories in her."

With the lead rope securely snapped to Emma's halter I looked deep into her right eye. She looked more relaxed than when I last saw her in Sonoma. I led her back to the grooming area under the overhang projecting out from the wood barn. I had to admit it. Emma looked neglected. I felt guilty that I'd let her get in this condition. Her face and legs were covered in black resin. I began the messy job of picking the tarry stuff off Emma's nose.

"Tarweed is such a pain to clean," I said, turning to Sue who watched the tedious removal.

She squatted next to Emma's left front leg and began to get the yucky goo off her pastern.

"Horses get coated with the stuff when they nose around for the more palatable grasses," she said. "Fortunately, not many of those plants are in my pasture so it shouldn't take long for her legs and nose to clean up. It's really disgusting stuff."

"She's quite the picture," I said. "With the tar on her nose and legs, a tee shirt over her face and bones sticking out everywhere I'm surprised that the neighbors haven't called the SPCA." I said it as a joke but felt the pang of reality.

"Oh, come on," Sue said laughing. "She's not that bad. I'm sure they've seen far worse. She's just thinner than you're used to."

I brushed Emma's coat with strong, long sweeps to bring back some of the life.

"She went downhill so fast," I said. "I don't think she would've made it through the winter up there. I'm grateful to have found your place."

"We'll take good care of her," Sue said smiling. She gently smoothed Emma's forelock.

When the muscles of my abdomen started to relax, I knew that Emma had found peace in her new home. I kissed her on the nose and said goodbye, satisfied she was getting the care she needed. Before hopping in my car, I scanned the rural setting of knobby hills cloaked in black oak, tan oak and laurel. The amount of undeveloped land this close to major metropolitan areas never ceased to fill me with gratitude for my good fortune for living in California.

Driving home through the winding turns forced me to slow down, enjoy the scenery and, more importantly, gave me time to think. I felt bad that Emma had to suffer for my mistakes in selection of homes. She would have never been sent to Sonoma if I had known it was such a bad choice. I couldn't have been happier with the care given by Sue and her veterinarian husband. My lungs let out a sigh emanating from the depths of my belly.

I called Carol after a couple of weeks went by. Just because I thought Sue's place was a good fit, didn't mean that Emma shared that view.

When Carol answered the phone, I feigned a cheery voice. I reasoned that people didn't generally want to know about your problems.

"Hey Emma, how are you doing?" I asked.

"I'm better now," Carol translated with more force in her voice at the end of the sentence.

"I'm so sorry that you got so thin," I said not hiding the concern in my voice.

"My weight isn't so bad," Carol translated, with a reassuring tone. "I'm not like the sad horses you watch on Animal Planet."

I laughed with relief. Perhaps Emma's physical form wasn't as much of a worry as I had believed. She was right. She was nowhere near the condition of the rescue horses I'd seen on television that weren't much more than walking skeletons.

"Sue told me you've been lying down a lot in the pasture," I said. "She said one of the retired horses stands over you like he's guarding you."

"He was keeping me company," Carol translated with sadness in her voice. "He listened to me. I was crying. I had a miserable time in Sonoma. I couldn't find anyone to be my friend and too many of the horses bullied me. They were odious."

"I'm so sorry," I said. Pangs of guilt scurried up and down my spine. "Not to change the subject, but, Carol, was 'odious' Emma's word or yours?"

"Those horses were just down right despicable and obnoxious," Carol said, laughing. "It's Emma's concept and my word for their base and contemptible behavior."

"Have you been studying for a vocabulary test?" I asked joining her in laughter.

"I was just trying to do justice to what Emma was telling me," Carol said, her giggle infectious.

"The other horses didn't like me," Carol translated for Emma switching to a serious tone. "They didn't get who I was. They kept hurting me. I tried to stay out of their way, but when I was least expecting it I would get kicked or bitten. I love you. I want to be with you."

"Emma, I feel bad. I'm so sorry," I said. "Carol, I guess I know why you chose the words you did. Emma, how did your eye get hurt?"

"When one of the horses kicked out at me," Carol translated with anger in her voice. "Gravel flew and hit my eye. It really hurt much more than the kick. I can't see as well out of that eye anymore."

"The experience in Sonoma was really awful for you," I said. "The personality of the other horses who were there seems to be the worst part."

"The people were alright," Carol translated. "The energy of the land felt good. I just didn't fit in."

"Do you like where you are now?" I asked.

"Breezy watches over me," Carol translated in a cheery voice. "He has lovely manners and is gentle. He's also intelligent. He tells me funny stories. I'm happy to have a friend."

"Emma, everyone needs a friend," Carol and I said simultaneously. We must have been having a mind meld.

I sat still for a while after we said our goodbyes. I knew that the social life of a horse is important, but I would never have imagined that in a herd of twenty horses Emma wouldn't have been able to find at least one friend. Just like us, horses want to be with companions whose dispositions match their own and who understand them. I wondered how often I neglected to provide good friends to animals in my care.

"Emma. Thank you for educating me to be a better caretaker," I said in a forceful voice, so Emma would be sure to hear me. "I want you to be happy."

I didn't need Carol to hear her answer.

"I know you do."

Chapter 36

Under Sue's watchful eye, Emma put on close to seventy-five pounds in a few weeks. Her coat gleamed in the sun. By the middle of winter, she was looking a little rotund. I had never seen her so filled out. Sue often came down to the barn when I showed up. Over the winter we became friends. In sharing the love of horses, we both did what we could to give them the best possible life. A horse that was newly arrived at Sue's ranch was extremely grouchy. She asked if I would talk to her to find out what was causing the bad temper.

I still didn't have much confidence in my abilities as an animal communicator. Nevertheless, Sue urged me to try. Standing next to the horse while she nibbled her hay, I cleared my mind.

"Do you feel pain anywhere?" I asked.

The dam broke. I received clear messages in feelings and words.

"My person does not know how much I hurt," the chestnut mare told me. "She got very impatient with me for going slow. How could I go fast when my feet hurt? She wanted me to jump over fences and go quickly over uneven ground. I couldn't. She got angry at me and hit me hard. After she got another horse, she put me here. She doesn't come out to see me. Who will love me? The shoes on my feet are making me sorer. Please take my shoes off."

Sue listened carefully to my translation of the big chestnut mare's story.

"That makes sense," she said stroking the side of the mare's neck. "The owner did eventing with the horse who started quitting in front of the fences. The vet diagnosed navicular disease so that explains her painful feet. The owner wants to keep shoes on her."

"Can you talk to her?" I asked. "Sneakers instead of metal shoes help with sore feet."

"She doesn't want to spend any more money on this horse than she has to," Sue said. "Sneakers are expensive. She never comes out here, so I think that I'll have the shoes taken off. She won't know the difference and the horse will be happier."

The disposition of the horse seemed to improve after our talk. As soon as Sue had the shoes removed, the mare looked far less miserable. I wasn't sure of the ethics of going against the wishes of the mare's owner. I told myself perhaps in the best interest of the horse, the ends justified the means.

With each new horse that came into her care, Sue called me to ask what would make them happiest. Besides the horses for which Sue provided care in her boarding business, she had several of her own riding horses and a few dozen goats. She loved goats and her passion led her to collect them from everywhere. Besides the goats, Sue had two dogs, two indoor cats, pet rats and various other animals.

Because of the number and variety of animals that were under Sue's watchful eye, we found that we would talk regularly on the phone about their conditions. Sue's cat, Aqua, had digestive problems and other physiologic challenges. I'd spoken to him a couple of times, sharing with Sue what I'd heard.

One day when I was driving home from work and I let my mind wander, I felt Aqua join me. She sent me a ghostly image of an emaciated cat that was other-worldly. She appeared dead or near dead. Her pallor was chalky, her eyes lifeless. I decided to call Sue to let her know Aqua had contacted me with a frightening image.

I tried to sound neutral.

"Sue," I said. "I don't want to scare you, but Aqua contacted me today."

"What did she say?" Sue said her pitch rising.

"It wasn't what she said - it was the image she sent me," I said. "She sent a picture of herself either dead or near dead."

"That's interesting," Sue replied. "I've been really worried about her. She's so sick. She's has lost too much weight. I'm afraid I'm losing her."

"By the picture she sent me, she's very ill," I said using a tone of caution.

"Thank you for letting me know," Sue said. Before she had a chance to say goodbye, Sue started softly crying. "She means the world to me. I'm going to do my best for her."

"Of course." I sent Sue and her cat loving thoughts.

Later, I learned Sue put Aqua on her bed that night surrounded by her husband and sons. They formed a prayer circle and directed as much love and positive energy as they could to the cat. The next day the cat started eating again. She regained her health and some weight. Sue thanked me profusely. She felt strongly that it was my warning and the love of the family that pulled her cat through her health crisis.

A few months later Sue called to tell me the latest news in her area. A few domestic animals had been mysteriously killed. The bodies had been badly mauled sometime during the night. It felt creepy. Was weird ritualistic killing going on? We had heard about some grisly animal sacrifices on the evening news in other parts of the country. After we made ourselves sick with conjectures, we concluded that we would feel a lot better if we steered the conversation to happier topics.

A week later Sue called to let me know what a local rancher had discovered. Cougars had been identified as the culprits of the slain animals. I settled myself into my chair to listen.

"I don't know why cougars would come out of the hills to hunt," Sue said, "when there are so many deer available. We usually don't spot any cougars at all. My understanding is that given a choice, cougars avoid both human contact and developed areas. I've been racking my brain and I can't imagine why they're going after penned animals that are basically in someone's backyard. Why wouldn't they stay in their own territory hunting the game they know? Why are they coming close to civilization?"

I leaned forward in my chair to get a better look at the hills in the open space bordering my home. Cougars had been spotted walking on the streets a couple of blocks away from where I lived. Cougars in my city didn't have much choice. The open spaces had dwindled and the connectors between them were paved roads. In Morgan Hill where Sue lived, there were tracts upon tracts of undeveloped land.

"I have no idea," I said leaning back in my chair.

"Well," Sue said with a rising pitch in her voice. "At least their prey has been farther down the valley, so my goats are safe."

The next time I called Carol, I asked Emma whether she could verify if cougars were in the area. Emma replied yes, but they didn't frighten her. She felt safe. She was big enough that she wouldn't be a target. I was relieved Emma felt secure. With dangerous animals on my mind, I took the opportunity to ask her about the rattlesnakes in the area. Emma said that they were around and of no concern. She didn't bother them and they didn't bother her.

A couple of weeks later I received another call from Sue as I was finishing up the dishes in the kitchen. Putting the dishcloth away, I sat down so I could give her my full attention.

Her voice seemed tense.

"A rancher who lives about a half mile from my home called me to tell me he lost one of his goats," she said. "He kept it in a small pen near his house. This is getting too close."

"That's alarming," I acknowledged, feeling her discomfort.

"I'm not only frightened for my goats, but I'm worried about the cougars," Sue said. "I'm really torn here. I don't want my goats hurt, but I don't want the cougars hurt either. The local ranchers are talking about applying for a permit to hunt and kill them. That would be such a waste. Deer are overrunning the area and desperately need thinning out."

I felt Emma's energy join me. She felt fine. I couldn't detect any stress from cougars. I sighed with relief that Emma wasn't worried.

"It sounds like an unfortunate situation," I empathized.

"What can you do to help?" Sue's voice became assertive.

I sat upright. "What?"

"Do something," Sue said.

My mouth dropped open. "What can I do?" I asked.

"Talk to the cougars," she said. "Tell them what's going to happen to them."

"I usually only speak to pets," I said. Adding some sarcasm, I continued. "You know, companion animals, the ones in relationship with humans."

"Why can't you talk to the cougars?" Sue pleaded.

I sat there and thought for a minute trying to find similarities in something I might have done.

"I know I don't have to meet the pet physically to hear what they have to say," I said, "but there's always been some form of connection to their person. I did talk to a captive dolphin once. He was staring straight at me and lived in a tiny pond at a hotel. There was no question who I was talking to. I've talked to gophers and other wildlife, but I came in contact with them. I've never tried to connect to a wild animal I've never seen or met. I wouldn't know how to do it."

"I'm sure you can do something," Sue insisted.

"No," I said gently. "I don't think so.

I didn't know what to do with Sue's request. Because it seemed so farfetched, I felt at a loss. All I could do was commiserate with her.

"The horses are safe and your dogs would probably come to the defense of the goats or at the very least sound an alarm," I said, ending the conversation with an attempt at a cheerful thought.

When Sue called me again, I heard desperation in her voice. She told me a neighbor's calf had been killed by the cougars.

"You have to do something," she urged. "I know you can."

I couldn't stand her distress. One of the problems of being empathetic is I can't easily block out someone else's emotions.

"Okay, okay," I said. "I'll try my best. I'm not hopeful and I'm not promising anything other than I'll try."

"I'm so happy," she said with immediate lightness in her voice. "I know you can do something."

I couldn't help but think that she and Carol both had high expectations of my capabilities.

"I'll do something this weekend," I said.

"Great," she said with relief.

On the weekend I put off fulfilling Sue's request for as long as I could. When Sunday afternoon slipped away, I knew I wouldn't be able to postpone it any longer. I sat down on my couch in the living room. Clearing my mind, I sat still and concentrated on my breath. I did my best to picture an image of a cougar. Each time I tried to force my mind to hold onto the image, my gaze wandered instead. The Japanese maple on my patio had turned color displaying a buttercream golden yellow, and the maple next door interlaced the branches of yellow with vibrant, orange and carmine leaves. My fingers traced the outline of leaves on the jacquard pattern on the cushions of the sofa. Anything to forestall this fruitless exercise.

I felt Emma join me. Her energy was supportive and strong. Perhaps she could help me as she had done many times before. I remembered one occasion where Emma helped connect me to a swan.

I worked in an office complex that was home to a water fowl sanctuary. On my lunch hour I would wander about the grounds feeding the wild Canada geese, ducks, and other migratory birds with the chicken scratch I had purchased from the local feed store. My office was probably the only one in the complex of 10,000 workers that harbored a fifty-pound sack of grain. All the other birds accepted food from me except a magnificent pair of mute swans. They were large, perfectly formed with pure white plumage. And very aloof. They seemed completely disengaged from human activities, content to inhabit their own private world. Whenever they swam by, I did my best to communicate with them and attract their attention. As they glided by, I had to accept that I didn't exist in their world. I loved them and was nurtured by their beauty. I ached to connect to them.

Then one day, as the larger of the two swans swam by, he turned his head and looked over his shoulder directly at me. He stared for a long moment almost quizzically. He slowed his pace and changed direction swimming a "U" turn to the edge of the pond where I was standing. I eased a handful of grain into the water near where he had stopped. He eyed me and then scooped up the seeds. That was the beginning of our relationship. Whenever the swans saw me, they swam to me, even from the opposite end of the small lake. At the edge of the pond they waddled out over the rocks heaving their heavy bodies out of the water. Then they would give me a most incredible greeting. They raised their heads with beaks pointed at the sky and made a fluttering sound with their breath. Then they lowered their heads and repeated the movement. One swan and then the other. The energy from their greeting made my muscles quiver with delight. I was honored by their acceptance.

Later I found out Emma made it happen. She proudly told me she was able to amplify my voice, so the swan could hear me. Her intervention intercepted the swan's train of thought, so the first contact could be made. Whenever my voice seemed too weak, Emma said she strengthened the signal and delivered the message.

The squawks of a band of wild turkeys trotting along the hill of the open space adjacent to my home snapped me back from my mind's wanderings. I could sit here all-day daydreaming and avoiding what I had promised to do. I reasoned that disappointing Sue was part of my reluctance. With a deep sigh, I brought my thoughts back to the present and cleared my mind.

I wondered if Emma could help. Suddenly I felt a different energy join me. The picture of two well-muscled cougars flashed through my mind. All I could think was, my God, I'm connected to the cougars. How amazing is that?

Then my body received their feelings. They were a bit skittish. I felt as if I was talking to moving shadows. Here, there and then gone. After a while they settled down a bit, getting more comfortable talking to me. They explained they were juveniles and that their mother had died before she could teach them how to hunt. Because they didn't have the necessary hunting skills to survive, they had to kill the animals that were trapped by pens and fences. They seemed open and receptive to talking to me. I didn't know what else to say to them other than I was sorry they had lost their mother. I warned them about the dangers of killing the ranchers' stock. Since they had no other way to get food, I couldn't ask them to stop killing the domestic animals. I thanked them for joining me and picked up the phone.

"Sue, you're never going to believe this," I said right after her hello.

"You talked to the cougars," Sue said without missing a beat.

I was stunned. "How did you know?" I asked.

"I knew that you could do it," she said with delight.

I told Sue what happened.

"Now you need to teach them how to hunt deer," she insisted.

"Just like Mom taught me," I quickly replied.

"Stop that. I know you can do it," she said with a voice full of authority.

"I suppose I could go look up cougar on Wikipedia and it will tell me how to hunt deer," I said barely masking my lack of enthusiasm.

"Don't be a brat," she warned.

"Let me remind you," I countered. "I'm just a translator. I don't have any magic powers."

"Think of something," she ordered me.

"Okay," I said. "How about you do some research on how cougars kill deer and then let me know."

Sue laughed, still refusing to give up the idea that I could help. I didn't understand how she could even think of asking me to do such an extraordinary thing. We shared a concern for the cougar's well-being in a world populated with unhappy ranchers and left it at that.

Because Sue's pressure was unrelenting and at the core I was concerned for the ranchers' animals and the wild cougars, I decided to give this matter some more thought. After all, I didn't believe I could talk to the cougars, yet I did. Why not see what might happen?

Once again, I responded to a promise I had made Sue. I plunked down in my living room, cleared my mind, relaxed and sat quietly. After a few moments I felt a presence join me. I had no idea who it was. I waited for a picture. No image was forthcoming. Even though I wasn't sure who it was, I was sure that whoever contacted me had something they wanted to communicate. Within moments I saw a picture of what looked like the floor of a forest. When I looked around, I saw I was lying on a tree limb several feet above the ground. Below me I saw a narrow path worn in the undergrowth. I saw a flicker, a hint of movement - a dark shadow. When the shadow came closer, I felt as if a deer was about to emerge. My muscles tensed as if I was about to leap. I was told when my body should lunge downward. How to spring and where to land on the shoulders of the deer. I felt where to grab the neck and how to use my weight. It all happened so quickly. I sat immobile, stunned. My breath left me. I had experienced a kill.

While I knew that I had received important information, it didn't come in a form that could be easily verbalized. It was more about feeling and muscle knowledge. Not wanting to let the strength of the message get lost over time, I summoned the juvenile cougars. As soon as I felt them join me, I shared with them the pictures and the bodily sensations I had been sent. They were very interested in and attentive to what I was showing them. I shared with them everything that had been sent to me, including how to spot a deer trail. When I was done, I said good-bye and wished them well. I felt them break the connection.

I sat still, thinking the whole thing was crazy. Here I was in my living room in a lovely, peaceful community in Walnut Creek, telling cougars in Morgan Hill how to kill deer. Who or what sent me the pictures wasn't revealed. My best guess was an old, wise cougar had somehow gotten connected to me. Maybe it was a spirit cougar. There was so much I didn't know about the workings of the animal world.

Over the next several months Sue kept track of the news. With immense relief she regularly reported that no more domestic animals were reported being killed after my last talk with the young cougars. She was even more excited when she read in the paper that the ranchers had dropped their plans to pursue a permit to destroy the cougars.

It could never be proved that the sudden change in behavior of the juvenile cougars was due to my communications with them. Sue, however, was sure of it - and my intuition chimed in with agreement. I was in awe at what could be done with animal communication. I couldn't deny what I'd experienced. As with other of my experiences, I didn't know how to integrate it into my everyday life. Who would believe me?

Chapter 37

Without warning Emma's stay in Morgan Hill was cut short. A serious injury affected Sue's ability to care for the retirement horses any longer. I got busy and on Craigslist I found a small barn in Martinez just over the border from Pleasant Hill and Lafayette. A visit to the small stable revealed that the owner/manager was diligent about caring for the horses. Emma would have her own stall and paddock and be fed as much as she wanted. Coincidentally there had been important changes in my life that would free me up to care for Emma myself.

The work to settle my parent's estates had at last concluded. Probate had been completed and my parents' house had been sold. I felt as if a major portion of the burden from that part of my life had been liberated. Much of the energy that I had needed for protection was freed. The need to interact with my sister was over.

A call to my financial advisor had confirmed that my portfolio would support me in my retirement, especially since I had saved a year's worth of living expenses and wouldn't have to draw down any funds for twelve months. Knowing that I would soon be leaving the toxic environment of my job had immediate impact on my anxieties. They rapidly diminished, leaving me the happiest I'd ever been in my life. I initiated the slow decrease in my medications so that I would be free of any prescription drugs.

My own problematic emotions wouldn't exacerbate Emma's. When I realized I would be leaving a difficult work environment behind me forever, I reveled in the freedom of approaching retirement. With just a few months away from making it happen, I invited Emma to join me in joy at the nearby barn I had found.

To get Emma trailered up to Martinez I contacted a boarder at the new barn who seemed kind and was willing to transport Emma for me. When Emma arrived at her new home, I walked her around the property including the small outdoor arena and round pen. Then I let her loose in her stall. She nosed around the walls and then explored her paddock. She inched her way up the incline checking out the perimeter. At the top she stopped and surveyed the area. She looked happy and proud.

The drive to the new barn from my home was less than twenty minutes. Seeing Emma regularly would now be possible. We could spend more time together at this quiet barn mostly visited by weekend riders. And within a few short months I would be retired.

Emma was fine the first day in her new home, as she often was, whenever I moved her. The second day she fretted. Her eyes looked wild. She paced back and forth in her paddock, up and the down the hill, rushing into her stall and barely putting on the brakes in front of the half-door. After the first few days, she seemed to be settling down, although she still had some attacks of fretting. Emma's pattern was familiar to me, so I wasn't too concerned about her pacing. Unfortunately, her behavior was new to others.

"Diana," the barn owner called out to me from her back porch, catching me as I was heading up to Emma's stall, "your horse doesn't look safe."

"It's only the end of her first week. Don't worry," I said coming back down the hill to face her. "This is what Emma does. Despite how scary she appears, Emma is simply expressing her own internal terrors. Nothing bad will happen."

"But she looks like she's going to jump out over her stall door," she said, the stress in her voice escalating. "She's frantic."

"In a few more days she should be okay. This is what she does to calm herself," I said, and stopped next to the steps of the back deck. "The weaving at her stall door releases endorphins. She's self-medicating. If she isn't running and screaming non-stop, nothing needs to be done."

The barn owner didn't look relieved. I didn't know how else to dispel her concerns. And it was no surprise when a couple of days later she called me out to the barn at 3:00 AM. Before leaving the house, I checked in with Emma. I didn't feel anything unusual. The only reason I made the trip out was to assuage the concerns of the barn owner. I walked up the hill to Emma's stall expecting to find nothing. The whites of Emma's eyes were showing when I aimed the flashlight at her face, but she was standing still in her stall. Because she wasn't pacing there really wasn't anything I could do so I turned around and went back home. Perhaps the barn owner simply wanted reassurance that I would respond to her request.

As soon as Emma's anxiety subsided, the next order of business was to get Natural Balance shoes on her. If she was back in town and her anxiety was low enough, I wanted the opportunity to ride her on a regular basis. The arena was smaller than a dressage short court but large enough to do a canter circle and a few strides of a lengthening. I needed a blacksmith who used Natural Balance shoes. Fate directed me to Lynne, who was willing to come out and see what she could do. Bending over to check out Emma's feet, Lynne shook her head. Her long sandy blonde hair fell away from her face when she stood up.

"Have you ever thought about keeping Emma barefoot?" she said releasing Emma's left front foot.

"I know Emma likes to feel the dirt between her toes, so to speak," I said unzipping my jacket to let in cooler air.

She picked up Emma's hoof pointing to the bottom of her foot.

"Her sole needs to be thicker and tougher," she said pressing her fingers into Emma's sole. "She would have a healthier foot if we kept her barefoot. What I recommend is getting boots for her. Whenever you exercise her, put on her boots for the extra protection. I'm pretty sure if you do this, she'll have great feet in six months."

I studied Lynne's face. Her explanation had been earnest. She believed in what she was recommending. I believed her too. Even though Emma had been barefoot for the last several months and I shouldn't have any reason to expect her to suddenly improve going forward, I at some level knew that this was the right path. Perhaps the monthly trimmings and the added stimulation of going back to work might make the difference.

"Okay," I said. "It works for me. I had just started using a bitless bridle with great success so why not try a new theory on my horse's feet. It feels like time for changes."

Lynne dropped her rasp, letting it join the files and knives neatly stored in her tool box. "I'll put you in my book and come out every month," she said pushing Emma's nose away from her pocket. "It may help you to know that I hear the horses too."

"You do?" I asked dumbfounded by this confession.

"I hear what they say," she said writing down our next appointment in her book. "I don't go around telling everybody, but I knew I could tell you."

"That's so awesome," I said untying Emma. "Thank you for letting me know." Wow, someone in the business who admits to hearing animals.

Two months later when Lynne was out at the barn to trim the feet of a few of the other horses, she telephoned me at home.

"Diana, your horse is weaving and is all stressed out," she said with urgency.

"That's not unusual," I said, sighing. "That's how she acts sometimes. These days she's obsessing on the horse across from her. Whenever he leaves his stall, she weaves. She'll settle down when he comes back. Is he gone from his stall?"

"Yes," Lynne replied.

"Remember," I said wondering why in the world she was calling me, "I told you Emma has anxiety attacks. She'll weave until she feels better. There's nothing to be concerned about. The endorphins will eventually kick in. She'll calm down."

"But she's really anxious," Lynne insisted.

"Yes," I said picturing what Emma looked like in a full panic attack and thinking this wasn't it. "I know. Trust me. It can get much worse."

"Have you ever tried to do something about it?" she asked.

I froze, stunned into silence. How could I possibly answer that question? Lynne's voice told me she was genuinely distressed by Emma's behavior. I had forgotten how it looked to other people. I guessed the years of dealing with it made me jaded. But her question hurled me into a distant place as I replayed everything in my mind I had tried.

"Do something about it?" I said once a little more control was restored. "Everything I know, everything any vet I ever met knows and everything any trainer whose help I have enlisted knows. Homeopathy, flower essences, acupuncture, TTouch, chiropractors, UC Davis vet school, hormones, prescription medications and antidepressants." I was embarrassed by the amount of energy that burst out at the recitation of my list. She was, after all, only trying to help.

"I know a vet that might be able to do something for Emma," Lynne said, clearly immune to my diatribe. "She's a different kind of vet."

I had heard similar statements before, but there was something about Lynne I trusted. My intuition said, go for it.

"That's great," I said, amazed that I really meant it. "What's her name and number?"

And so, I called and made an appointment with Cheryl Schwartz, DVM. She was available and willing to travel from Alameda.

I greeted Cheryl at the barn. She was a tiny thing. Short blonde hair and wide, open expressive eyes. For the middle of winter, she had a gorgeous tan. From our phone conversation I felt attuned to her methods of treatment. Now that she was standing in front of me I could feel her energy. It felt comfortable. I let her know I used telepathic animal communication to get better details of what Emma was experiencing. She seemed to know exactly what I was talking about.

I led Emma out of her stall and walked her to the little sand arena. Cheryl greeted her with respect. She talked directly to Emma as if Emma understood every word.

Wow, Lynne is right. This vet is different.

Cheryl started doing energy work on Emma. She put tuning forks near different points on Emma's body. At other times she would run her hands over Emma starting at her poll and proceeding over her back and rump and down to her hind hooves.

"Emma is experiencing terror," Cheryl said looking over to me.

"How do you know?" I asked not hiding my surprise.

"I hear the horses myself," she said turning back to Emma.

"You mean telepathically?" I asked, my ears perking up.

"Yes," she said smiling at me.

"Wow," I said literally jumping up and down. "A vet who works with alternative medicine and can get feedback directly from the horse's mouth. It makes diagnosis so much easier."

Cheryl looked at me and smiled. She turned back to Emma.

"There's a lot of sadness," Cheryl said running her hands over Emma's flanks, "surrounding her reproductive organs."

"Emma," I said stepping closer to Cheryl, "reabsorbed a foal once. And on another occasion was unable to conceive."

"I'm not sure why she's sad," Cheryl said wrinkling her brow, "and I don't think Emma knows either."

"Cheryl," I said looking her in the eye, "I'm not sure you understand how appreciative I am. Not only do you believe in animal communication, you can do it yourself. I'm used to making up strange stories about how I know of Emma's symptoms that aren't visibly perceived."

Cheryl moved the tuning fork to another point on Emma's flank.

"I think I know." Cheryl looked up at me, her pixie-like face beaming.

Over the next few weeks Cheryl was able to improve Emma's anxiety level. At last Emma could venture across the gravel side road and eat grass on the vacant lot next door. Up until then Emma would immediately pull on me to take her back as soon as we stepped one pace out the front gate. To see her contentedly eating grass warmed my heart. I knew how much Emma loved green grass. For goodness sakes, horses should be able to graze on fresh grass. What a testament to Emma's internal hell that she hadn't been able to do something that was perfectly innate to horses.

To help Emma's anxiety even more, Cheryl prescribed the homeopathic remedy stramonium 20 C. Even though the remedy was intended to help with rage, Cheryl explained that anxiety and rage are closely related. Cheryl thought this remedy might be worth trying. She required I contact my vet to have potent tranquilizers on hand in case Emma acted out. A temporary, intense expression of the symptoms being treated was one of the possible side effects of homeopathic treatments. Twelve hundred pounds of horse out of control with blind rage could do a lot of damage with hooves and teeth. Emma respected fences during her panic attacks. She might not with this remedy.

A few clicks on Amazon.com and I found the link to the Hahnemann clinic for homeopathic remedies. I followed up with a quick call to my local vet for the tranquilizers. Next step for Emma's recovery was in place.

A couple of days later and before I had received the remedy in the mail, Cheryl called to say in good conscience she couldn't recommend using this treatment. No vet she contacted had ever used it with horses – it was simply taking too big a risk. The potential to release a profound rage in a horse could be extremely dangerous.

Cheryl didn't want anyone or Emma getting hurt. She knew of a case where a German shepherd had been administered the remedy and if the owner hadn't been a highly experienced professional trainer the dog would have landed its attack. Cheryl once again stressed I not administer the remedy.

I heard what she said and thought about it. I wondered what Emma would want Ever since I had learned about animal communication, Emma played an active role in her own health care.

I sat down in my living room and quieted my mind. I summoned Emma. I waited for her to join me.

"Emma," I said as soon as I felt her energy, "do you want to take the risks Cheryl described associated with this remedy?" I asked.

"I don't have much of a life now," Emma said. I could feel her sadness. "I'm so tired of living in terror. I want to do it."

"OK, I'll see you at the barn tomorrow with vial in hand," I said.

The next day I slipped the little round sugar pellets of the remedy into the side of Emma's mouth. I stood next to her in her stall observing every little movement. My feet got tired. After ten minutes I retrieved a plastic lawn chair and sat with her in her stall. As soon as she showed any sign of acting on her rage, I was ready. The syringes filled with a couple of heavy-duty tranquilizers rested in my pocket.

Once Emma got used to my being in her stall and had sniffed me everywhere she could reach, she stepped back and dropped her head and cocked her hip. I watched as she seemed to doze. My body relaxed and my breathing matched the slow rise and fall of Emma's flank. The flies buzzed overhead and the horse next door stomped his foot. As my body succumbed to the warmth of the afternoon sun, I felt as if I might nod off. I let out a deep breath.

I was yanked out of my quiet contemplation when with no warning Emma jerked her head around. She bit at her shoulder and grabbed her skin with gnashing teeth. My instincts wrenched me into action. I vaulted up, heart racing and snatched the syringe out of my pocket. I took my eyes off Emma long enough to pop the cap off the needle. When I glanced back at Emma, I stiffened into immobility. She had aimed for and dislodged a biting fly and now was scratching the area with her teeth. I sighed and shook my head at my reaction. I put the cap back on the needle and plopped back down on the chair. Emma took a step over and plunged her nose into her bucket to see if she had missed any grain from her earlier snack. Bucket licked clean once again, Emma dawdled over to her manger to scrounge for tiny bits of hay she may overlooked. I sighed and took deep breaths. I was pretty sure I heard Emma laughing.

I waited another half hour and then headed home after I was convinced that Emma was fine. I didn't sleep well that night half expecting to get a call from the barn manager.

I was relieved when no one called that night and nothing outrageous happened the next day or the day after.

A few weeks later I called Carol. I wanted more details than I was picking up on.

"It's a miracle," Carol translated for Emma. "Rage attacks that came ripping through my body were released. Instead of my needing to act out and attack something, the rage just went 'poof.' Please find another drug that will make my anxiety do the same thing."

"Emma, that's huge progress," I said, tears forming in the corners of my eyes. "I'm proud of you for wanting to take the remedy and I am grateful for the benign outcome."

When I hung up with Carol, I called Cheryl.

"I heard what you said about the stramonium," I said, controlling my enthusiasm. "Emma and I discussed it and it was Emma's decision to take it. I was all prepared with tranquilizers. Nothing happened."

"That's great news," Cheryl said with palpable relief.

"Emma has done really well and says her rage is gone. Now she wants a treatment for her anxiety and panic attacks. I'm glad that we helped her with her rage, but it has been the anxiety that's the most debilitating. It's her anxiety that keeps me from riding her on the trail. She's been doing well in the arena and rarely has an attack there. As long as I keep her close to the barn she holds it together."

"I'm determined to get you two enjoying the hills," Cheryl said. I heard her sigh. "Trail riding is my goal for you both."

"Wow, that would be a miracle," I said, imagining a safe trail ride on Emma.

"The next thing to try is stramonium 200 C," Cheryl said. "It's a higher potency. I'm really glad you didn't tell me in advance you were going ahead with the stramonium 20C. I would've been worried sick."

When I hung up the phone with Cheryl, I heard Emma say, "Do it."

When I received the higher potency remedy from the Hahnemann Clinic, I gave it to Emma. Again, I hung around to see if it created any strong affects. It didn't.

Emma seemed to stay in process for several weeks. Her face morphed much like Jim Carrey's at his best. One emotion expressed itself and then another and another. Her facial expression was constantly changing. The number and variety of changes were eerie to watch. I could only hope when she was done processing her anxiety would be extinguished forever.

When the remedy seemed to have finished its work, I waited for the first pleasant day to test whether Emma's anxiety was really gone. The test would be easy. I only needed to walk her a couple of blocks down the main road towards Briones Park. She was always beset by a panic attack at the corner of the main road and the driveway to the park entrance. Although she could never identify the inciting trigger at that intersection, its predictability was guaranteed.

With each step down the road, my heart beat faster. Emma stopped to eat some grass. That's a great sign. If she's relaxed enough to eat grass on a path away from home, this remedy may have done the trick. She grazed for a few minutes and then I urged her on. We entered the second block. She stared straight ahead. One step, two steps, three steps closer to the side road leading to the entrance to the park. Despite the potholes and fallen branches strewn across the path and needing to watch where I put my feet, I kept my eyes on Emma.

We were ten feet from the turn. Would she get past this spot? I held my breath as we closed the gap. Two feet from the intersection, her head shot up, her body tensed and I saw the whites of her eyes. She froze. She had gone from calm to high anxiety in a couple of seconds. Misery and disappointment took turns engulfing my body.

I turned Emma around. Her level of tension was so attenuated that she felt like an iron bar. When she pulled on the lead rope, I gave it a quick jerk to stop the lunge forward. She tossed her head, lightened her front end and threatened to rear. I struggled to get her safely home, before she completely lost it. Nothing had changed. She was just as panicked as ever.

As soon as we returned to her stall she settled down. I stood and watched her for a few minutes. She remained calm. I was grateful that I hadn't triggered a long-lasting panic attack. I gave her some grain and said goodbye.

On the drive home I felt tired and numb. Would this scenario ever have a different ending?

Chapter 38

With retirement I regained energy and focused even more of my attention on seeking resources that might benefit Emma's rehabilitation. During a dinner with friends I was introduced to a chiropractor who suggested she might be able to help Emma's anxiety. She explained that her work was at an energy level and that she didn't do hands on skeletal manipulation. I reasoned that this work would support what Cheryl was doing and I made an appointment. Cheryl was researching the next remedy to try with Emma so at this time Emma was not in process or about to be treated.

When the chiropractor came out to the barn, she explained her methods to me. She would use me as a surrogate to ask Emma questions. Her queries of Emma would be answered by muscle testing my arm for the "yes" or "no" response.

I was fascinated by this process. Although muscle testing wasn't a new concept for me, I hadn't been introduced to the idea of using a surrogate before. When I was told that I could ask any question I wanted, I gave it some thought. What first came to mind was how Emma's anxiety might have started. I knew that when she was a couple of weeks in utero both the owner and ranch hand at her home had been brutally murdered. When I had done research on the internet I couldn't find any more information than what I already had known second hand from others. I wondered if this horrific crime had any impact on Emma. This might be a good way to learn about Emma's past.

Emma had not been able to talk about her earliest history through telepathic animal communication. By using muscle testing, we might access a different part of her memory. I was stunned by the answers. Not only had Emma's mother been aware of the murders, she also lived in constant terror that she would be harmed. She knew the person who had committed the two murders and felt that he would come back to kill her. Her terror influenced the developing fetus. I had no way of knowing whether this was accurate until a few years later I found confirmation when internet research yielded a summary of the court records of the murder trial. The murderer had been the previous caretaker of the horses and had returned to ask for his job back. When it was explained that the position had been filled, he beat and murdered the owner and beat, raped and murdered the current caretaker. No one explained to Emma's mother that the murderer had been arrested, tried and sentenced. No one told her that she was safe. Emma had been gestated and then born into an environment of extreme fear. Her sensitivities made the experience even more horrendous for her.

From the chiropractor I learned other details of Emma's early life. Tears flowed down my cheeks and I embraced Emma. Our lives of terror were so similar that I was also weeping for myself.

A week later I heard from Cheryl. She had identified the next remedy she wanted to try. I made an appointment for Emma's next treatment.

As I drove out to the barn I couldn't help but appreciate that Cheryl was persistent enough to keep trying.

"Don't be discouraged," Cheryl counseled, as she opened her bag. "Finding the right homeopathic remedy takes time. I haven't given up and neither should you. There's no reason why this beautiful horse and you can't enjoy your retirements in the lovely park next door."

"Okay," I said, and ran my hand over Emma's neck, taking a moment to enjoy the shine of her coat as the morning sun highlighted golden flecks in the brown.

"She may be twenty-three years old," Cheryl said, pausing with the tuning fork in her hand, "but she doesn't look it and she's perfectly sound."

"She still moves with a lot of spring and suspension," I said, picturing Emma's bouncy, ground covering trot.

Emma stood motionless as Cheryl glided the tuning fork across her body. The breeze stirred the fine dust on the gravel paths surrounding the grooming area. I stifled a sneeze when my nose tickled.

"First I want to have a couple of more sessions to work on Emma energetically," Cheryl said, turning to retrieve her acupuncture needles. "Then let's give her the homeopathic remedy cupric metallicum."

I listened to Cheryl's words and felt her energy of enthusiasm and encouragement. I checked in with how I was feeling. One more try to cure Emma of her anxiety attacks. No excitement or happy anticipation accompanied the possibility that we had at last found a solution to Emma's suffering. Too many attempts that either helped for a short time or not at all had exhausted my reservoir of hope like the desert sun diminishing a puddle left from a summer rain. Slow but continual.

After I talked myself into a more positive frame of mind I said, "I will try and not turn my back on hope."

Cheryl smiled, patted me on the shoulder and packed up her tools.

After the final session of Cheryl's energy work on Emma, I ordered the cupric metallicum from the Hahnemann Clinic. As usual the administration went well. I watched Emma for the first few days. I saw no change in countenance or behavior. I wondered if the remedy had done anything. I could have tested to see if the remedy was successful by leading her outside and down the road. I was aware that I conjured up one excuse after another. A few weeks passed before I forced myself to go to the barn with the intention of taking that fateful two block walk.

I had an appointment with Cheryl coming up. I couldn't see her again and have her ask me how it was going and not have an answer.

Good thing embarrassment is a motivation. With all her support and determination, I could at least step up and do my part.

With a dry mouth and a peculiar whiplash between dread and anticipation, I led Emma out of her stall and down the road to her "crisis corner." She looked relaxed, but then, she had the last time we started down this road. I couldn't force myself to take anything more than small, mincing steps. I couldn't hurry. My feet had a life of their own and they wouldn't obey.

I was afraid to know. As we neared the dreaded intersection, the "T" junction that always precipitated a panic attack in Emma, I held my breath. My toes scuffed the ground. I couldn't breathe. Emma slowed her pace to little more than a crawl. She looked with interest at the horses pastured on the hillside to the right. One step. Two steps. When we rounded the corner and we stepped onto the driveway leading to the Briones Park entrance, my lungs were ready to burst. I gasped air. Could this be real? Emma continued walking with her head in a relaxed position, stretched out.

"Oh my God," I said, my heart leaping up and bounding out of my body. "You didn't react." But of course, my skepticism made me wonder if this was an anomaly or a true behavior change that might last.

With each week that passed, Emma seemed to be more settled and at a deeper peace. Her expression didn't lose that doe-eyed softness that communicated a contented horse. I began to trust that the remedy had altered her emotional landscape. I would drive home from the barn thanking God for at last giving my horse the life she deserved.

As the months slipped by, I became more confident that Emma's panic attacks were a thing of the past. Unlike the prescriptions of Western medicine, homeopathy seemed to offer up lasting solutions. Although Emma still had mild bouts of anxiety at times, they were nothing like those flights into a world of terror that had so badly tormented her. These episodes of anxiety seemed to be short-lived and more like what a normal horse might do when frightened by something.

Emma seemed to delight in life and with a predictable emotional calm she could connect to more of her human friends on a more consistent level. The joy she felt swept over and around me and nurtured me. There had been so many years of anguish. How wonderful that Emma could enjoy her retirement years.

Children came out to visit Emma and enjoy pony rides on her. One little girl drew the sweetest picture of her riding Emma, a rainbow spanning the sky and a big red heart in place of the sun. Adults came out as well to visit Emma. Special ones, dear ones, those who knew of Emma's struggles and who loved her. Life was at last kind to this big-hearted horse.

Chapter 39

One cloudy winter afternoon, I quit my house cleaning and eased down to give my body a much-needed rest. I had been thinking that I wanted to talk to Emma. We hadn't chatted in a while. While cleaning, a wistful energy had spread across my mind, putting me in a reflective mood. I had been rummaging around in my closet to organize the containers that been abandoned for one reason or another. In a back corner I found a box that had been long forgotten and whose contents had awakened a deep yearning. I wanted to share some thoughts. I cleared my mind, breathed deep, dropped my energy and waited for Emma to join me. I felt the weight of the box on my legs and listened to the mournful song of a bird, perhaps a hermit thrush, in the pine trees in the open space bordering the front of my home. When I felt a blast of love, I knew Emma and I were connected.

"Emma, our years together have taught me that a partnership invites you into the life of the other at a very intimate level." I took a deep breath. Images from poignant moments in our life together flitted through my mind. I paused to fully experience with each memory the associated emotion. I let the memories continue their journey across the horizon of my inner reality. "Your anxiety wasn't just your problem. It was our problem."

A sparrow swooped down across my patio and lit on a branch of the Japanese Maple whose sheltering arms protected me throughout the seasons. The sparrow cocked his head and chittered away. A pair of towees trotted across the sparkling stone tiles of my patio. I loved those birds; they seemed less fearful and more social than their other feathered companions.

"I never would have survived in this world without you," Emma replied, a strong voice in my mind. "I loved you from the first day I saw you and knew I at last had a chance to be happy."

"I love hearing that," I said and felt my heart glow. "Any lingering or problematic symptoms from the homeopathic remedies?"

"Nope," Emma replied with joy in her voice. "I'm doing peachy."

"Your twenty-fifth birthday has made me think about our journey together," I said, sliding the lid off the box on my lap. "Your body is well past middle-age. It's always remarkable when an eighteen-year-old horse competes at the higher levels. At the FEI Dressage World Cup last year, I watched the best horses and riders in the world. Their horses were in their prime. The elegance and magic of the performances sent me into a world of ecstasy. With each exquisite test, my heart ached. You, more than anyone, know how hard it has been for me to give up dressage."

"My behavior wasn't under my control. I couldn't help it," I heard Emma say. "I loved dressage too, and the connection it gave us."

Emma's sadness stilled my heart.

"I know. You always did your best," I said. I peeled back the tissue paper revealing the contents of the box. I stroked the cheek straps and brow band of the double bridle that had been cleaned and retired to the box many years before. I had never used this bridle with Emma. This bridle was reserved for training and competition at the higher levels of dressage. This bridle with its well-crafted black leather edged in white trim had been very special to me. Lilo Fore, my instructor, had purchased it for me in Germany. When she returned from her trip, she had presented it to me in a ceremony saying that I had earned the right to use the double bridle. My seat and hands were educated. The bridle held a lot of significance. I rewrapped it in tissue paper and nestled it back in the box. I wasn't ready to part with it.

"Emma, both of us are on the other side of middle age. My back isn't as flexible as it once was. Your knees were injected with Legend to ease the discomfort created by arthritis. We're the over-the-hill gang."

"I'm still pretty spry," Emma said sending me a picture of her with her heels well above her head in an exuberant kick.

"Even at your age you're still no beginner's horse." I said, laughing and imagined Emma frolicking around the arena. "You are my best friend and what a gift to have found you," I sent a wave of delicious golden puffs of love to Emma. "I couldn't do the sport I love, but I wouldn't trade our life together for anything."

"Ah shucks," Emma replied blasting me right back with love.

I sat still, letting the warmth of her love infuse my body.

"Look at how much you've taught me," I said, feeling my eyes moisten. "Eighteen years ago I didn't know anything about animal communication. Now here we are chatting like a couple of old friends over tea. The world has changed too. Who would have thought that both your vet and blacksmith would be capable of experiencing your voice? How amazing is that? Do you remember how people made fun of me?"

"Yes," Emma said, her voice filled with mirth and incredulity.

"They called me nuts," I felt the pain of the name-calling. "Behind my back they referred to me as the 'Emma says' woman."

"People are very complex," Emma said. "I don't understand them. You were only trying to help. I also remember you were the first one they ran to whenever they had an unsolvable problem with their horse."

"That was a hoot," I said laughing. "How ludicrous. It seemed as if the people who made the most fun of me were the first to consult me.

If I had a nickel for every time someone asked me, 'What does Emma have to say about this or that?' I would have retired years ago."

"You did ask me about a lot of things," I heard Emma respond.

"Sometimes I wonder what our lives are about," I said feeling a little nostalgic. "The only thing I know for sure is that my life has been far richer because of my association with you. The world will never be the same for me."

"As long as you need a horse in your life, I will continue to reincarnate as a horse," Emma pledged, sending me another waft of love.

My heart quickened.

"That is so sweet," I said looking at Emma's photograph on my side table, "but you need to be on your own path and not worry about mine."

"We've been together for a lot of lives," Emma reminded me.

"Remember when you gave me the ride of my life for a Mother's Day present?" I said. "You said that the horses had been talking among themselves trying to decide what to give their person. They wanted to honor them in a special way. At the time it seemed so far-fetched. Today I know better."

"I'm grateful you're my person," Emma said, sending warmth so strong I had to unbutton my sweater.

"As long as we're reminiscing, I've always wondered why your show name was sent to me." I stared out of my living room window at the ridgeline of the hillside as if looking for an answer. A couple of squirrels cavorted around the trunk of an aspen as if they were engaged in a joyful game of tag.

"Do you remember? Right after I got you I went to sleep meditating on what I should name you. When I woke up in the morning I clearly heard a voice say, 'Emma,' 'Emissary.' The two definitions I found in the dictionary for emissary have always intrigued me – 'a secret agent' was the first definition and 'one sent on a mission for another' was the second. I think I've figured out the secret agent part. I believe you're a secret agent for the Divine, because you've always done your best to model forgiveness, generosity, kindness and love. You've taught me to trust my heart, accept commitment and risk a relationship with intimacy. But I haven't figured out what the mission is. What mission have you been sent on?"

I could feel Emma's mood turn serious.

"Since the beginning of time," I heard Emma say, "A special bond has existed between humans and horse. Humans have felt the love of horse consciously but have been unaware of how deep the bond goes. Horse has worked alongside man, but there is so much more. Man does not fully know how encompassing our devotion is."

"That sounds huge, archetypal," I said trying to absorb what Emma had just said.

"It is," Emma said as she often did when things were just so.

"But what's the mission?"

"Our job is to bring into human consciousness the fullness of the bond between horse and man. What man has known unconsciously since the beginning of the horse/human relationship, we must bring into full human consciousness. We have to expand their knowing," Emma said.

"That sounds huge, Emma," I said shaking my head.

"That's our work together this life," Emma said.

"So, how are we going to do that?" I asked, laughing. "Write a book? Make a movie?"

"Don't worry," I heard Emma reply. "I'll help you."

Epilogue

Emma's legacy has ensured that my relationship to horses has continued to evolve. My goal is to deepen my understanding of their behaviors, motivations and emotional needs.

Since my association with Emma I have experienced other horses. Although more typical in their behavior, they presented challenges to bring them the happiness they deserved. My horsemanship improved with each encounter.

Even if no more than a short story, there are more experiences to be shared. My mare Etta suffered terribly from PTSD caused by unconscious humans. Her recovery took years through homeopathy, cranial sacral work and myofascial release. Other stories need to be told such as my brief experience with a four year old race horse who was delivered directly to my door step from Golden Gate Fields.

As ever my goal is to educate myself and share with other humans the way of the horse.

www.ingramcontent.com/pod-product-compliance
Lightning Source LLC
LaVergne TN
LVHW041606070426
835507LV00008B/157